INDIAN TRIBES IN TRANSITION

India has witnessed a sea change in its social structure and political culture since Independence. Despite the developmental model that the country opted for, the hangover of the Raj continued to encourage fissiparous tendencies dividing the Indian populace on the basis of religion, ethnicity and caste hierarchy.

This book argues for the need to develop a fresh approach to dismantling the stereotypes that have boxed the study of India's tribal communities. It underlines the significance of region-specific strategies in place of an overarching umbrella scheme for all Indian tribes. The author studies tribes in the context of changing political and social identity, gender, extremism, caste dimensions and development issues, and offers a new perspective on tribes to accommodate the diversity and transformations within culture over time and through globalization.

Lucid, accessible and rooted in contemporary realities, this volume will be of great interest to scholars and researchers of sociology and social anthropology, tribal studies, subaltern and Third World studies, and politics.

Yogesh Atal is Professor Emeritus at the Madhya Pradesh Institute of Social Science Research, Ujjain, and member of the Indian National Commission for Co-operation with UNESCO, Ministry of Human Resource Development, Government of India. He was appointed by UNESCO as its Regional Adviser for Social and Human Sciences in Asia and the Pacific and retired as Principal Director in 1997.

INDIAN TRIBES IN TRANSITION

The need for reorientation

Yogesh Atal

NEW DELHI LONDON NEW YORK

First published 2016
by Routledge
2 Park Square, Milton Park, Abingdon, Oxon OX14 4RN

and by Routledge
711 Third Avenue, New York, NY 10017

Routledge is an imprint of the Taylor & Francis Group, an informa business

© 2016 Yogesh Atal

The right of Yogesh Atal to be identified as author of this work has been asserted by him in accordance with sections 77 and 78 of the Copyright, Designs and Patents Act 1988.

All rights reserved. No part of this book may be reprinted or reproduced or utilised in any form or by any electronic, mechanical, or other means, now known or hereafter invented, including photocopying and recording, or in any information storage or retrieval system, without permission in writing from the publishers.

Trademark notice: Product or corporate names may be trademarks or registered trademarks, and are used only for identification and explanation without intent to infringe.

British Library Cataloguing-in-Publication Data
A catalogue record for this book is available from the British Library

Library of Congress Cataloging-in-Publication Data
A catalog record has been requested for this book

ISBN: 978-1-138-96077-0 (hbk)
ISBN: 978-1-315-66019-6 (ebk)

Typeset in Sabon
by Apex CoVantage, LLC

CONTENTS

Introduction	1
1 Anthropology today and tomorrow: a tribute to Professor S. C. Dube	6
2 Defining 'tribe': a conceptual crisis	24
3 Socio-cultural dimensions of development	50
4 Issues in tribal development	61
5 Social science input to Man and the Biosphere Programme (MAB) of UNESCO	73
6 Sustainable rural and tribal development	85
7 Tribal studies: need for reorientation	95
8 March of tribal women	110
9 Concern for indigenous knowledge	121
10 Tribal unrest, state politics and empowerment in contemporary India	129
11 Anthropological perspective to study youth in Asia	139

CONTENTS

12 Ethics in research and research in ethics 159

13 Anthropology and the future of humankind 173

Bibliography 187
Index 189

INTRODUCTION

This is a collection of my essays written in the past few years in response to invitations by various institutions to serve as keynote addresses to the national-level seminars and conferences on different aspects of tribal development and connected anthropological researches in India.

I sincerely feel the need to promote thinking and research on a significant, though grossly neglected, part of our multicultural society – the tribals. Of late, there is some decline in anthropological research on tribes, although people from other disciplines have begun showing interest in them. That is why some of the universities, particularly in the North-East, have both the department of anthropology and the institute of tribal studies. In addition, some of the states have set up tribal research institutes. However, these institutes which started with much fanfare are now dwindling structures with poor and ill-trained staff, generally headed by bureaucrats and statisticians who have no commitment either to research or to the welfare of the tribals. Most tribal research institutes have been reduced to tribal museums. There is a need to revamp these centres of research with fresh perspectives and well-trained scholars with a multidisciplinary orientation.

It should, however, be noted that social science research in this country began with the study of the tribes. Defining anthropology as the 'study of other cultures', British scholars – that included not only trained anthropologists but also administrators and missionaries – found India a good site for anthropological research. Their writings constitute a significant part of literature on Tribal India. But anthropology of those times had a different orientation. It was the queer, the exotic and the primitive aspect of the lives of the tribes that attracted alien ethnographers who described these cultures in the idiom of 'eternal present', giving the impression that they are non-changing. Not only this, the authors showed so much concern for the tribal cultures that

1

they feared their disappearance with the onslaught of modernization. Their plea for the preservation of tribal cultures was so very eloquent and forceful that they were criticized for keeping the tribes as 'anthropological zoos'. The policy formulated for the tribes by Verrier Elwin at the behest of Pandit Jawaharlal Nehru was called *A Philosophy for NEFA*. That 'philosophy' clearly ordained to protect the tribals from outside influences. However, Elwin responded to the mounting criticism by denying his – or for that matter of the colonialists' – intentions to keep them in a zoo. By the wisdom of the hindsight one can now say that the philosophy advocated was part of the British strategy to 'divide and rule'. In our enthusiasm, created by the euphoria of independence, we unquestioningly adopted the 'manifest' intentions and allowed the creation of vested interests in the name of 'tribes' and so-called oppressed classes merging in them several primordial groups of different hues and fostering separate identities. Independent India pursued the dual policy of separate identities of the so-called backward groups – tribes and 'lower' castes – and promoting national integration. If gaining independence meant partition of India along communal lines – partial acceptance of a two-nation theory – it also meant encouraging vested interests along caste and tribal lines. Strangely, India of the 1950s was divided into Urban, Rural and Tribal segments. While the first two groups were geographical, the third group was based on autochthonous character of the populace. However, a liberal interpretation of the word 'tribal' was then employed in terms of the remote and isolated location of the various tribal communities.

It is a historical fact that in the beginning only anthropologists studied the tribes; other social sciences showed complete indifference towards them. Moreover, the students of tribal societies were expatriates, and the discipline of anthropology was described as the study of 'other cultures'.

The consequence has been the dearth of non-anthropological, discipline-specific studies in the earlier years. As the discipline of anthropology began making roots in India, Indians also started studying the tribes, but these researchers, too, were non-tribals.

It was, in a way, a mixed blessing: the students focussing on the tribal studies developed an interdisciplinary approach and attempted to cover all aspects of tribal culture and society. The cultures were viewed holistically. Such an emphasis led to the distinction between sociology and anthropology. Sociologists were regarded as those that studied their own society and anthropologists were regarded as those who studied tribal societies. Besides, the holistic approach in anthropology

INTRODUCTION

also meant that a student graduating in that discipline also studied and researched subject matters related to physical anthropology and prehistoric archaeology.

Strangely enough, at the present stage of the development of social sciences, the emphasis on holistic approach and on interdisciplinarity – the approaches that anthropology mothered and nourished – is also adopted by other social sciences. It must, however, be said that the 'ideological underpinnings' of anthropology of the colonial times were rather different. Holistic approach was used to emphasize that all parts of the culture are so intertwined that any change brought therein may disrupt their integration. Ethnographies were used to demonstrate the non-changing character of these societies and to classify them in the category of the primitives and the backward so that they received a separate treatment. This approach somehow prevented the tribal groups from joining the so-called mainstream of Indian society.

Today the situation has changed. In the last 50 years, tribes have been studied more by the Indians than the non-Indians. And in their studies, disciplines other than anthropology have been increasingly involved, with the result that the recent studies of the tribal areas have varied orientations. The tribals themselves have changed significantly in their social demographic characteristics. They are no longer preliterate, and their life ways do not correspond to the descriptions of earlier ethnographies. Literacy, urbanism, connectivity and participation in the national political process are some of the indicators on which tribal development can be rated. No doubt, there are deficits on all these fronts in each of the 700-odd tribes listed in the State Schedule,[1] but none of the tribal groups today corresponds to the ideal type of a primitive society of the nineteenth century. Lumping them together may be administratively convenient, but it is sociologically absurd. There is nothing like a separate Tribal India. Tribes are scattered in different parts of the country, they belong to different racial stocks and speech communities and they live in varied habitats. Their contacts with the neighbouring settlements have broken their isolation, and they have thrown leadership which effectively partakes in Indian polity.

It is sad that while the discipline of anthropology is growing in the country as is evidenced by the number of teaching departments or the number of anthropology graduates, not much research is taking place in the tribal areas. Way back in 1973, when I was Director at the ICSSR, we brought out a brochure identifying fresh priorities for anthropological research in the hope of giving a spurt to research in

3

INTRODUCTION

the tribal areas. Unfortunately, very few responded to the call. The need for return to the tribal areas with a fresh agenda for research is valid even today.

But we must acknowledge the fact that in some of the so-called tribal areas, particularly in the North-East, literacy statistics are far better than in many non-tribal zones. The universities established there have departments of various social science disciplines and they all engage in empirical research in the local areas. Thus, they have not only the departments of anthropology but also of sociology and even 'tribal studies'. Even the departments of political science, economics and education are carrying out research amongst the local tribal communities. The local students doing anthropological study of their own communities are now said to be doing 'auto-anthropology'.

Such a scenario demands a careful review of the prevailing concepts, research orientations and theoretical formulations.

This book of essays is meant to trigger a debate on the manner in which we look at the tribes. Through various angles I have argued that the myth of Tribal India should be broken to facilitate the integration of various tribal groups into the general stream of Indian society. I firmly believe that the word 'tribe' imposed by the colonial masters on the local colonial societies is, at best, a transitional category. It is absurd to lump together all the 700-odd communities into a common box and design a common strategy for development. It also needs to be reviewed whether we view all change and development as 'killer' of indigenous cultures.

In all these essays delivered as keynote addresses or inaugural lectures at various seminars, I have raised these issues to put across my views and to press the demand for a fresh perspective that is non-colonial, non-separatist and unbiased.

I know that many would disagree and would plead for the continuance of the colonial practice. But I am confident that there will be others who will see merit in my plea and commit themselves to respond to the re-invitation to anthropology to visit the field that has given them their academic identity.

In the end, I would like to express my gratitude to my colleagues who prompted me to write these essays by inviting me to the seminars organized by them: Professor S.N. Choudhury of Barkatullah University, Bhopal; Professor A.K. Danda, Member Secretary of INCAA (Indian National Confederation and the Academy of Anthropologists); Professor V.R. Rao, former Director of Anthropological Survey of India and now Professor of Anthropology at the Delhi University; and

INTRODUCTION

Professor K. K. Misra, former Director of the Indira Gandhi National Museum of Man and simultaneously Director of the Anthropological Survey of India.

In preparing the manuscript for the press, I have been helped by Professor Sunil K. Choudhary, Department of Political Science, Delhi University. I am indeed grateful for his readiness to assist and for his critical comments.

Note

1 In 2001 the Census listed 664 Scheduled Tribes; this number increased to 705 in the 2011 Census enumeration.

1

ANTHROPOLOGY TODAY AND TOMORROW: A TRIBUTE TO PROFESSOR S. C. DUBE

I S. C. Dube and his legacy

In his conversations, Dube always described himself as a 'home-spun social scientist',[1] because his formal degree was in political science, although he earned his doctorate in anthropology. Like him, his wife, Leelaji, also moved to anthropology and produced excellent monographs on the *Gond Woman* and on *Matriliny and Islam* in Lakshadweep. His two sons – Mukul and Saurabh – did their degrees in sociology and history, respectively – but both display anthropological orientation in their work. Anthropology was a part of his family culture. Concluding his piece titled 'The Journey So Far' in the *Festschrift* that I edited in his honour, he wrote: 'our house is open to young colleagues who seek to discuss their ideas and projects, and many of them receive our warm welcome'.[2]

I am alluding to this aspect of Dube's intellectual profile here with a purpose. In Dube's lifetime there were several occasions when some lesser-known enthusiasts of the discipline questioned his credentials. He was on the faculty of the Department of Political Science at Lucknow University, but was working for his doctoral degree in anthropology. Professor D. N. Majumdar invited him to share some teaching load in the newly established Department of Anthropology, and also to assist him in the editing of the *Eastern Anthropologist*. Professor Dube's book on folklore was published from here, and it is here that he did his monograph on *The Kamar*. In fact, when Professor Majumdar suddenly passed away in 1959, there were hopes of his return to this place to succeed Majumdar, but somehow it did not happen. I recall another instance where I proposed his name for an examinership and the head of the department raised the question of his academic credentials!

ANTHROPOLOGY TODAY AND TOMORROW

More important is the point that those who pioneered teaching and research in anthropology in India, as also elsewhere, came from different disciplines. Since anthropology was not taught at Lucknow in the 1930s, Professor D. N. Majumdar was roped in as lecturer in primitive economics in the Department of Economics whose professors – Radha Kamal Muherjee and D. P. Mukerji – smuggled in sociology and became its first tutors. In Calcutta, Professor Nirmal Kumar Bose moved from geography to do anthropology and became its notable contributor. S. C. Roy, who started *Man in India*, was, I am told, a lawyer. In later years, many young anthropologists gained acceptance and worldwide acclaim as sociologists – M. N. Srinivas, T. N. Madan, Andre Beteille, to name a few. As a truly interdisciplinary discipline anthropology kept its doors open to other specializations and, unlike many other subjects, it did not become 'endogamous'. Hybridity has been its strength and, I believe, it should be maintained. In this context, I feel happy that INCAA did not raise any such doubts while honouring Professor Dube.

Saurabh, Professor Dube's son, has crisply summed up Dube's intellectual journey in a piece he did for him. To quote:

> Initiated into the academy through the tribal anthropology of the 1940s, Dube was a major player in the village studies boom of the 1950s, straddling scholarship and administration over the 1960s, primarily occupying higher positions in academic bureaucracy in the 1970s and 1980s, and dedicating himself to political-cultural writing in Hindi after the mid 1980s. At each step, Dube's interests and presence could not be simply compartmentalized into discrete arenas, easily divided into different roles.

Not founder of any particular 'school', not a narrow specialist, a wanderer in search of new pastures, an investigator of the contemporary against the backdrop of history and with a vision of the future, Professor Dube had an enormous circle of friends, colleagues and admirers. Among the important trailblazers in Indian sociology and anthropology Professor Dube occupies a place of prominence. Professor Dube's intellectual journey almost coincides with the journey of Indian sociology and anthropology in the country.

Earning B.A. honours in political science, Professor Dube got his first teaching assignment in his *alma mater* – Hislop College affiliated to Nagpur University. From there, he moved to Lucknow as a

7

lecturer in the Department of Political Science, where, as I mentioned earlier, he worked closely with Professor Majumdar in setting up the new Department of Anthropology. Recognition of his talent and work within few years of his graduation resulted in his 'transfer of residence' to Osmania University, Hyderabad, where the Sociology Department was established with active involvement of Professor Christoph von Fürer Haimendorf – a noted anthropologist who did his field work among Indian tribes of Central India and the North-East.

Not only did Professor Dube move geographically from Lucknow to Hyderabad, he also made a transition academically from tribal studies to the study of village communities. The village of Shamirpet, in the vicinage of Hyderabad, became internationally known through his *Indian Village*, incidentally the first full-length monograph to appear in print on an Indian village. That study also posted a new landmark as it was based on team research, unlike ethnographic researches carried out by lone scholars.

Dube was involved in yet another team research in the villages of Rankhandi-Jhaberan area of Western Uttar Pradesh, popularly known as the Cornell-Lucknow Project. Cornell University picked him from there for a stint as a Visiting Professor of Far Eastern Studies. At Cornell, he wrote his third major book, *India's Changing Villages*. This book again heralded a new era of the studies on 'Directed Cultural Change'.

Upon his return from Cornell, Dube joined the Nagpur station of the AnSI for a brief spell, and then in 1957, at the relatively younger age of 35, he moved to the University of Sagar as the first professor in the newly created Department of Anthropology.[3] My association with him began from there in 1957 and remained till he breathed his last.

While at Sagar, Professor Dube carried out two research projects for the Planning Commission, Government of India on: (i) *Leadership, Communication, and Decision-Making* in the villages of North Madhya Pradesh and (ii) *Cultural Factors in Rural Health and Hygiene*. Both were completed but reports on them somehow never got published. I had the good fortune of working in the first project immediately upon the completion of my M.A.

Only after 3 years of his stay at Sagar, Professor Dube joined, in 1960, the Central Institute for Research and Training in Community Development at Mussoorie. Mainly through his efforts the institute was restructured as the National Institute of Community Development (NICD)[4] with its new location in Hyderabad. His 4 year sojourn at the institute helped in mobilizing several young scholars from various social science disciplines to do research on the processes of directed cultural change in Village India.

His return to the academe, after a close 'participant observation' of the running of bureaucracy and of the process of policymaking, influenced his teaching. Back in Sagar, he drastically revised the courses and introduced new ones on communication, political sociology and modernization. He renamed the department as that of Anthropology and Sociology. His departure to Shimla in 1971, as the Director of the Indian Institute of Advanced Study, was not only his adieu to Sagar; it also, unfortunately, orphaned social anthropology there. The department split into Sociology and Anthropology; and the Anthropology Department became virtually the Department of Physical Anthropology, with no one on the permanent staff to teach social anthropology; the Sociology Department also returned to the set pattern sacrificing the unique character that it had adorned under Professor Dube's leadership. It is indeed a sad story.

After his tenure at the Indian Institute of Advanced Study, he became the founding Director of the G. B. Pant Institute of Social Research in Allahabad. He left that institute to become the vice chancellor of Jammu University. Then he became National Fellow of the Indian Council of Social Science Research (ICSSR). At the same time, he participated in a United Nations University Project on 'Socio-Cultural Development Alternatives in a Changing World (SCA)' during 1978–1982. For this project, he wrote a book titled *Modernization and Development: The Search for Alternative Paradigms* (Zed books, London, 1988). This book is a sequel to his previous book *Explanation and Management of Change* (McGraw Hill, New York, 1974).

In 1980, he joined the United Nations Asia-Pacific Development Center (APDC) in Malaysia as a consultant. There he did another book, *Development Perspectives for the 1980s*. His last official assignment was as Chairman, Madhya Pradesh Higher Education Commission.

Dube never displayed much enthusiasm for theory, with the result that his reviewers talked of his 'lucid style', implying thereby that there was absence of theory in his work. He discouraged 'narcissistic intellection and the feverish search for theory' for, he felt that, such 'theory, often phoney, distracts attention from larger issues of public policy. . . . Theory is important, but the search for theory at the cost of human concerns is very disconcerting. . . . I am all too aware of the limitations of empiricism, but I am more distrustful of theorizing without a solid data base'.

Quite individual and distinctive in style, Professor Dube was very versatile; he was a prolific writer and an eloquent speaker both in English and in Hindi. As a teacher, he enthralled his students and inspired them to work and explore unchartered territories. As a frontiersman, he did not create a 'school' of his own. His doors were open to all; even those who were not his formal students felt at home with him. He showed his genuine enthusiasm over the achievements not only of his colleagues and students but even of those who may have been his opponents. Wherever he went, he spotted the sparks and encouraged them to become torches. Ultra-modern in his lifestyle, dubbed as a 'deluxe professor', Dube was a teacher in the true Indian tradition. A great intellectual, an inspiring teacher, a generous human being and a secular Indian, Dube was distinctly different.

II   The beginnings of anthropology

With this brief eschatological excursion into the life and works of Professor Dube, let me now turn to the main theme.

I wish to focus on Anthropology's new agenda for *India*.

As a backgrounder let us first re-look at the beginnings of our discipline.

The birth of anthropology in the second half of the nineteenth century was, in a way, a product of colonialism and the Industrial Revolution. The Industrial Revolution opened the gateway for the people of the West to the countries of the Third World. Adventurers, researchers, merchants and missionaries got the opportunity to be exposed to different cultures and civilizations. It is the queer and the exotic of the non-Western cultures that attracted attention. The different flora and fauna, and the primitiveness of many societies, offered new material to those scholars who were engaged in the task of developing evolutionary theories of change.

Students of natural history and anthropology welcomed the opportunity to carry out investigations of their subject matter in strange settings to further exemplify the theory of evolution as developed by Charles Darwin in his *On the Origin of Species*. The key concepts of *Natural selection* and *Survival of the Fittest* used by Darwin to explicate his theory of evolution were found useful in building an evolutionary ladder for human societies putting the savages at the bottom, barbarians in the middle and the civilized peoples at the top. The colonial administrators used this framework to justify their superiority and the legitimacy of their rule over the colonies. One of the followers of

ANTHROPOLOGY TODAY AND TOMORROW

Darwin, Francis Galton, saw merit in the process of natural selection and developed ideas about the power of hereditary influence. Virtually ignoring the existence of cultural processes, Galton developed his science of *Eugenics*, and made misleading generalizations regarding racial superiority.

When Darwin's theory of evolution was published, there was little understanding about human cultures. Those studying human society were guided by biological determinism, and later by geographical determinism. Human behaviour was regarded as a product of one's biology and of compulsions of the geographical environment. Anthropologists brought in the concept of *Culture* as socially inherited way of life and regarded it as determinant of most human behaviour.

Scholars working to develop a general theory of evolution focussed on human society, or human civilization as a whole, attempted various generalizations about the origin of society based on their limited knowledge. Included in this category are students of history and of ethnology. The ethnologists were differentiated from ethnographers. The latter took to describing the 'actually existing structures of societies' that were considered to be primitive, representing, in a sense, the earlier ladders of the currently advanced societies of the West.

The forerunners of anthropology came from disciplines as varied as biology and geology on the one hand, and psychology, philosophy, history, law and economics on the other. They all contributed to the new discipline which came to be known as ethnology, or general anthropology.

People of my generation received such interdisciplinary orientation. To quote Max Gluckman and Fred Eggan from their *Introduction* to the four-volume ASA monographs[5]:

> Outwardly the common mark of social, cultural, and psychological anthropology was that they all continued to be comparative and cross-cultural in outlook, with an emphasis on the small-scale tribal societies of the world, and for many years the study of such a society was virtually the initiation ceremony which admitted a scholar into the ranks of anthropology.
>
> (1966: xi)

As the discipline grew, its professionalization began with the posting of boundaries of a distinct area of study, and its membership becoming restricted to those socialized within the endogamous territory of

ANTHROPOLOGY TODAY AND TOMORROW

anthropology. But this group itself began to show the signs of gradual compartmentalization, like the *phratry* or *moiety*. To quote Gluckman and Eggan again:

> By the 1930s the different disciplines were beginning to separate from one another . . . [And as] each anthropological discipline separated out, its practitioners turned to other subjects . . . Physical anthropologists depended more on the biological sciences; psychological anthropologists . . . on psychology . . . and psychiatry; and social anthropologists on sociology, history, political science, law and economics. Cultural anthropologists alone continued to draw on the biological, psychological, and sociological sciences.
>
> (ibid.)

When my generation entered the university to specialize in anthropology in India in the late 1950s, the orientation of general anthropology continued in the sense that we had to offer papers in prehistory, archaeology and physical anthropology; we also learnt serology, anthropometry, dermatoglyphics and even photography. It was not only Hooton's *Up from the Ape* but also Henry Gray's magnum opus, *Anatomy*, that were part of our compulsory reading.

Anthropology, in the understanding of a commoner, was, however, equated with the study of tribes. Not only did we have a full paper on Tribal India, all theory papers in social anthropology made references to, and provided examples from, tribes from different parts of the world as well. Anthropology came to be known as the study of the *Primitive* and the *Past*. Specializations did exist in the departments, and laboratories for anthropological research became part of the infrastructure. But as we grew in the profession, separation between physical and social anthropology began occurring on a large scale. Those of us specializing in social anthropology were naturally getting exposed to other social sciences, especially sociology; our work on Village India brought us closer to rural sociologists and caught the attention of the policymakers and planners who were engaged in the massive programme of Community Development.

Delivering the First D. N. Majumdar Memorial Lecture in 1972, Dube foresaw the contours of a newly developing paradigm. Let me quote:

> By and large, academic anthropology in India continues to maintain a semblance of the classical 'grand design' and

12

ANTHROPOLOGY TODAY AND TOMORROW

keeps within its fold cultural and social anthropology, physical anthropology, and prehistory. It is becoming increasingly evident, however, that this federal character will not last. Ethno-linguistics could never become as effective a part of anthropology in India as it did in the United States. Now prehistory is discovering its natural affinity with archaeology and is slowly being absorbed into that discipline. Physical anthropology remains attached to cultural anthropology and is not making a determined bid to find a place for itself among the life sciences. This has contributed to its retardation. Anthropology and sociology have come closer in spite of the presence, in both these disciplines, of purists who make a deliberate attempt to avoid the pollution of their 'own' subject by the other. Evidently, these purists are fighting a losing battle. With anthropologists seeking a new and larger unit of study the fusion of social anthropology and sociology is imminent. If we have to move from micro to macro studies this is both necessary and desirable. Nostalgia for the academic tradition and false pride in disciplinary labels are bound to be counter-productive. Those who care for understanding are increasingly rejecting the artificial disciplinary boundaries. Vested interests, rather than reason, appear to account for the continuing clash.[6]

What Professor Dube predicted then has come out to be true. But the profession did not heed to his caution about the creation of artificial boundaries. He was not opposed to specializations and, for that purpose, to developing alliances with relevant disciplines from biological or social sciences. But what is emerging today is the tendency to insulate the apertures. As one reviews the professional demography of the departments of anthropology today in India, one comes to a rather dismal conclusion that the separation has led to a relative neglect of social anthropology. There is a need to review this situation and to work out strategy for a rapprochement.

III   Anthropology for tomorrow

For a growing and flourishing discipline it is necessary to periodically review the achievements of the past and chart out a path for the future.

We must give credit to our seniors who foresaw a new role for anthropology and took the first steps to accommodate new concerns which lent them to anthropological treatment. Majumdar took his students every summer to Jaunsar-Bawar for the study of Khasa who were at that time not included in the category of the tribes. Both he and Dube participated in Cornell-Lucknow Project that studied the impact of community development in Rankhandi-Jhaberan area of Uttar Pradesh. Madan went to study the Kashmiri Pandits in a village; K. S. Mathur and Brij Raj Chauhan studied villages in Madhya Pradesh and Rajasthan, respectively. Srinivas studied the people of Coorg and then a Mysore village pseudonymed Rampura. A number of anthropologists from UK and USA came to study India's villages. Their studies were published as ethnographies. Their researches followed the technique of observation – both participant and non-participant. However, they were different from tribal ethnographies in the sense that in them the village was treated as a community in place of an ethnic group. A tribe lives in several villages and the anthropologists described them as if the entire tribal territory was one living space. The culture of the tribe was described in the idiom of the eternal present.

The village attracted attention for two reasons: (i) it was a microcosm, an easily isolable unit, suitable for observation and (ii) it became a target for social change; the delay in its study would have meant loss of the opportunity to describe the relatively 'non-changing' community. Village studies laid the foundations of rural sociology in India, with all its pioneers hailing from anthropology.

Social anthropology, thus, moved from the study of small and simple societies to the study of complex societies and civilizations. We began our journey as a discipline to reconstruct the past; in the post-independent era we joined the national efforts in the improvement of our present through planned development; now is the time when anthropology is invited, like any other social sciences, to participate in the fashioning of our future.

Reviewing the achievements of the development decades towards the conclusion of the last century, the United Nations acknowledged that economic development alone is not enough. It endorsed the need to bring back 'culture' to the centre stage. It gave the slogan 'Think globally, act locally'. The movement of the indigenous populations throughout the world, the concern about indigenous systems of knowledge and the acknowledgement of the need to maintain cultural diversity just as the need to preserve biodiversity are signalling a redefinition of our role as anthropologists.

If the birth of anthropology was necessitated by colonization and facilitated by the Industrial Revolution, the reorientation of it

ANTHROPOLOGY TODAY AND TOMORROW

today is necessitated by globalization and facilitated by Information Revolution.

In laying down priorities and developing a doable agenda it is necessary to keep in mind what is expected of us by the society and what are our capabilities to deliver. In terms of the latter, it can be said that today the indigenous manpower trained in various fields of anthropology is much larger than what it was when the discipline was struggling to gain entry into the Indian academe in the 1940s and 1950s. Even in the late 1950s, India had a limited number of centres teaching anthropology; today that number has greatly swollen. Along with the numerical growth of departments and practitioners of the discipline, there has also been bifurcation in terms of narrow specializations, particularly in the field of physical anthropology with a greater slant towards human biology compared to palaeontology and prehistoric archaeology.

Social anthropologists, likewise, have moved away from the study of the tribes to other areas including rural and urban studies, health and hygiene, the study of professions and development-related topics of national concern. Such studies have brought them closer to sociology. Such interdisciplinary transactions have enriched our theoretical apparatus resulting in conceptual clarifications and paradigmatic formulations. Information Revolution has greatly facilitated the arrival and use of machine culture – digital cameras, voice recording devices, laptops for writing field notes, mobile phones overcoming hurdles in communication, big computers for mass storage of data and their easy and quick retrieval and new software facilitating complicated multivariate operations. All this has contributed to the evolution of an efficient methodology for data collection, storage, analysis and report writing. It has broken the traditional isolation of the anthropologist working in remote and inaccessible settlements. These developments have not only affected the work culture of a social anthropologist but also, and perhaps more significantly, eased the task of those specializing in the new areas, such as genomics. Visits to the tribal areas – the traditional territory for anthropological field research – are now much easier with improvements in transportation – roads, railways and even airstrips for landing helicopters. These areas are now frequently visited not only by anthropologists from abroad, or other parts of the country to which they now belong, but have opened out to others as well. No doubts, there are still some areas that are comparatively inaccessible, and thus maintain the semblance of the underdeveloped region. But such barriers are being broken. Not only outsiders enter

ANTHROPOLOGY TODAY AND TOMORROW

such zones, but the insiders also make forays in the neighbouring regions. Such interactions have changed their cultural profiles, and enlarged their worldview – *Weltanschauung*.

Arrival of new technology in the area of research, however, has also raised new questions of ethics. Technology extends the limits of the 'possible', but societal considerations restrict the domain of the 'desirable'. What is technologically feasible may not always be socially desirable. In deciding about the agenda this consideration becomes quite crucial.

Against this backdrop, the practitioners of the discipline will have to judge the admissibility of demands made by the society. Available technology, trained manpower and level of theoretical sophistication in the discipline should determine the contours of our doable agenda. It is also significant to note that with the expansion of education in these areas, there are *indigenous* scholars trained not only in anthropology but also in other social sciences. For such anthropologists hailing from the tribal societies a new term, *auto-anthropologist*, is now in vogue. Thus, tribes are being studied not only by the discipline of anthropology but by other social sciences as well, and the researchers are both insiders and outsiders – the latter category of outsiders includes both the non-tribal nationals and the expatriate researchers. There is, thus, a need to revisit our old concerns with a fresh perspective.

Let me begin with a personal experience.

In the year 2007, I was invited by the Government of Rajasthan to serve on a Three-Member Committee set up to examine the candidature of the Gujjars as a tribe. The agitators insisted that the committee should have one anthropologist as a member. Since I come from Rajasthan, and happen to be an anthropologist, I was roped in. For me, it was a good opportunity to demonstrate how anthropology can be of help in such a situation of crisis. However, when I started searching relevant literature, I found to my dismay that while the Gujjars in Rajasthan were agitating for a number of years there were no studies carried out on this community in that state – no PhD, no research project undertaken by any university or the Tribal Research Institute, or by the Anthropological Survey of India (AnSI), which has a regional station in Udaipur. The AnSI's *Peoples of India* was of no help either; it had a sweeping two-page generalized description, partly a rehash of what I wrote about this community in my book *The Changing Frontiers of Caste*. Neither the Tribal Research Institute nor the Station of the AnSI, both based in Udaipur, thought it advisable to investigate the matter. Anthropology was expected to provide a dependable answer,

16

ANTHROPOLOGY TODAY AND TOMORROW

but it had nothing to offer. In view of the demand for tribal status by the Gujjar community, anthropologists should have, on their own, taken the initiative to undertake such a study. I surmise that since the Gujjars are not listed as a Scheduled Tribe this community was ignored. I am told that since this community, practising Islam and living in the state of Jammu and Kashmir, has, of late, been given tribal status, it has now become eligible for anthropological research!

In saying this, I am making three points: (i) Our subject matter is decided by the official definition (a group is a tribe if it is listed in the Schedule); (ii) Anthropology has not offered a commonly agreed definition of the concept of Tribe; and (iii) anthropologists in India have, in recent years, generally neglected the study of the tribes, and moved to other areas and peoples.

Let me take the last point first. In 1973–74, the Indian Council of Social Science Research issued a fresh set of priorities for research in various social science disciplines. The priorities recommended for the tribal studies by the expert team included *restudies* of those tribes which had been studied previously – and mostly – by foreign anthropologists. The ICSSR felt that the monographs have become dated. The communities studied have been undergoing substantial changes with the result that the descriptions available in the earlier monographs appear to be esoteric. The restudies of these communities will prepare their present profile and help gauge the changes that have occurred during the interregnum. In addition, the committee also recommended new ethnographic studies of the tribes that were not studied earlier. ICSSR was prepared to fund such research and encourage younger teachers and anthropology students to carry out field work in them. Today when we assess the work done in the past 30 years, we find that nothing significant has been done to improve our baseline data relative to tribes in India. Of course, more specialized works are being produced; for example, there is an excellent study of the Angami Nagas done by N.K. Das titled *Kinship, Politics and Law in Naga Society* (1993). There is also a first-rate monograph by Vinay K. Srivastava on the Raikas of Rajasthan that earned him a PhD from Cambridge in the 1990s, but it focussed on the religious aspects of this semi-nomadic tribe.

Old ethnographies present profiles of non-changing societies, but the very same societies today look vastly different from those stationary profiles. As living societies they are in the throes of change and they have discarded several stereotypes about them. But where is the empirical evidence? The government has put all of them in a single

17

category of ST, to dub them as backward; and we unquestioningly accept such characterization.

A review of tribal studies for the fourth round of ICSSR Survey of Research in Sociology and Social Anthropology brought out the fact that there is decline of interest in the conventional field of anthropology. Of course, during this period some encyclopaedias on tribal societies have appeared. Also the People of India Project of the AnSI covered the tribal communities. In addition, some good pictorial – in fact, costly coffee table – books done by professional photographers, in league with anthropologists, who provided the script, have also come to the market. But most research is reported as articles and communications in professional journals such as *Man in India* and *Eastern Anthropologist*. Even here, the number of articles on social anthropological aspects of tribals is falling. The survey revealed that only 67.11 per cent of the articles published in *Man in India* during 1993–2002 and 18.9 per cent articles published in *Eastern Anthropologist* during the period 1988–2001 related to the tribals.

I must also mention that while interest in tribal studies amongst the social anthropologists is generally declining, other social scientists have taken up studies of specific aspects of tribes, particularly those related to development. Additionally, there is now emergence of what is called 'auto-anthropology'. Such scholars have not only brought in the 'insider view' but also challenged the very definition of the discipline of anthropology – as 'the study of other cultures'.

This leads me to my second point, namely lack of uniformity in the use of the concept of Tribe. Ethnographies written in the idiom of 'eternal present' regarded these population groups as 'non-changing'. Since they attracted the attention of the pioneering anthropologists visiting remote areas as being very different and perhaps representing the earlier stage of their society's own evolution they just dubbed them as 'primitive' and 'preliterate' without bothering to furnish a definition. As a consequence, anthropology became a study of 'other cultures' – cultures other than one's own. When Indian anthropologists started studying Indian tribes and villages, they somehow challenged that definition of the discipline because they were, in a way, studying their own culture – a multicultural outfit called *indigenous civilization*.

Without questioning the nomenclature, anthropologists took those groups as subject matter of their study which were officially designated as tribes. It is interesting that in the 1931 Census, which had recorded castes for the last time, a list of the tribes is given. But even in

ANTHROPOLOGY TODAY AND TOMORROW

this Census, the groups that were identified by a distinct tribal name were classified in terms of their religion. Only those that were not converted to any religion – Christianity, Islam, Hinduism or Jainism – were called Tribals. Hutton went to the extent of calling tribal religions as residuals that were yet to enter the temple of Hinduism. G. S. Ghurye also advocated this line of reasoning.

When independent India adopted its new Constitution that made provision for the listing of tribes in a special Schedule, the officialdom took recourse to the Census and listed all the tribes registered therein. In doing so, they ignored the finer distinction made by the Census Commissioners. If you look at the 1931 Census you will find that these groups were classified on the basis of their religion and only the non-converts were classified as tribals, the primitives. But the official listing of STs included all those that bore the tribal name by clubbing the converts with the animists. Thus, a total of 19,116,498 (19.1 million), divided into 212 tribes, got listed as population of Tribal India, constituting 5.36 per cent of the total Indian population in 1951. In undivided India of 1941, this percentage was 7.8 – the deficit of 1951 represented that section which became part of Pakistan (both East and West). Today, the number of tribes listed as ST has burgeoned to around 700, and represents a little more than 8 per cent of the total population. The increase in the number of tribes[7] is attributable to separate state-wise listing of the same tribe and inclusion of several other groups which claimed a tribal status. In the process, a group bearing the same name, and claiming the same origin, has become a non-tribe in some states. But we lack anthropological evidence to justify such exclusions. It is the state that has the prerogative to class a group as a tribe, or deny such a claim.

It is for the purpose of granting a tribal status to a claimant group that the question of defining a tribe has now become significant. Unfortunately, anthropology did not provide an answer, as it did not bother to fashion one.

Dube listed six features as descriptors of a tribe, but that was hardly a definition in the real sense of the term.

The government took note of Dube's formulation and came up with the following criteria to judge the candidature of a group for the tribal status: (1) Primitive traits, (2) Distinctive culture, (3) Geographical isolation, (4) Shyness of contact and (5) Backwardness. These criteria are not employed for those who are already listed as ST. If applied, many of them, to be sure, will have to be de-scheduled. Moreover, these official criteria are too vague to judge the candidature of any group.

19

In effect, a tribe, in the Indian context, is the one that is included in the official Schedule. As anthropologists we have accepted the official definition. This is rather unfortunate. Students of tribal studies take up those groups which enjoy government recognition without bothering about a scientific definition that would be universally applicable. The implication is clear: academic research is carried out along political lines without raising crucial issues. It is, in my opinion, the task of the researcher to point out flaws in the policy and offer guidelines rather than toe the official line.

We need to remind ourselves that while early anthropologists studied tribes as non-changing phenomena, there was an underlying assumption that these are already a part of the evolutionary ladder and are likely to move away to a different destination like the developed societies. A tribal status is, thus, a transitional status in the same manner as, for example, youth is. In due course of time, a group has to give up the tribal status and assume the status waiting for it at another destination. In other words, we need to ask the pertinent question: *When does a Tribe cease to be a Tribe?* If we took recourse to history, each one of us can claim to have belonged to one tribe or the other just as the Gujjars are doing today, even after enjoying the status of a Hindu or a Muslim caste for several generations. We need to insist that there cannot be a path reversal, or moving backward. It is wrong to assume that once a tribal is always a tribal.

Today's India cannot be classed into the neat categories of Urban, Rural and Tribal. While the first two are residential categories, the third one is an ethnic or a racial category. That is why tribes can also be classified into urban and rural; certainly sections of them that still remain less mobile – socially or spatially – may need special assistance to move out of their insulation, but this cannot be the case for the entire community.

It is in this sense that the clubbing together of all statistics for the 8 per cent of the population designated as 'tribal' serves little purpose. How can we, as students of culture, accept such merger into an administratively convenient category? Are we not still thinking in terms of preserving anthropological zoos?

Whenever we talk of issues related to tribal development in academic seminars, we adopt the tone of preservation and highlight the so-called evil effects of modernization, and now of globalization. I am of the view that there is a need to differentiate between two concerns, namely that of recording for our posterity the prevailing patterns of behaviour and elements of material culture as part of human history, and that of documenting the process of change and transformation

ANTHROPOLOGY TODAY AND TOMORROW

that various communities are undergoing. As cultural relativists we must abstain from giving judgement about what is good and what is bad. Our study of the indigenous knowledge – be it about the stars and the clouds, or about the herbs and medicines, or the skills of cultivating the land – should not be done with the intent of its glorification and claiming it to be superior to scientific knowledge of the modern times. Where it is indeed superior, it must be widely adopted and universalized, but where it is mundane, it needs to be replaced. If a tribal patient is suffering from a malady that can be successfully cured by an outside intervention, it will be fruitless to propagate an ineffective indigenous treatment. As researchers, we are neither the protagonists of tradition nor adversaries of modernity.

Historians of knowledge generally fall into two categories: the *adumbrationists* who attribute everything to the past, to tradition, and do not acknowledge any novelty of innovation; and the *palimpsests* that refuse to acknowledge the shoulders of the past on which the novelty is mounted. Time has come when the fruitless debate on tradition versus modernity needs to be closed. Let us accept that we cannot recreate our past and live in it; and also that the present and the future require the foundations of the past. It is the amalgam of the old and the new that defines our present and would fashion our future.

A politically desirable continuity of the confusion should, in my view, not become the basis for objective portrayal of the existing reality. It is time that we, as social scientists, propose the definition of tribe as a *transitional* structural unit and focus our attention on the study of the processes of its transformation into a larger society as well as its assimilation as a subset in a larger social system.

These developments require a change in the paradigm for the study of tribes. We must return to the tribes but not with the burden of the past. There is a need to understand India's tribal population not as isolated communities but as groups assimilating in the broader assemblage of the Indian society. There is a need to describe their present and contrast it with their past as depicted in the old ethnographies to see the differences in their profiles and to trace the path through which they have crossed the passing years.

It seems to me paradoxical that while the treatment of tribes as 'anthropological zoos' was rejected way back in the 1950s, as anthropologists we still continue to highlight their 'exotic' character they themselves despise, and museumize their cultural products. We become advocates of 'preservation' as if we have vested interest in their alleged 'backwardness'.

Recent researches have also indicated that while cultural considerations are important we must not become advocates of non-change. The key concerns regarding the futures of cultures are generally expressed in questions such as these: Will economic and technological progress destroy the cultural diversity and bastardize our cultures? Will we witness a return of intolerant chauvinism that would make cultures retreat to their shells? Will there be a judicious fit between the old and the new? Where are we going? Can we change the course?

Those who take the pessimistic view of the future of cultures feel that all cultures will lose their pristine nature through hybridization and will be reduced to their ornamental roles. The optimists, on the other hand, feel that cultural communities will plunge into their indigenous roots and come up with their own recipes for survival and advancement. Alongside of social activists, several of us in the profession have adopted the role of 'preservationists'. Their guiding motto is: 'preserve', 'protect' and 'renovate'. 'Change' does not exist in their vocabulary; Culture, to them, is a mere museum of tradition. Their protests against culture contacts notwithstanding, what has happened even in regard to the tribal groups the world over is quite astonishing: no tribe has remained completely *insulated* from the outside world maintaining its pristine, exotic existence, and many of the material cultural traits of various non-Western societies have travelled far and wide to become showpieces in modern drawing rooms.

Anthropological literature exhibits a peculiar ambivalence towards 'change'. Interestingly enough, whatever we have by way of literature on culture–development interface[8] is mainly anecdotal. There are narrations of stories of (mainly) failures highlighting the importance of the cultural factors. But no guidelines exist as to how to plan a change that will not meet a failure. Similarly, the planners have also not yet improved their planning protocol to incorporate the cultural variable in the planning process to ensure that it will not cause hindrance. We all recognize that there is a cultural dimension to development but we feel ill-equipped to handle it. One may ask: does disappearance of certain cultural traits amount to the destruction of a culture? If the answer is in the affirmative, then we may pose the question: how does culture grow? Or, is culture just another name for the deadwood? I would submit the point that changes occurring in the ambit of culture do not always erase its identity; it may, however, confuse its identification. Accretion and attrition are the processes that operate in all living cultures. That is how cultures grow and express their vitality.

ANTHROPOLOGY TODAY AND TOMORROW

Anthropology of today should change its course to answer the questions of tomorrow. Rather than remain clogged in the past it must move towards the frontiers of future.

Notes

1 This was to forestall the objections of some puritans. In fact, one of them called him, in an essay written long after Dube's death, 'a self-selected anthropologist'.
2 See *Understanding Indian Society*, edited by Yogesh Atal, p. 42.
3 Before 1957, Sagar University had a joint department named Anthropo-geography headed by a British. In 1957, it was split into two independent Departments of Anthropology and Geography. Professor Dube was the first incumbent of the newly created Department of Anthropology.
4 Now renamed as NIRD – National Institute of Rural Development.
5 Edited by Michael Banton and published by Tavistock in 1966.
6 S.C. Dube, *Social Sciences in Changing Society: D. N. Majumdar Memorial Lectures 1972*, Ethnographic and Folk Culture Society, Lucknow, 1973, p. 49.
7 Without affecting the percentage.
8 See, for example, Yogesh Atal, ed., *Culture-Development Interface*, New Delhi, Vikas Publishing House, 1991.

2

DEFINING 'TRIBE'

A conceptual crisis[1]

Preliminaries

Time and again I have reiterated the need to reorient our approaches and perspectives. Old theories and their attendant concepts are gradually losing their utility. Their proclaimed universality is being challenged by the emerging structures and patterns, and changing social structures. Such a situation demands not only more refined conceptual frameworks but also better informed perspectives to make meaningful analyses and offer doable prescriptions to the policymakers and planners.

I take this opportunity to elaborate my deep concern over the issue of the definition of Tribe. And in doing so, I shall like to take you to a brief sojourn in the past of the discipline of anthropology so that you can appreciate the urgent need for the rethink of the paradigm. I suspect that most of the speakers at this Seminar might have not felt the need for such an exercise. In fact, in their enthusiasm for the so-called poor and backward brethren, they might come up with easily acceptable recipes and prescriptions in the old mode of thinking. Hopefully, my presentation would shake up this complacence.

I

The birth of anthropology in the second-half of the nineteenth century was in a way necessitated by colonialism and its growth was facilitated by the Industrial Revolution. Described as general anthropology, it included physical anthropology, prehistoric anthropology and social or cultural anthropology with due accommodation in it of philosophical and psychological anthropology. As Max Gluckman and Fred Eggan admitted in their *Introduction* to the four-volume ASA monographs (edited by Michael Banton and published by Tavistock in 1966),

> by the 1930s the different disciplines were beginning to separate from one another. . . . [And as] each anthropological discipline separated out, its practitioners turned to other subjects. . . . Physical anthropologists depended more on the biological sciences; psychological anthropologists . . . on psychology . . . and psychiatry; and social anthropologists on sociology, history, political science, law and economics. Cultural anthropologists alone continued to draw on the biological, psychological, and sociological sciences. (1966: xi)

When my generation entered the university to specialize in anthropology in India, the orientation of general anthropology continued in the sense that we had to offer papers in prehistory, archaeology and physical anthropology; we also learnt serology, anthropometry, dermatoglyphics and even photography. Hooton's *Up from the Ape* and Grey's magnum opus, *Anatomy*, were compulsory reading even for those specializing in *social* anthropology. The senior batch of students in our department of anthropogeography was taken by the then professor Lt. Col. G. R. Gyre[2] to the Bastar region in Central India to give them direct exposure to tribal life, and the geographical milieu of their settlement.[3] It was then believed that no one could claim to be an anthropologist who has not studied the tribes.

But things began changing. While the focus on the tribes continued, the scope of the discipline was extended to cover the communities constituting part of rural India. We were directed to conduct field work in the villages. Thus, both Tribal India and rural India became the subject matter of anthropological studies.

Specializations did exist in the departments, and laboratories for anthropological research became part of the infrastructure. But as we grew in the profession, separation between physical and social anthropology began occurring on a large scale. Those of us specializing in social anthropology were naturally getting exposed to other social sciences, especially sociology; our work on Village India brought us closer to rural sociologists, and caught the attention of the policymakers and planners who were engaged in the massive programme of community development. The changes that occurred in post-independent India began erasing the distinction between the tribal and rural regions. The tribal habitats began transforming into urban and rural, and the size

DEFINING 'TRIBE': A CONCEPTUAL CRISIS

and number of groups living in the so-called tribal – meaning remote – areas began shrinking.

At that time, the so-called puritans in anthropology treated us – social anthropologists exploring non-tribal territories – as 'defectors', and the puritans in sociology regarded us as 'intruders' into their area of investigation. Social anthropologists did not, however, use any derogatory term, in retort, for the physical anthropologists who were going down from Humans to Lemurs and Langoors, or moving closer to biological sciences. I am also not sure whether they were regarded as 'intruders' in those disciplines. The decades of 1960s and 1970s were characterized by discussions and debates on such separation and defections. It was heartening for us that some of the prominent social anthropologists were held as sociologists of international renown. I must confess that I do not oppose to any such tag – sociologist or anthropologist – attached to me. In fact, I am quite comfortable when people introduce me as a social scientist.

However, as I see the professional demography of the departments of anthropology today in India, I come to the rather dismal conclusion that the separation between its various branches, due to over-specialization, has led to a relative neglect of social anthropology. Recently when I was invited by the vice chancellor of a prestigious university – where I was the first to start teaching social anthropology in the early 1960s – to address the staff and students of anthropology department, I noticed that the physical anthropology staff virtually boycotted the event. There are also departments in other universities where social anthropology is taught by outsiders hired on a lecture-to-lecture basis. A discipline that grew out of an interdisciplinary coalition of ideas and got the distinction of being specialist on tribal studies is now caged in its own web. Its greater affinity to biological sciences is distancing it from the study of those societies that were uniquely their domain.

I say this not to undermine the new signposts in the long journey of this discipline. Social anthropology has moved from the study of small and simple societies to the study of complex societies and civilizations. It is contributing its bit to the newly developing management sciences. What is worrying is that in the process it has virtually given up its old concern, namely the focus on the tribes – and this applies to both physical and social anthropologists. I might also add that this hiatus is being filled by specialists from other disciplines – political science, public administration, economics and geography, for example. One also notices a new development. In Arunachal Pradesh – a state in the North-East consisting mostly of tribal people – has now a Central

26

DEFINING 'TRIBE': A CONCEPTUAL CRISIS

University which has three separate departments, namely Anthropology, Sociology and Tribal Studies – all focussing primarily on the tribes. I am told that all the three departments carry out researches amongst the tribes! and yet the departments are headed by an anthropologist, a sociologist and an economist (he is now replaced by a linguist), respectively. Thus, tribes are now being studied by three different, yet overlapping, perspectives. And the subject matter, namely the tribes, no longer corresponds to the stereotypical image of their being primitive, remotely located and exotic, although their distinctive cultural identities are still maintained. Arunachal Pradesh has twenty-four tribal groups and yet they belong to a common state and a common nation. The state is now pluri-tribal.

A shift in the orientation of social anthropology is, certainly, not attributable solely to the increasing dominance of physical anthropology. The changes that are occurring in the tribal societies and the new challenges for application of anthropology to other areas of social interaction are equally responsible for the changing character of anthropology – both physical and social.

II

As anthropology began its journey it came to be defined as the study of the 'past' and the 'primitive'. Evolutionary theories of the nineteenth century raised questions about the Origin of Man, and the voyages to distant lands facilitated by the Industrial Revolution of the times exposed the scholars to a variety of flora and fauna. The early encounters with the simple people, living exotic cultures, intrigued the scholars. Comparing them with their own culture they regarded them as 'primitive' and placed them at the lower rungs of the evolutionary ladder. The 'present' of these 'primitive' societies was regarded as some stage of their own 'past'. George Peter Murdock called them *Our Primitive Contemporaries*.[4] Such a conceptualization gave strength to the colonial regimes to justify their rule by using the twin criteria offered by Darwin, namely *Survival of the Fittest* and *Struggle for Existence* in his well-known book *On the Origin of Species*. Apart from such justification, the colonialists also wanted to understand their 'culture' – in the anthropological sense of 'way of life' – to be able to better administer them; and thus anthropology came to be defined as the study of 'other cultures'. At that time, ethnographies paid more attention to description, and less to theorizing. Ethnology, on the other hand, adopted the path of comparison and classification;

27

in doing so, both the ethnographers and the ethnologists almost took the definition of the Tribe for granted and refined constituent concepts related to family, kinship, religion, magic etc.

With the end of colonial era and the growing *Globalization* and *Information Revolution*, a new orientation for anthropology is now in order. The focus is shifting from the past to the present and to the future; and the processes of Westernization, Modernization and now of Globalization have brought in remarkable changes in the profiles of all cultures – primitive or modern. Ethnographies written in the idiom of 'eternal present' have become dated, and the tribal societies that were the subject matter of anthropology demand a new diction and a new grammar for their reportage. There is a demand for a definition of society that is universally applicable to all societies – be they modern or primitive, living or dead. And in that definition, the definition of the prefix 'Tribal' is being sought.

This is what I call re-invitation to anthropology. It is a call to revisit its original interest and to contribute to the understanding of the change occurring in them. We must remember that whatever might be the private – that is internal to the discipline – image of ours, the public image of anthropology still remains the same, namely the specialized study of the tribes.

The need to return to tribes was felt in Indian anthropology even in the 1970s. As Director of the Indian Council of Social Science Research, I convened a group to identify priorities for research in the field of anthropology. The group expressed its concern over the diminishing interest in the study of tribes, and also underlined the need for restudies as old ethnographies did not match the emerging profiles of several tribal cultures in India.

But not much was added in the subsequent years to our literature on the tribes from an anthropological perspective, although scholars belonging to other social science disciplines also began taking interest in them, thus breaking the monopoly of anthropology.

III

Why the need to return to the Tribes? This is a legitimate question. Let me answer that question briefly in the Indian context.

When the Constitution for independent India was being drafted, the Constituent Assembly agreed, after a long discussion, that there is a need for special provisions for the so-called oppressed castes (a British coinage for the Census to lump together all the castes that

DEFINING 'TRIBE': A CONCEPTUAL CRISIS

were regarded as having a lower rank in the religious hierarchy of castes, and were considered as victims of oppression by the castes of the higher *Varna*). There was a lack of unanimity initially on inclusion of such a provision in the Constitution, but finally it was agreed that such groups may be given special privileges for the first few years. It was then agreed that two schedules be prepared, one for the tribes, and the other for the so-called oppressed castes – the adjective was first used by the Census authorities.

Although it was a temporary measure, politics of the latter days made it difficult to withdraw such a provision. The consequence has been in the form of not only continued postponement of the provision, but rising demand from many groups to be included in the special categories of the Scheduled Tribes (STs) and Scheduled Castes (SCs). In fact, to satiate the demands of many others who did not qualify for any of the abovementioned two categories, a new category of 'Other Backward Classes' was created. For this purpose, a commission was set up under the chairmanship of Kaka Kalelkar.

However, the demand for inclusion in the category of ST or SC by some groups has continuously been rising. Some have succeeded in getting such a status. Others are still agitating for it.

The most recent instance of such a demand is that of the Gujjars of Rajasthan seeking the status of a Scheduled Tribe. The demand was first raised in 1961, but it took a violent turn 20 years later, in 1981, and led to massive campaigns and huge rallies in the first decade of this century with horrifying incidents of violent clashes and death of agitators and policemen in the confrontations. While Gujjars demanded a tribal status, those already included in the tribal category strongly opposed this move. Others in the general public remained either neutral or joined one of the two camps.

It is in this context that the need was felt to create defining criteria for judging the admissibility of new claimants to any of the three categories. While the admissibility in the SC and OBC categories were somewhat simpler,[5] problems arose in the case of a claim for the tribal status by a new group not earlier considered as a Tribe.

The Constitution of Indian Republic, thus, recognizes the existence of tribes and has a Schedule listing them for special treatment to facilitate their entry into the mainstream and enjoy the fruits of development. While taking this step, hailed by all as a well-intentioned policy, little attention was paid to the definition of the word 'Tribe'. Perhaps the need was not felt as tribes were listed in the Censuses since 1891. The 1931 Census – regarded as the last Census that had enumerated population by caste – has listed 'Primitive Tribes'; the list of 1935 talks of 'Backward Tribes'. Lifting these entries the Government of India prepared the Schedule in accordance with the new Constitution, and included all tribal groups without any exception, thus erasing a distinction between a Tribe and a Scheduled Tribe.

It must be said that the Census authorities of the British times recognized that already many tribal groups were converting into other religions and felt the need to separate them from those who still remain animists. It is such groups living in remote areas and practising animism that were described as primitive and backward. While the generic name continued for all such groups, statistics for each such subgroup was separately tabulated and presented in 1921 and 1931 Censuses.

Thus, Bhils of Rajasthan, for example, were classified into Christian, Hindus, Jain, Muslims and Tribals; similarly, Garasia (गरा

सिया) and Mina (मीणा) were classified into Hindu, Muslim and Tribals, the implication being that those who have opted for another religion have moved to the non-tribal category. Only the non-converts were called the tribals.

This classification changed their demographic profile, as is shown in Table 2.1.

It is reported that in 1931 Census, more than 76 per cent of all Bhils were returned as Hindus as against 19 per cent at the previous Census, conducted in 1921. It is interesting that in all the three groups, namely Bhil, Garasia and Meena, the size of the tribal population was reduced substantially because of the entry of its members into other religious groups. Only 3.35 per cent of the Meenas, numbering 20,336, were returned as 'tribals'. Among the other two groups, the percentage of those that remained tribal came down to 23.62 (Bhils) and 24.10 (Garasias), respectively. It was a retrograde step but now this distinction has been erased and the entire ethnic group bearing the common name has been redesignated as a Tribe. This is denial of the process of assimilation

Table 2.1 Proportion of non-converts in key ethnic groups in Rajasthan 1931 Census

Ethnic group	Total population	Tribal segment	% tribal
Bhil	655,647	198,005	23.62
Garasia	29,231	8,258	24.10
Mina/Meena	607,369	20,336	3.35

DEFINING 'TRIBE': A CONCEPTUAL CRISIS

identified by the Census of 1931 in the following words: 'Bhils are practically all found in Mewar and the Southern states. In spite of a hazy tradition that they originally came from the North, they are really among the earliest inhabitants of this part of the Agency and in the more accessible localities are rapidly becoming Hinduised'. What is more striking is the fact that the Meenas who were treated as residual tribals, constituting a meagre 3.35 per cent in 1931 population, regained a tribal status for the entire population known by the generic name Meena. Even the traditional distinction between *Jagirdaar* Meena and *Chowkidar* eena was erased in post-independence India. It is this fact that enraged the Gujjars of Rajasthan who demanded identical treatment. While they accentuated their demand by seeking a tribal status for all, the latent agenda was to seek ouster of the Meenas from the tribal category on grounds of identical status. The Gujjars also became fiefs and kings of small territories, although they entered the Indian territory at different times as shepherds and cowherds from the Middle East and Eastern Europe.

A peculiar thing happened in case of Uttar Pradesh where no ST groups were listed initially, but later the Khasa of Jaunsar-Bawar, and the Gonds and Cheros of Mirzapur District have been included in the Schedule meant for the Tribes. Incidentally, the Gonds are regarded as Tribes and found in many states – Madhya Pradesh, Chhattisgarh, Jharkhand, Uttar Pradesh and Andhra Pradesh – but they are now treated as separate tribes in terms of administrative and constitutional definition. The Khasas of Jaunsar-Bawar are an exclusive group and anthropologists had been studying them as a tribe practising polyandry, but the then chief minister of Uttar Pradesh insisted on non-inclusion of any of its endogamous groups as tribes. The practice of polyandry among the Khasas was comparable to the instance in the Hindu Epic *Mahabharat* where the five Pandav brothers shared a common wife, Draupadi. This was an instance to deny the practice of polyandry as a 'tribal practice'. It is much later that the Khasas are now accorded a tribal status.

The proliferation of the number of Tribes in the ST category is, thus, partly a consequence of this policy and partly of admitting additional groups heeding to their demand for a tribal status; these included not only the Muslim converts but also castes, thereby ignoring the fine distinction made in the Constitution under Article 366(25). Granting of tribal status to Muslim Gujjars of Jammu and Kashmir in the late twentieth century is a glaring example of undermining the provision of the Constitution. This political act encouraged the Gujjars of Rajasthan to intensify their agitation for the tribal status. It is interesting

31

to note that while Gujjar leaders from other states offered support to their agitating brethren in Rajasthan, they themselves have not opted for this route.

The definitional crisis emerged when some of the communities which hitherto were considered as a 'caste' and which functioned as a caste unit in multi-caste settings of the village and the region began seeking admission in the category of Tribe. The provisions of reservation and special privileges granted to STs and SCs instigated a reverse process of returning to the roots and of preferring to have the tag of the 'primitive'.

Technically speaking, considered as a transitory category in social evolution, a tribe can only move out and become a subsystem of a broader group, but cannot return to the earlier stage of evolution.

Let me allude to the Indian Constitution in this regard.

The Constitution has made the provision for declaration of the Scheduled Tribes in Article 342 which reads as under:

Article 342 of the Indian Constitution:

(1) The President may with respect to any State or Union territory, and where it is a State, after consultation with the Governor, thereof, by public notification, specify the tribes or tribal communities or part or groups within tribes or tribal communities which shall for the purposes of this Constitution be deemed to be Scheduled Tribes in relation to that State or Union territory, as the case may be.

(2) Parliament may by law include in or exclude from the list of Scheduled Tribes specified in a notification issued under clause (1) any tribe or tribal community or part of group within any tribe or tribal community, but save as aforesaid a notification issued under the said clause shall not be varied by any subsequent notification.

Article 366 (25) defines the Schedule Tribes as follows:

'Scheduled Tribe' means such Tribes or Tribal committees or parts of groups within such Tribes or Tribal committees as are deemed under article 342 to be Scheduled Tribe for the purposes of this Constitution.

This is a tautological definition, as it does not specifically mention the qualifying characteristics other than the provisions of Article 342.

DEFINING 'TRIBE': A CONCEPTUAL CRISIS

Compared to this, Article 366(24) defines the Scheduled Castes as follows:

'Scheduled Castes' means such castes, races or tribes or parts of or groups within such castes, races or tribes as are deemed under article 341 to be Scheduled Castes for the purposes of this Constitution.[6]

When the officialdom was asked to draw the first list of tribes for inclusion in the Schedule the distinction of 'primitive' or 'backward' was conveniently ignored and the entire group bearing the tribal name was included.

It is important to note that there is no indigenous word for *tribe* in any of the Indian languages. In Sanskrit, there is a word *Aatavika Jana* [आटविक् जन] – meaning *Banvasi* or forest dwellers – which was used to denote agglomeration of individuals with specific territorial, kinship and cultural patterns. Prior to the colonial period, they were also commonly referred to as a *Jati* [जाति] – caste. But the colonial administration began calling them tribes, and differentiated them from the other groups on the basis of animism. In this category, some food gathering groups and shifting cultivators were also included, though they lived closer to the villages. In the decennial censuses, they were first called 'forest tribes'. In the 1931 Census, they were named as 'primitive tribes'. In 1935, the British began calling them as 'backward tribes'.

IV

When societies were classified into civilized and uncivilized – as savage or barbaric – the question of defining Tribe did not arise. All uncivilized societies were *preliterate*, implying the absence of writing in them. That meant that the transmission of culture was through oral tradition, and the history of the society went as far back as human memory could take it. Beyond this was prehistory. With absence of history, oral transmission of society's knowledge pool to the younger generation, elementary technology and greater dependence on nature for survival and faith in the supernatural described their way of life. Living in small hordes, and unaware of the world outside the narrow confines of the community, the geographically and socially isolated communities defined themselves as residents of a given territory, and as belonging to a specific racial stock. Such groups became the subject matter of study of the anthropologists who came to these societies as a

33

consequence of colonization. In this sense, tribals were also described as non-Western cultures.

Problems arose when countries like India were colonized. Described as an indigenous civilization, India got divided into the civilized and uncivilized sections, but belonging to the non-Western part of human civilization. In India, the original inhabitants got pushed into the remote tribal tracts by the groups that migrated from abroad at different phases of its history – as nomads and pastoralists, as invaders who became conquerors of parts of the vast territory of India. Many such groups who came from the Middle East, Eastern Europe and Mongolia came as adventurers or nomads and gradually got assimilated with the local populace. This involved initial confrontation, accommodation and finally integration into the main stream. Historians of the nineteenth century – mostly foreign, and primarily administrators or military officers of the Raj – called all such migrating groups as tribes – because of their common origin and a distinct identity. But they also acknowledged the process of their gradual assimilation into the Hindu fold.

What was happening to the original inhabitants – the *Adivasis* – in terms of cultural contact resulting into so-called Hinduization (also conversion to Islam and Christianity) was also happening to other communities that arrived later from abroad. There may be different stories about their place of origin, but all authorities agree that they arrived in India before the Mughals and spread to different parts of the country and even conquered the territories which they ruled. During the course of history regimes changed due to internecine wars and outside invasions. And the migrating communities settled in different parts, adopting local cultures, contributing to them some of their own cultural traits, including religious beliefs and practices. They were also treated as a 'caste' in multi-caste villages where most of them have settled as agriculturists, along with the pursuit of their hereditary occupation as graziers/herdsmen. In Southern Rajasthan, a group/caste of Gairies (spelt as GAYARY) is known for herding sheep and goats. Gujjars also have their herds along with cattle. It is believed that those Gujjars who remained shepherds became, in due course of time, a different caste of Gadaria or Giary, and the Gujjars took to cultivation. But both are settled agriculturists without the characteristic of transhumance. Going by the 1931 Census definition, they are the castes, despite difficulties of fitting them into the Varna scheme. Sociologists and anthropologists have long acknowledged the point that caste hierarchy in traditional terms is not possible. Both attributional and interactional theories of caste ranking are employed by them in specific village contexts to get an

DEFINING 'TRIBE': A CONCEPTUAL CRISIS

idea of the village social stratification. The practice of child marriage, widow remarriage (*Nata*) and bride price are common to all castes that belong to lower ladders of caste hierarchy. Caste Panchayats are also a common feature of all castes, and not just of the Gujjars. So is the case with death feasts and elaborate eschatological rituals.

Commenting on the situation in the 1930s, J. H. Hutton wrote:

> It will be understood then that one important function of Caste, perhaps the most important of all functions, and the one which above all others makes caste in India an unique institution, is, or has been, to integrate Indian society, to weld into one community the various competing if not incompatible groups composing it. Some of these groups have been occupational or religious. Others, and this is more important, have been national, political and tribal societies that must otherwise have either been absorbed and transformed or remained as unadjusted and possibly subversive elements. Generally speaking, conquered peoples and their conquerors blend into one society in which one or other element may in the long run predominate.
>
> (Hutton, 1961: 119)

If one were to look at the internal structure of caste and a tribal group, one would find considerable similarity. Both are endogamous and both have internal divisions that are exogamous – call them *gotra* (गोत्र), or clan, or a cluster of clans such as *phratry* or *moiety*. What distinguishes them is the fact that the tribe is a systemic whole while a caste is a *unit* of the wider social system – more appropriately a caste system or *Jati vyavastha* (जाति व्यवस्था). Generally speaking, a tribe is not further divided into endogamous groups, whereas caste system consists of a number of castes that are endogamous and these interact with other groups within the system. It is only hierarchy in the religious sphere that makes their positions higher or lower, or similar. Just as the Hindus have four *Varnas* (चतुर्वर्ण) in which a number of endogamous groups called castes (*Jatis* जातियां) are located, the Muslims are also divided not only as Shia and Sunni, but also as Syed, Sheikh, Mughal and Pathan. Not only these groups are endogamous among the Muslims, endogamy among them is so strong that the circle of preferred marriages is reduced to the parental family as they allow not only cross-cousin but also parallel cousin marriages, and marriages between mother's brother (MoBr) and sister's daughter (SiDa). The converts to Christianity and to Islam from the Hindu fold have carried

DEFINING 'TRIBE': A CONCEPTUAL CRISIS

their caste with them and they continue to practise endogamy at that level. These facts suggest that caste as a structural category is not confined to the Hindus only; also, while caste may be characteristic of a pan-Hindu culture, effective caste functions at the regional level. People bearing the same caste name, or practising the same traditional occupation, but belonging to other regions, constitute separate endogamous groups. Of course, such insulation is now breaking and fresh marital apertures are being created.

One consequence of increasing interaction between communities and regions and the developing phenomenon of co-living in the same habitat has been the transformation of a section of the tribal community into a caste like unity in the village social structure.

It is also to be noted that a caste is a horizontal unity joining several villages of the vicinage in northern India. While a village is defined as a vertical unity of several castes, it may be noted that any caste in a given village is represented by only a few families and most of which are lineally related, and that is the reason that village exogamy is observed; but that is not observed in a town or city where a caste may be represented by several clans and lineages.

It is important to note that while the definition of scheduled caste in the Indian Constitution specifically mentions that 'the castes, races or tribes or parts of or groups within castes, races or tribes' could be notified for inclusion in the category of Scheduled Castes, the scope for eligibility in the category of Scheduled Tribes is limited only to 'the tribes or tribal communities or part or groups within tribes or tribal communities'. Implicit in the formulation is the point that those groups that were included in the category of tribes in the Census of 1931 and in the following decennial censuses qualify for inclusion in the category of Scheduled Tribes.

In such circumstances, the definition of tribe is indeed problematic. There is merit in Lokur Committee's remark that in India the 'tribes are in transition'. Some social anthropologists called it a Tribe-Caste Continuum. Hutton said that the Tribal religion in India is that which has not yet been built into the temple of Hinduism.

All acknowledge that the Constitution has refrained from giving a definition of the concept of 'Tribe'. Scholars in social sciences have begun accepting those included in the List of Scheduled Tribes as a Tribe, without bothering whether it meets sociological criteria or not. That is administrative convenience. Wrong judgements by the state governments in hurriedly furnishing lists for inclusion in the ST and SC categories have created several anomalies, and these were tried to be

DEFINING 'TRIBE': A CONCEPTUAL CRISIS

corrected through appointment of various committees. Even the criteria evolved for judging the eligibility of a group for a tribal status are vague. Following five criteria are given for eligibility:

1 Indication of primitive traits.
2 Distinctive culture.
3 Geographical isolation.
4 Shyness of contact with the larger community.
5 Backwardness.

It appears that the basic distinction, as is made in the context of USA, Australia and New Zealand, between the tribals and the non-tribals is the criterion of 'indigeneity'. The tribals are the indigenous people, also known as 'autochthonous'. During the debates of the Constituent Assembly – drafting the Constitution of the Republic of India – a tribal leader, Jaipal Singh, asked President Rajendra Prasad:

I wish that you would issue instructions to your Translation Committee that the translation of Scheduled Tribes should be Adivasi (meaning original inhabitants or indigenous peoples). The word Adivasi has a grace. . . . Why this old abusive epithet of Banjati (forest dwellers) being used.

Even the SC&ST Commission, in its 1961 Report, stated that Scheduled Tribes are known as indigenous peoples under international law. There are people who believe that the word 'primitive' is antithetical to the universally recognized principles of dignity for, and equality of, all human beings. These problems notwithstanding, the AnSI prepared an initial list of 6,748 communities in India. Of these, 461 were tribal, having 172 segments, comprising 8.1 per cent of the total population of the country. This number is much larger than the original figure of 212 given in the 1951 Census when the tribal population constituted around 6 per cent of the Indian population. These have created several anomalies.

Let us examine each of the criteria employed by the government in determining the status of a group as a tribe.

Objectively speaking, the first criterion – namely indication of primitive traits – is broad enough to cover all the other criteria: the primitives are those who have a distinct culture of their own, live in relative isolation and, therefore, fight shy of contacts with the outsiders, and, as a consequence of their isolation, they have remained

37

backward. What, then, are the additional 'primitive' characteristics to be included in the first criterion?

Primitiveness of a community is a comparative term, as it is opposed to modernity – yet another term which is variously defined. Broadly speaking, primitiveness indicates the lingering state of backwardness of a group and its inability to catch up with the mainstream in terms of socio-economic development. Primitiveness may be attributed to lack of education, narrow worldview or a *Weltanschauung*, ethnocentrism, cultural prejudices, lifestyle and socio-economic inequities. No present-day society, however backward and underdeveloped, fits the nineteenth-century stereotype of a 'primitive', Stone Age culture. Construction of approach roads, opening of schools, use of modern means of agriculture (such as tractors, chemical fertilizers), use of national currency for monetary transactions replacing barter and even the use of radio transistors, and now the mobile phones, have changed the material cultural profile of the so-called primitive communities. What then are the key component variables of the concept 'Primitive'?

The same is the difficulty with the concept of 'Distinct Culture'. Can one not argue that the primitiveness, as implied in the first criterion, will result in a distinct culture? Also, a distinct culture does not always have to be primitive.

The criterion of 'Geographical Isolation' is also untenable. With increasing connectivity caused by tremendous improvements in the area of transportation and communication, there are a few islands of relative isolation with difficulty of access. Revolutionary changes brought about by advances in Information Technology have broken the communication barriers and reduced isolation. Democratic governance in the country has greatly contributed to the breakdown of isolation. The electoral process involves campaigning by various candidates in their respective constituencies including the village communities that are otherwise not regularly contacted. Such contacts not only break geographical isolation but also help enlarge cognitive horizons of the common people. They come to know of political parties, leaders and political issues. And they are also dragged into the political process either as fellow campaigners or as candidates for posts in different legislative bodies and local self-governments, such as Panchayat *Samitis* and Panchayats or co-operative societies. No doubt, geography still hinders effective interaction in some areas, but the situation is vastly different from the days when savagery and barbarism perpetuated because of lack of contact. Today, even the tribes have been politicized. In the North-East, the country had to face separatist movements led by

DEFINING 'TRIBE': A CONCEPTUAL CRISIS

the indigenous people. Support is sought and is given to the Naxalites by members of several tribal communities in Central India. While such acts damage the prospects of national unity and integration, they are indicative of their political participation and breakdown of seclusion.

No groups fight 'shy of contact' with others. Of course, shyness as a social norm of courtesy towards elders, or amongst people of opposite sex, is not to be confused with shyness that was exhibited by the people living in the non-civilized world when they were confronted with the outsiders – colonial rulers or the research investigators. That is a matter of past. Sale of rural products, such as dairy items and cash crops in urban markets, by these claimants of tribal status clearly indicates the entry of these people in the regional economy.

It is the concept of Backwardness that seems, however, to provide a dependable list of variables for developing a suitable index. But this might as well apply to many other non-tribal village communities. Backwardness is either an attribute of a *territorial* community or of individual families within it, and not of any *biotic* community. There are tribal areas in the North-East which are urban, and there are many individuals belonging to the so-called tribal groups in other regions in Central India who have excelled in business, academics or politics.

These have created several anomalies. Bakarwal Gujjars studied prior to 1991 were studied as a nomadic Muslim caste in Jammu and Kashmir, but now they have been designated as a Scheduled Tribe. The Rabari are a Scheduled Tribe in Gujarat and is included in the category of 'Other Backward Classes' in Rajasthan. The old state of Hyderabad did not recognize Yenadis, Yerukulas and Sugalis as tribes, but Andhra State recognized them. Similarly, Gaddis are treated as an ST, but in Punjab they are recognized as a tribe only in the scheduled areas but they do not live in such areas.

It was in response to the criticism that the lists of SCs and STs were not rational and had several anomalies that the Government of India set up in June 1965 a three-member committee under the chairmanship of Mr B. N. Lokur (other members were A. D. Pandey and N. Sundaram) to advise the government on the proposals received for revising the 'existing lists' of SCs and STs; and to advise whether 'where a caste or a tribe is listed as SC or ST in relation to a particular area in a State or a Union Territory, members of that Caste or Tribe residing (i) in other areas within the same state or Union Territory, (ii) in other States or Union Territories should be recognized as belonging to Scheduled Caste or Scheduled tribe'. It will thus be seen that the Lokur Committee was not asked to furnish a fresh definition of the

DEFINING 'TRIBE': A CONCEPTUAL CRISIS

tribe. It was to examine the historical and 'scientific' background of over 800 tribal communities and caste groups and assessment of their social, educational and economic conditions with a view 'to determining their eligibility to be specified in the lists of Scheduled Castes and Scheduled Tribes'. All this huge task by a team of three persons was performed within three months of the constitution of the Committee! Despite the quick job the Committee had done – the credibility of which can be questioned – the Committee made one significant observation:

> In considering fresh proposals for inclusion in the list, it was noted that care was necessary in drawing up the schedule in order to ensure that communities which had been assimilated in the general population were not at this stage invested with an artificial distinctiveness as tribes, and that communities which might be regarded as tribes by reason of their social organization and general way of life but which were really not primitive should not now be treated as primitive.

In fact, the Lokur Committee noted that 'even the social scientists have found it difficult to evolve a universally acceptable definition of a Tribe'. Moreover, the problem in case of India is more complex because here the 'tribes are in Transition'. In para 12, it said: 'We have considered that tribes whose members have by and large mixed up with the general population are not eligible to be in the list of Scheduled Tribes'. The Lokur Committee had taken note of the fact that the special privileges granted to these groups have created a vested interest in them to remain classified as 'backward'.

Some observations made by the Lokur Committee in this regard are important to be reproduced here:

1. In several States, we have come across a multitude of organizations of castes and tribes, a few even at the all India level, whose main object is to secure a place in the lists of Scheduled Castes and Scheduled Tribes. The motivation for the growth of such organizations arises from what may be called the very attractive 'package deal' of special facilities and benefits that are provided for communities included in the Schedules. (para 13)

2. It has been in evidence for some time that a lion's share of the various benefits and concessions earmarked for the

DEFINING 'TRIBE': A CONCEPTUAL CRISIS

> Scheduled Castes and Scheduled Tribes is appropriated by the numerically larger and politically well organized communities. The smaller and more backward communities have tended to get lost in democratic processes, though most deserving of the special aid. (para 14)
>
> 3 While we appreciate the necessity of providing special assistance for the uplift of the Scheduled Castes and Scheduled Tribes until they rise to the average stratum of society, we regret to note that the listing of these castes and tribes has more or less created vested interests and has tended to damp to some extent personal effort and enterprise to improve one's position and fortune. Inclusion in the lists is regarded more as a coveted prize than as a reflection of backwardness. (para 15)
>
> 4 . . . prominent social workers, political leaders outside the fold of Scheduled Castes and Scheduled Tribes and a large number of officials . . . asserted that . . . the time has come to do away gradually with these privileged classes, particularly in view of the increasing demand for inclusion therein, and to organize development schemes without reference to castes and tribes . . . that the emphasis should be on the gradual elimination of the larger and more advanced communities from these lists, and on focusing greater attention on the really backward sections, preferably by applying an economic yardstick. (para 15)

The Draft Tribal Policy Statement, released sometime in 2007, also says:

> Not only is the number of individual tribes scheduled under the Constitution quite large (standing today at 700 State specific Scheduled Tribes), but also because the heterogeneity is immense. Each tribe is distinct from the other with, usually, separate languages and dialects, customs and cultural practices and life styles. . . . Despite this diversity, tribal communities do have similarities, though broad generic ones. They are known to dwell in compact areas, follow a community way of living in harmony with nature, and have a uniqueness of culture, distinctive customs and traditions, and beliefs which are simple, direct and non-acquisitive by nature.[7]

DEFINING 'TRIBE': A CONCEPTUAL CRISIS

The Policy statement also said that 'the backwardness of tribal areas is partially due to their geographical isolation due to the *rugged, mountainous and forested terrain* of the major tribal areas of the plateau and the North East. The social and physical infrastructure in the tribal areas is inadequate and at a much lower level than the rest of the areas. Moreover, the data which is available for the state as a whole or district-wise gives a misleading picture, as it does not reflect the very skewed distribution within the districts/State. There are extremely backward ST areas within States witnessing high growth rates'.

The key question that is behind such agitations is the very definition of the word Tribe and its distinction from Caste. It was natural that people looked towards anthropology for an authoritative response. Sadly enough, the discipline had no firm answer to provide. It is intriguing that in all the commissions and committees set up by the Government of India from Kaka Kalelkar in 1950s to B. P. Mandal in the 1980s, no anthropologist or sociologist was ever appointed as a full member. The Mandal Commission did take the assistance of Professor M. N. Srinivas, but it was only for designing a questionnaire! He was treated as an expert and not a member of the Commission.

The Mandal Commission issued three questionnaires, one each for the state governments, central ministries and departments and the general public; the latter questionnaire was published in leading English and vernacular papers of each state, and also widely distributed in meetings held during the Commission's tour to various states. However, the response was quite poor. Only 1,872 questionnaires were received back from the public. The Commission received 2,638 representations from public men and voluntary organizations. The Commission visited 84 district headquarters, but went only to 37 villages![8] In all, 171 meetings were held where the Commission heard the views of the interested parties. In addition, a panel of 15 experts prepared a research design for the country-wide socio-educational field survey. For this survey the panel recommended '1% purposive sample of villages at district level'. But in view of the limitations of time, this plan had to be dropped and instead '100% coverage of two villages and one urban block in each district of the country was considered to be quite adequate' (p. 55). Thus, the survey covered three settlements each from 405 districts, making a total of 1,215 settlements.

The consequences of the Mandal Report are there in front of us. People challenging these reports signified their dissent on the definition on the one hand, and registered their protest against the policy of reservation, on the other.

DEFINING 'TRIBE': A CONCEPTUAL CRISIS

Over the years, the number of tribes listed in the Schedule has burgeoned to more than 700, although the percentage of population covered by ST category is around 8, not much different from the 1951 figure, taking cognizance of the fact of population growth. This increase in number of tribal communities, I must mention, is mainly caused by state-wise recognition of the tribal groups – in other words, subgroups of tribals have been given separate region-based identities with the result that a group that is considered a tribe in one state might have been denied that status in another.

However, for some unknown reasons such status was accorded to the Muslim Gujjars in both the states, namely Himachal Pradesh and Jammu and Kashmir. Using the example of the two states, as also comparing their lifestyle with the Meenas of Rajasthan, the Gujjars of that state put forth their claim once again in the 1990s. Heeding to the demand of the agitating group, the Government of Rajasthan set up a High-Powered Committee consisting of a retired judge, an IAS officer of senior rank and a social scientist. Thus, for the first time in the history of independent India, a social scientist was made a full member to examine the case of a single community in the context of a single state, and full six months were given to the Committee to submit its report. Surprisingly for me, the onus fell on me to serve on the Committee as an expert social scientist. I should emphasize the point that the assignment came to me without any political connection or party affiliation. The fact that I come from Rajasthan and that I had studied a multi-caste village in Mewar that had Gujjars as the numerically preponderant group must have influenced this decision. I regarded this assignment as a re-invitation to anthropology and I decided to face this challenge. Incidentally, the representative of the Meena community did file an appeal before the High Court asking it to have a representative of the AnSI on the Committee; perhaps they were not aware of my credentials!

I must mention that the new Tribal Policy draft document, issued by the Government of India in July 2006, acknowledged the redundancy of the five criteria. It boldly asserts: 'all these broad criteria are not applicable to Scheduled Tribes today. Some of the terms used (e.g. primitive traits, backwardness) are also, in today's context, pejorative and need to be replaced with terms that are not derogatory' (para 1.2). In para 20.4, it says that 'other more accurate criteria need to be fixed'. It is significant that the Tribal Policy acknowledged the need for a process of 'descheduling' so as 'to exclude those communities who have by and large caught up with the general population. Exclusion of the creamy layer among the Scheduled Tribes from the benefits of reservation has never been seriously considered. As we move towards, and try to ensure, greater social justice, it would be necessary to give this matter more attention and work out an acceptable system' (para 20.6).

Social situation in India has drastically changed over the years with several forces of change – planned or unplanned, endogenous or exogenous. And the change has touched all sections of our society be they urban, rural or even tribal. If we stuck to our old definition then we should be prepared to take out those groups which earlier matched the definition but are now metamorphosed. To invent a new definition to suit the vested interests of the concerned groups is an exercise of little value. If the intentions of our Constitution makers were to include only the backward among the tribes in the Schedule and make specific provisions for them so that their backwardness is removed, then we should develop objective criteria for descheduling the groups, or individual families, that have shown improvement, and at the same time disallow entry of fresh groups on false pretexts. To insist on retention of the primitive traits is nothing more than conspiring to keep certain groups backward for all times. In today's context, tribal areas of the past can also easily be classified into urban, rural and even tribal. In many groups the claim of being tribal is of historical significance only. Many individuals or families who belonged to these groups but who have changed their personal and social profile by acquiring good education, better employment or a political stature should voluntarily opt out rather than wait for their ouster as a 'creamy layer'.

It is amply clear that the intention of the founding fathers of our Constitution was only to remove the backwardness of the groups, and not of preserving them as exhibits in an 'anthropological zoo'. But the approach they followed of identifying specific groups rather than geographical areas as backward was at fault. In areas where the two coincided the problem did not arise, but in backward regions where people belonging to different groups were discriminated along lines of caste or tribe, this strategy has failed. Rather than looking towards future, this policy has encouraged several groups to engage themselves in re-inventing their pasts. The groups who had moved towards acceptance of the elements of 'Great Traditions' of India, to use Robert Redfield's term, and putting claims for a higher status in the Hindu caste hierarchy, are taking a U-turn towards parochialization. When Gujjars of Rajasthan, for example, were asked to furnish evidence of their being tribal, using the official five criteria they dug out whatever to them looked like primitive or tribal. They referred to their dressing pattern – but that was no

DEFINING 'TRIBE': A CONCEPTUAL CRISIS

different from other villagers in the same setting. They insisted on their being non-vegetarians whereas traditionally they are a vegetarian caste. They claimed to be addicted to drinking when, in fact, teetotalism is the community norm. They asserted that they were believers in witchcraft and black and white magic, but this was no different amongst other village dwellers: worship of Bheru – a Hindu god – whose priest enters into a trance – is a common feature of rural Rajasthan and of course, the priest is always a Gujjar. It is also interesting to mention here that in the Hindu temples of Charbhujaji only a Gujjar serves as the *Pujari*. The myth of Devnarayan contains references to Hindu gods and goddesses. To prove their being tribal, they even mentioned the prevalence of polyandry as if all tribes are supposed to be polyandrous. All this indicates the ambiguity that is found amongst the claimants as to what defines a 'Tribe'. Dressing pattern, food habits, superstition and marriage practices are not enough indicators for a tribal status.

Our field visits to twenty districts in Rajasthan which have preponderance of Gujjars uncovered the fact that despite name semblance, people using the Gujjar name belong to different endogamous groups, speak different dialects and are not only pastorals but also agriculturists, and some of them have distanced themselves as a ruling class. The word 'Gujjar' is an umbrella concept, perhaps referring to whosoever was a herdsman. The gotras among them include Hun and Kashana (an abrupt version of Kushan) indicating their entry with these two invading groups. Similarly, of the two divisions of the Gujjar, namely Lor and Khari, the latter can be traced to Iran where they are still known by this name and are primarily herdsmen. Gujjar group has taken the character of a Varna in the sense that like other Varnas, the Gujjars are also divided into several castes, and, leaving aside a small group in the District of Bikaner, all regard themselves as Hindus. However, we found some of the areas in the eastern part of Rajasthan where the lifestyle of the inhabitants could match the criteria of primitiveness. But then, these were the sites where people of other castes were also residing, and thus well deserving of the special benefits. As a specific geographical sub-region such sites need development inputs without any discussion on the definition of the word 'tribe'.

The question that arises is: at what stage does a tribe cease to be a Tribe? Is it that a Tribe remains a tribe forever? It can be argued that all segments of the world population have remained tribe at one stage or another, and in due course of time, they merged their identities to form part of one or the other civilization. The concern for development basically implies efforts to break down isolation, expand

45

their *Weltanschauung*, expose them to the developments in science and technology and to ensure their participation in the national life. But if the doling out of privileges and a paternalistic attitude of charity continue, they would only reinforce tribal solidarity and usurpation of benefits coming from the outside by the rich and powerful among them with total denial of these to their poor brethren. In other words, the time has come where poverty or backwardness needs to be treated as an 'economic' phenomenon rather than as an 'ascribed' status.

We must admit that both the words 'caste' and 'tribe' are non-indigenous terms that were used by the foreign writers while describing the Indian social structure as they understood it. That is the reason that the word 'caste' is loosely used to refer to different kind of groupings ranging from Varna to Jatis, and even gotra (*Rishigotras*, i.e. eponymous clans, and *Laukikgotras*) and to groups of people hailing from a particular region (such as Punjabis, Madrasis, Bengalis[9]). Similarly, there is no indigenous word for tribe. In vernacular languages, all endogamous groups were referred to by the word *Jati*; later prefixes like *Van* (forest) or *Jan* (folk) were used for the forest dwelling groups. Some others preferred the word *Adivasi* for them to acknowledge their autochthonous and aboriginal character (oldest inhabitants).[10] This appellation was officially employed in 1948[11] but this was replaced by *Vanyajati* or *Banvasi* by those who were interested in asserting that the majority group living in the Indian subcontinent is also original to this land, and, therefore, this epithet should not remain confined to the backward communities still leading a jungle life.[12]

While working on caste in the 1950s I also struggled with the problem of differentiating between caste and tribe, as the village in Mewar that I chose for my study had not only the castes, including the Gujjar, but also representatives of the Bhil tribe who were treated as a caste and who distinguished themselves from the tribal Bhils by calling themselves as *Gametis* (village dwellers) and occupationally identified as Chowkidars (watchmen). It was then that I wrote an article on the 'Tribe-Caste Question'.[13] In terms of core characteristics of a caste that I worked out, following S. F. Nadel, the Gametis qualified to be a caste as a unit in the caste system of the village. From this it occurred that the distinguishing attribute of a tribe is found at the level of the system and not as a unit. When a section of a tribe moves to be a part of the multi-caste village, it assumes the characteristic of a caste as a unit. But when the tribe lives a separate existence it has the core characteristic of being endogamous, but does not possess the feature of inter-caste relationships (hierarchy or occupational specialization, or commensal

DEFINING 'TRIBE': A CONCEPTUAL CRISIS

restrictions etc.). I still feel that the distinction I offered then has validity even now. But my submission offered then went unnoticed which was not surprising in a country where status in the academic hierarchy decides the fate of a point of view.

In that article, I underlined the fact of continuous cultural contact amongst the tribals and the neighbouring members of the majority community, and suggested that the tribes should be seen as belonging to different stations in a continuum, and proposed the following classification[14]:

I   Tribal Communities Living in Their Original Habitat

    A   *Relatively Isolated*: Retaining most of the characteristics of their social organization, despite some culture contact (the Kadars)

    B   *Two or More Tribal Groups Living in the Same Area*: Such groups maintain mutual contact, and yet remain isolated from other non-tribal groups, demonstrating some sort of cultural symbiosis (the Todas, Kotas and Badagas)

    C   *Living with Other Tribal/Religious Groups in the Same Community*: These have the subtypes:

        (i)   Followers of their own religion, retaining most of the characteristics of their social organization and culture

        (ii)   While remaining separate from other religious groups, accept the leadership and domination of the other groups

        (iii)   Those moving towards Hinduization

        (iv)   Hinduized

            1   Tribes that have been forced the degraded status of untouchables

            2   Those enjoying high status

            3   Those assigned status in the ranges of the Hindu hierarchy

        (v)   Baptized in religions other than Hindu

            1   Towards conversion

            2   Converts

II   Tribal Groups Living Away from Their Original Habitat

    1   *Settled in Neighbouring Villages*: These could also be classified into five categories as in I (c):

DEFINING 'TRIBE': A CONCEPTUAL CRISIS

(i) Followers of their own religion, retaining most of the characteristics of their social organization and culture

    a   While remaining separate from other religious groups, accept the leadership and domination of the other groups

    b   Those moving towards Hinduization

    c   Hinduized

        (1) Tribes that have been forced the degraded status of untouchables

        (2) Those enjoying high status

        (3) Those assigned status in the ranges of the Hindu hierarchy

(ii) Baptized in religions other than Hindu

    (1) Towards conversion

    (2) Converts

2   *Living in separate villages in other areas*, such as Bhoksa of Nainital

3   *Settled in industrial centres or cities, or in tea plantations, military recruits, and others*

This distinction of the original habitat, seems to me, to be very much relevant in the sense that such groups are not migratory, and therefore, there is greater degree of territorial attachment. Like the Maoris in New Zealand, such indigenous people have ancestral claims, and despite their getting modernized their autochthonous roots cannot be challenged. As against these, the migrating communities lose their attachment to their parental land and show greater degree of adaptability. All those who constitute the mainstream have a queer mix of the Great tradition and the little parochial traditions. Their being tribal is a matter of past ; that is why Col. Tod or Sherring calling all groups – Rajputs, Brahmans, Gujjars – tribes becomes less significant in the context of today because they have entered the fold of civilization and even contributed to its richness. Even illiteracy does not block this transition. Those who are part of the civilization also have stratification in social, economic and political terms.

It is time that that the points raised here are given serious consideration by the students of Tribe. The task of defining should not be left to the bureaucracy or the political elite. It must satisfy scientific criteria and should be universally applicable. In doing so, we have to keep in mind that Tribe is a transitory category; once people move out to other destinations they lose the tribal status and become an advanced group.

Notes

1 This is a revised version of the Rajiv Gandhi Memorial Lecture Delivered at the Barkatullah University, Bhopal, 11 February 2009. I am grateful to Barkatullah University for kindly inviting me once again to share my views and concerns relative to social sciences in general and their utility in understanding the processes of change that our country is currently experiencing.

2 He was a military man but did his doctoral work on *Ethno-paleo Pathology of Polish-German Frontiers*.

3 In 1957, the Department was split into two – the Department of Geography, headed by Professor Muzaffar Ali (who came from Aligarh), and Professor S. C. Dube (who left the Nagpur Station of the Anthropological Survey of India to join the University, becoming the first University Professor at the age of 35).

4 This book by Murdock was published in 1934 by the Macmillan Company, New York.

5 It may be noted that Kalelkar was opposed to the idea of having the OBC category. Also that his Report was never put before the Parliament.

6 This clearly indicates that while the tribes can be included in the category of Scheduled Castes, none of the castes can be included in the category of Scheduled Tribe. The implication is clear. A tribe is a category that emerged earlier than the caste in social evolution, and therefore it can only enter into a category that arrived later and thus graduate to a different status, namely that of becoming a subsystemic unit of a broader social formation. But once classified as a caste it can return to a previous position that is lower in the evolutionary ladder. It is also possible that a tribal society becomes larger and the subgroups within it become endogamous in character and thus the entire Tribe may transform into a caste system.

7 See http://tribal.gov.in (accessed on 15 March 2015).

8 In a country where the number of villages is more than half a million.

9 It is interesting to note that in some of the older Reports on Backward Classes have mentioned Bengalis as a caste, even in the context of Rajasthan.

10 In the Indonesian and Malaysian language, aboriginal groups are called *Orang Asli* – meaning original people.

11 The Government of India published a book by that name at that time.

12 The replacement of the term *Adivasi* was disputed during the debates of the Constituent Assembly – drafting the Constitution of the Republic of India. A tribal leader, Jaipal Singh, asked President Rajendra Prasad: 'I wish that you would issue instructions to your Translation Committee that the translation of Scheduled Tribes should be Adivasi (meaning original inhabitants or indigenous peoples). The word Adivasi has a grace. . . . Why this old abusive epithet of Banjati (forest dwellers) being used . . .'.

13 Yogesh Atal, 'The Tribe-Caste Question'; *Bulletin of the Bihar Tribal Research Institute*, Vol. V, No. 1.

14 Ibid.

3
SOCIO-CULTURAL DIMENSIONS OF DEVELOPMENT

The conclusion of the Second World War ushered in an era of reconstruction and development – reconstruction of Europe that was devastated by war, and development of the countries of the Third World getting freed from the yoke of European colonialism. In one word, it was a process of decolonization affecting both the colonialists and the colonies. This was the period when the colonialists had to withdraw from their erstwhile colonies and to develop new equations with the emerging new nations. The new nations had to rapidly respond to the rising revolution of expectations from the people by initiating a process of planned development to bring about changes in the economy, polity and society.

Having severely suffered from the devastating war, the countries of Europe took immediate measures to bring in normalcy in their social and cultural life. They also realized that it was no longer possible for them to contain the rising tide of nationalism in the colonies governed by them. That is why they took steps to reconstruct their infrastructures and rejuvenate their cultures on the one hand, and to decolonize the non-Western world on the other. Decolonization entailed not only a process of transfer of power to the natives but also a process of building new nations. While the West had to reconstruct their cultural ruins, the non-West had to initiate a process of constructing anew the infrastructure that was needed to run a modern society.

The concept of *reconstruction*, which emerged in the aftermath of the Second World War, related more to the Western world where the devastating war led to the destruction of cultural property and ruined a number of cultural institutions including educational institutions. Against this, the countries coming out of the colonial yoke had to engage in the project to come out of continuing underdevelopment. The other concept, namely *development*, became a synonym for

SOCIO-CULTURAL DIMENSIONS OF DEVELOPMENT

nation building. While in the West, reconstruction exercise focussed on the culture, the non-West embarked upon a programme of economic development. Reconstruction meant cultural reconstitution, and development came to signify nation building that involved social and political development and economic growth. It is this twin concern that was reflected in the fuller name of the World Bank, that is, the International Bank for Reconstruction and Development or IBRD.

After half a century's effort of the world community to attain the twin goals of reconstruction and development, several efforts are now being made to assess the gains and failures so that future strategies can be chalked out to make up for the deficits.

I

It is common knowledge that during the colonial period, the colonizers focussed more on the *cultures* of their colonies, rather than on their economic development. This was guided by two considerations: theoretical and practical administrative. The prevailing social theory of the times was Evolutionary – drawing inspirations from the Darwinian contributions to biology. Scholars found in the primitive, non-western societies evidence of the earlier stages of evolution of societies and cultures. They tried to put them on the evolutionary ladder at a lower step than their own to justify their own superiority. Borrowing from Darwin the concepts of *struggle for existence* and *survival of the fittest* they advanced the view that the non-West has lagged behind in its struggle for existence and has surrendered itself to the 'fittest'. The colonialists regarded themselves as a 'superior' race and took upon themselves the task of helping the primitives to climb the evolutionary ladder treating the West as the 'positive reference group'. Cultural development, in the conception of the colonialists, was a process through which natives gave up, at the instance of the West, their own practices and customs and adopted elements of Western Civilization. Of course, there were some scholars and administrators who wanted the native cultures to be 'preserved', that is, to be left untouched by the winds of change coming from the West. These people were criticized for having the ill-intention of treating the tribal cultures as 'anthropological zoos' – as exemplars of the queer and the exotic – so that curious tourists can come and visit them. More articulate amongst the protagonists for the preservation of tribal cultures put different and more convincing arguments to support their stand.

51

The practical-administrative interest in the native cultures was guided by the consideration of governance; to govern the colonies better, they needed to know their cultures – their language, behaviour, habits, traditions and even the customary law – all in the domain of anthropology. To be sure, they were not so much concerned about changing the primitive cultures as about the understanding of them. The changes that they introduced were those that were regarded as instrumental in keeping a stronghold on the natives. To prove their superiority, they highlighted those aspects of the native culture which they regarded as primitive and undesirable. There existed certain ambivalence towards native cultures – criticism of undesirable practices, and maintenance of the exotic forms of behaviour. All this was, now said with the wisdom of the hindsight, 'false philanthropy'.

This period witnessed a number of changes in the non-Western world. And they were described by the umbrella concept of 'westernization' or 'modernization'. Rising rates of literacy, urbanization, industrialization, and conversion to Christianity were regarded as useful indicators of the twin processes of westernization and modernization.

II

The attainment of independence led to the change of orientation towards social and cultural change. The focus of the new administration by the nationals moved from maintaining law and order and 'keeping the natives subservient' to accelerating the process of economic and social development. Of course, this orientation gave further support to the processes of westernization and modernization, but created multiplicity of positive reference groups located abroad. It is striking that those very cultural changes that the colonial masters initiated to strengthen their foothold in the colonies helped the natives in developing a front against the colonialists. They not only used the exposure to the West to stage a revolt against the alien rule; but also took steps both to decry some of their own traditions that were retrogressive, and to revive many of the traditions that they regarded useful in fostering solidarity.

The national leadership adopted an economic agenda for development. To hasten the process so as to 'keep up with the Joneses' – that is, to follow the path of Western development – they had to depend on external support. With the arrival of IBRD to provide financial support, and the setting up of agencies under the umbrella of the United

SOCIO-CULTURAL DIMENSIONS OF DEVELOPMENT

Nations, such support was available from a variety of sources, and not only from the colonial masters. This support came in the form of men (as experts), machines (modern technology), money and modern system of management – both of business and of the government. Externally induced but nationally approved programme of change began to characterize what came to be known as the Western paradigm of development.

In this paradigm, there was marginal place for culture. At best, culture was regarded only as an instrumentality, not an aim of development that was defined in economistic terms. Foreign experts (all invariably Western) enthusiastically tried to transplant their institutions, and their machinery in strange settings with a view to increasing productivity. While doing so, they did not realize the power of culture to reject or accept outside elements. Its role as gatekeeper was rather ignored.

Many of these narrow specialists were unfamiliar with local cultures, or with anthropological approaches that were developed during the colonial rule that focussed on the holistic character of culture and hinted at the integrative nature of cultural traits and complexes. Social scientists, other than anthropologists, entered the arena of tribal societies at a later date only to study the impact of change or to explain the failures of an innovation. Being ethnocentric, they regarded their cultures superior and were convinced that the 'low level cultures' can be lifted up by wholesale transfer of material artefacts and 'high ideals' of the advanced societies. In brief, imitation of the West and uncritical acceptance of so-called Western ideas and technology was regarded as process of modernization. Any obstacle to such interchange was regarded as dysfunctional and undesirable. All analyses of change thus used culture as a variable to explain the failure of a project, or non-acceptance of an innovation. Culture was regarded either as an *obstacle* to development, or as a *victim* of development.

It is much later, almost after five decades of development, that the social scientists realized the need for the inclusion of culture in the planning process. But nobody offered just how this can be done. What was available was not the methodology of how to pay due regard to culture. What the social science studies of the phenomenon of change offered was only post-mortem of failed events – all invariably indicating that it was the neglect of the cultural factor that was responsible for the costly failure of a good intentioned change brought from without. Social sciences began clamouring, in the late 1970s, for the inclusion of the socio-cultural factors in planning, but they were not ready with the recipe. Even today the situation remains more or less the same.

III

The decade of 1970s ushered in an era of disenchantment, resulting in the shift in emphases of the development paradigm. First came the need for the reintroduction of the concept of *endogenous development*, then the emphasis shifted to *sustainable development*; later, the international community introduced the concept of *human resource development*. In all of these proposals the importance of the human factor was emphasized. Understood broadly, the human factor is a part of the concept of culture – after all, it is culture that transforms the biological brute of *Homo sapiens* into a social animal.

The stocktaking exercises initiated under the aegis of the United Nations have highlighted the concerns related to population growth, environmental crises, gender issues and default on the social development front. More important is the point that for the first time a consensus emerged that piecemeal and sectoral approach to development is hazardous, and that there is a need for a *united thrust*. As a result, all agencies of the United Nations system joined hands to commonly evolve a programme of action to implement the various commitments made at the world conferences on different aspects of development, held in Copenhagen in 1995. It was for the first time that the world community recognized that there cannot be a single cure for a social ailment that may be commonly shared by many societies. Common problems need not necessarily have common solutions. While we have to think globally, we must act locally, we are told. There is a clear recognition of the cultural specificities and a recommendation that solutions to problems of social development should be sought in the light of those specificities. What may work in a given situation may not work in another.

Towards the end of the last century, we have learnt one great lesson: neither the Western capitalism nor the Eastern communism holds the key to success. While people in the non-communist world rejoiced at the collapse of the Soviet Union, and thus almost a demise of communism, they did not fail to notice that even the non-communist world did not succeed on the social development front. It is important that the World Summit for Social Development identified three main issues for discussion: *poverty, unemployment* and *growing tendencies towards social disintegration of societies*. The main reason behind the selection of

SOCIO-CULTURAL DIMENSIONS OF DEVELOPMENT

these three issues for discussion in the Summit on Social Development was the point that these problems confronted all societies, be they of North or South, rich or poor, tribal or 'civilized', capitalist or communist. Since economic development could not arrest these tendencies – in fact, it even gave rise to them – it could not be considered as the cure for these ailments. In this regard, one is reminded of the views of Professor Amartya Sen – the Indian economist who was awarded Nobel Prize. His study of the famines clearly indicated that they were caused not by the paucity of economic resources, but by other, and more potent, non-economic factors. While all for globalization – a trend that is now almost irreversible – Sen has been advocating the need to focus on education, health and other social sectors.

Chilean ambassador Somavia – the pioneering force behind the holding of the Social Development Summit – acknowledged the fact that such a summit was unthinkable during the period of Cold War. Neither party to that war accepted any deficits on the social front. But the end of the Cold War, with the disintegration of the Soviet Union, changed the scenario. The West felt the need to review its welfarist approach, and the former communist countries also began cutting public expenditure on the social sector. It now appears that the welfarist approach of the West was an answer to the socialistic stance of the communist states. That is why now they feel that the State is unable to bear the rising cost on welfare and will like the market forces to operate. The decline in the social sector expenditure in the former communist states, likewise, has caused unprecedented unemployment, and increased the ranks of the poor, not sparing even the intelligentsia. The former communist states that denied the existence of poverty now openly acknowledge the growing phenomenon of poverty. Poverty in these countries cannot be understood in the prevailing paradigms emanating from the West. The cultural context and the historical experience of these *Economies in Transition* are very different from those of India, or other countries of the Third World. In these cultures, ethnicity-based identification is resurfacing to cut across class-based identities that were forged during the communist era. Clearly, these communities feel that the communist ideology had eroded their cultural identities and superimposed the economic calculus of development. Strangely enough, even the capitalist mode of development also gave primacy to the economic factor and regarded traditions as functionless vestiges. Both these strategies contributed to the, what may be called, *museumization* of culture. Neglect of the cultural factor led not only to the failure of these strategies but also to politicized culture in the process. It will indeed be instructive to explore this phenomenon in a cross-cultural framework.

This emerging context gives a special meaning to the phrase 'Socio-Cultural Dimensions of Development'. The World Commission on Culture and Development, set up by UNESCO and the United Nations under the chairmanship of Javier Perez de Cuellar, focussed on this aspect and, as the title of the report of the Commission suggests, it underlines *Our Creative Diversity* (UNESCO, 1995). The report argues that culture is to be seen not only 'as a servant of ends, but as the social basis for the ends themselves. We cannot begin to understand the so-called 'cultural dimension of development' without taking note of each of these two roles of culture' (UNESCO, 1995: 24).

The key question is: how do we bring culture in the development process? There are three different views on the issue of culture–development interface:

1   Use of native ideologies/religious faiths in promoting development. This approach suggests that a justification for change may be sought in the native categories of thought. The analysis of the indigenous ideologies may indicate that native cultures are not opposed to change, but that they are not prepared for *all kinds of* change. That change which is in tune with the native ideology is always acceptable.

2   Developed societies are using this paradigm of culture–development interface in the context of newly emerging issues of national integration caused by massive international migration. The colonial phase created many *pluricultural* societies by amalgamating different regional regimes, and also introducing populations from other cultures – e.g. through indentured labour. Now the West is experiencing a form of 'reverse colonization'. The homogeneity of the European states is giving way to heterogeneity caused by a plurality of cultures arriving through migration. In these contexts, the new phenomenon of what I have christened *sandwich cultures* (Atal, 1989) has become significant. In these societies, the word 'culture' is used almost as a synonym of 'ethnic groups' and efforts are being made to ensure that the dominant culture of the host society maintains its position.

3   Another perspective is to examine the relationship between exogenous development and indigenous culture. Such an approach hints at the discrepancy between traditional norms and values and the values of industrial life, and it highlights the adverse impact of new technologies in accentuating inequalities.

SOCIO-CULTURAL DIMENSIONS OF DEVELOPMENT

While there is so much talk of the role of culture, there are several methodological questions that need to be properly addressed. Let these be briefly discussed.

- How to construct culture? And how to deduce it?

  While culture has been the subject matter of anthropology, there is still considerable grey area relative to its definition. Describing culture as a way of life of the people makes it very difficult for an analyst to draw the contours of culture particularly of plural societies. The various claimants to the core of a given culture require careful scrutiny, and acceptance by the members of the society. The insider-outsider perspectives on culture do not always tally; each of these carries its own biases. Moreover, it is not only the outsiders who may have differing views and perspectives – as the outsiders have different origins – differences abound even among the insiders. In the context of India, Srinivas referred to the 'book-view' and the 'upper-caste view' which are again related only to the Hindu segment of Indian society when he underlined the need for field work at the grassroots to get the empirical view of the existing reality. Present criticism of the Hindu view of society as being 'Manuvadi' by the Dalit leadership is an instance of the disagreement that prevails. Also are the problems of distinguishing between the prescribed and the prevailing, and the prevailing and the desirable. Who defines the desirable? What are the good values to be imparted and what values to be rejected? Dube's criticism of characterization of Indian traditions is pertinent in this regard:

  > In describing the Hindu ethos there has been an unjustifiable emphasis on religion, ritual and spiritualism. After all, Hinduism did not produce only *Dharmasastras*; it also produced *Arthasastras* (works dealing with the science of economics and statecraft), and *Kamasastras* (works dealing with the science of love and bodily pleasures). Similarly, Buddhism did regard *nirvana* as the ultimate objective but without neglecting intermediate concerns governing the everyday life of the people. . . . The egalitarian emphasis in Islam constitutes one of its significant characteristics. It encouraged economic pursuits, with one important provision that a part of the earnings were to be earmarked in the forms of *zakat* and *sadaqa* for collective good. (Dube, 1990:10–11)

- How to separate culture from ideology?

  While there is an agreement that ideology and culture are two separate entities, they are also so much intertwined that it poses problems for the analyst to extricate them from each other. People of the same culture may subscribe to different ideologies – home-grown or imported from abroad. Their followers may establish cultural parallels to justify their attachment to them and to attract new followers. In yet another sense, the totality of ideologies in vogue in a given society may be considered as components of a heterogeneous culture. Can culture be regarded as an ideology of conservatism, and ideology as a culture of forward-looking? A good deal of conceptual analysis and methodological sophistication is needed to clarify this relationship and to see their respective roles in the process of development.

- Whose culture is being referred to, particularly in a multicultural context?

  This point has been clarified in the previous queries. Suffice it to say that modern societies are facing the crises of managing the multiplicity. The conflicts among various subcultural identities are becoming more prominent, and the whole paradigm of core and periphery is under severe scrutiny. When talking about the cultural factor this question assumes special significance.

- Who wants to save culture, and what culture?

  This question is related about the desirability of change. There are situations where the people themselves wish to bring about change but outside agencies intervene to save the cultures. Environmentalists speaking on behalf of the poor have led several movements to halt the process of modernization be it promotion of tourism, building of dams, construction of hydro-electricity projects or introduction of alternatives to swidden cultivation.

- Is culture an alternative to exogenous development?

  It will be wrong to assume that those who plead for the place of culture are opposed to any change inspired from the outside. What is implied is the point that no culture accepts any change without its proper screening and its acceptance depends upon its compatibility with the prevailing infrastructure. A culture is an organic unity and it responds to changes brought from the outside as a functioning whole. A careful preparation is needed to receive foreign elements so that the host culture does not lose its identity and assigns a proper place to the immigrant cultural trait to ensure its integration in the new milieu.

How, then, to view culture in the context of development? Generally, scholars have tried to analyse the influence of development on culture and the role of culture in influencing development. But treating culture as a living entity, developmental process is to be viewed as part of the cultural process. Viewed thus, it is not a question of either/or. The old approach to preserve/save culture also needs to be reviewed. One needs to ask the question: does disappearance of certain cultural traits amount to the erosion of culture, or its total destruction? The phenomenon of cultural growth will be inexplicable if this process did not involve both attrition and accretion processes. Changes occurring in the ambit of culture do not, need not, erase its identity. Fifty years of development experience has clearly indicated that cultures possess different degrees of *resilience* – like a bamboo they might bend when they are hit by a gush of wind, but are able to rise again – bending is not equivalent of breaking.

Cultures around the world have experienced significant changes, mostly caused by the so-called development exercises, carefully planned and meticulously implemented. But despite these changes cultures have not lost their individual identities; in fact, what has occurred in the past decades is a rising revolution of identities. Cultures have remained distinctly identifiable, even though their demographic composition and ethnic constitution have significantly altered, and their material cultural profiles are drastically different from what they have been a few decades ago. All this goes to suggest that westernization, modernization and now globalization, do not ensure homogenization of cultures. What happens is a growth of complexity of individual cultures with multiple layers consisting of elements of international culture, emergent national culture – deriving from its civilizational base and giving the country its cultural identity, and regional-parochial cultures. A quote from Claude Levi-Strauss is very apt for what I am trying to say:

> The notion of world civilization can only be accepted . . . as a sort of limiting concept or as an epitome of a highly complex process. There is not, and can never be, a world civilization in the absolute sense in which the term is often used, since

SOCIO-CULTURAL DIMENSIONS OF DEVELOPMENT

civilization implies, and indeed consists in, the co-existence of cultures exhibiting the maximum possible diversities. A world civilization could, in fact, represent no more than a world-wide coalition of cultures, each of which would preserve its own originality.

(UNESCO, 1995: 29)

It is wrong to assume that traditions are static and unchanging. The vast reservoir of tradition possessed by ancient cultures provides support not only for the maintenance of status quo but also for radical reconstruction and imaginative innovation. The false dichotomy of tradition and modernity posited by the Western scholarship has to be discarded in favour of treating cultures as dynamic entities acting to preserve the good in human heritage and constantly innovating to enrich human life.

4

ISSUES IN TRIBAL DEVELOPMENT[1]

More than 60 years after independence, and with a history of major development efforts at the state level carried out to change the socio-economic profile of the country, it is perhaps useful to look back and take stock of our achievements and failures. Our country being predominantly rural – both in terms of our population residing in rural areas and our economy being mainly agricultural – it was natural that our planners and policymakers gave priority to rural and tribal development. While important strides have been made towards urbanization and industrialization, India still continues to be primarily rural, and population projections suggest that more than half of our population is going to be rural even after crossing the first-half of the twenty-first century.

I believe it is this context that gives significance to this Seminar. I am hopeful that the deliberations here would not just be the rehash of what we already know about our development experience – the inadequacies and the frustrations – but would help develop guidelines for a new blueprint for future action.

I have carefully studied the guidelines prepared for this Seminar. It appears from the Note that the organizers are interested in (i) the clarification of some basic conceptual categories, (ii) highlighting the great damage that has been done to our tribal cultures and (iii) assessing their present socio-economic and health status. This is the order in which the concerns have been expressed in the guidelines. However, the undercurrent in the entire Note is that of dissatisfaction with the development strategy which, according to the organizers, has done a good deal of damage to the tribals.

Despite this, I detect some sort of ambivalence regarding development in the Note: it seems that while the need for development is not denied, the organizers appear to be unhappy with the consequences that development has caused.

61

I wish to pick up this thread to elaborate my point. The conceptual issue that the organizers have raised relates to the definition of the word 'Tribe', but the concerns that are expressed in the subsequent paragraphs relate to the word 'Development'. I shall dwell upon both the conceptual categories, but reverse the order. First, let me talk about the concept of 'Development'. The Outline supplied by the organizers for this Seminar does not suggest a definition of this concept, nor does it refute any of the prevailing definitions. It has provided a long list of adverse consequences of development which are summed up in one phrase: *Cultural Degeneration*. The tribals are described as 'victims of civilization' who have lost their religion and their dialects, who now suffer from landlessness and alcoholism which has forced them to beggary. And all this has been caused by culture contact, impact of Hinduism and Christianity, Forest Acts of 1865, migration, industrialization and urbanization, development projects, NGO intervention, consumer culture and advancing globalization. It gives an impression that development has done nothing positive, as if the development efforts have further worsened the life of the tribals. Implicit in it seems to be the plea that the process needs to be halted almost instantly.

Such a characterization makes an interesting copy for a political statement, but makes one wonder as to what kind of future do we envisage for our tribal brethren.

What do we mean by development? The very fact that the development exercise is an *exogenous effort* to bring about culture change, and what we are doing here is also an *outsider review*, can we talk of insulation from culture contact? Or, are we advocating complete stoppage of any outside influence and a return for the primitive to his pristine purity? If we are concerned about his health, his poverty and his limited world view and wish to provide him with better nutrition and Medicare, improved means of earning a livelihood, and widened cognitive horizons, how do we do it? Do we still wish to keep him in the proverbial 'anthropological zoo'? Is the tribal leading an idyllic lifestyle worthy of our emulation? Or do we intend to bring him out of poverty, and of isolated existence? Should the tribal be deprived of the fruits of modern civilization, of advancements in science and technology? Should he remain where he has remained all through, or need we help him develop empathy to relate himself with the wider world?

When one turns to the other concern – namely their current status – one finds that the backward condition of the tribals is the worrying factor. Perhaps here one finds the hidden allegation that development has not reached its target audience. Taken seriously, this complaint

ISSUES IN TRIBAL DEVELOPMENT

signifies a demand for development. It says that despite so many years of development, there are still pockets of underdevelopment. And the Seminar is invited to suggest mechanisms through which such a deficit can be corrected.

Clearly, there is ambivalence regarding development. We detest development and we demand development. There will be no one in this audience who will not wish a better life for the tribals living in remote areas and pursuing a primitive way of life. And yet there will be many amongst us who would also wish to eulogize tribal cultures and the traditional stock of knowledge they possess, advocating not only its preservation but also its promotion.

Sometime back I had the opportunity of addressing a similar Seminar held in this very city and the university on Indigenous Knowledge (IK). In that Seminar also I raised a somewhat uncomfortable question as to the purpose of gathering data on Indigenous Knowledge.

The AnSI is now engaged in a massive project on what it calls Traditional Knowledge (TK). Since I am also associated with that project let me share the questions that I have posed before the research team in order to have a clear direction.

Any such exercise, to my mind, can be prompted by several considerations.

First, in the 1960s, for example, there was a movement in favour of what was named as *Urgent Anthropology*. The supporters of that movement had argued that we are living in an era of rapid social change, under the influence of which there is a real danger of disappearance of not only several cultural traits but also many small primitive communities – that may not survive or get submerged into larger entities losing their own identity. The movement, therefore, focussed on the 'dying' cultural traits and cultural communities and wanted them to be studied and recorded for posterity, and for the professional interest, before it was too late. Not studying them now, they argued, would mean never studying them as they would disappear from the world scene. This genuine concern for recording important aspects of human civilization is understandable. It was motivated by sheer academic interest, and not by any ideology that celebrates the past and the primitive. Work on TK or IK can, thus, be a fulfilment of the objective of Urgent Anthropology.

There can be, second, a set of people who sincerely feel that the primitive way of life is ideal and deserves to be preserved. This is what the proponents of anthropological zoos in fact intended; of course, some alleged that they were more eager to save the subject matter of

63

their study rather than the welfare of the people they studied. This charge was countered by the likes of Verrier Elwin who thought that uncontrolled contacts with the outside world have led to the unfortunate exploitation of the tribals, who were rendered homeless in their own homes. The worry over cultural degeneration expressed in the Seminar Outline clearly follows this line of argumentation.

Third, there are others who think that the vast canvas of Human Civilization has been enriched, in a variety of ways, by the multitude of cultures. There is a need, according to them, to give due credit to each society and culture for its contribution, and that learning should not be a one-way process where the tribals are at the receiving end and the so-called modern societies are at the giving end. There is much good in the traditional knowledge that can be used for the general good of Human society as a whole and should not be neglected simply because of its origin. This may relate to, for example, tribal pharmacopoeia, and even treatment of some ailments. In the general field of agriculture and horticulture, such knowledge may be immense and vastly scattered which needs to be collected and catalogued. It would, however, be wrong to plead that such TK can replace all other modern knowledge, or that modern knowledge has no place in the tribal setting. Acknowledegment of the multiplicity of cultures and, therefore, plurality of the TK bases should disallow cultural chauvinism. Anthropology's strength has been the emphasis on *cultural relativity*.

We need to come out of the either-or kind of dichotomy.

Let me now turn to the concept of Tribe by briefly alluding to the recent crisis in Rajasthan where one of the castes raised hell to be reclassified as a Tribe. I am referring to the case of the Gujjars. In the year 2007, a caste that has been rising upward in the Hindu hierarchy chose to go downhill to be counted amongst the backward groups as it found that the benefits of development are accruing to the tribals, and they have special privileges in the Indian polity which are denied to it because of its 'alleged' high status. This incidence refutes to a certain extent the allegation that the benefits of development had not reached the tribals. The Gujjar leadership spared no effort to prove that the powerful tribal group of the Meenas in Rajasthan have captured all major positions of power in the government machinery as was indicated by their number in IAS, IPS and the State Public Services, in which the number of the Gujjars was nearly nil.

Since I had the onerous task of serving on the High-Powered Committee – popularly known as Chopra Committee – appointed by the Government of Rajasthan to examine the claim of the Gujjars for a Scheduled Tribe status – I had scanned all official records relative to the definition of the word 'tribe' in the Indian context.

Even anthropologists, for whom tribes had been a subject matter of study, have not developed a universally acceptable definition of tribe. When societies were classified into civilized and uncivilized – as savage or barbaric – the task was simpler. All uncivilized societies were *preliterate*, meaning thereby the absence of writing. That meant that the transmission of culture was through oral tradition, and the history of the society went as far back as human memory could take it; beyond this was prehistory. With absence of history, oral transmission of society's knowledge pool to the younger generation, elementary technology and greater dependence on nature for survival and faith in the supernatural described their way of life. Living in small hordes, and unaware of the world outside the narrow confines of the community, the geographically and socially isolated communities defined themselves as residents of a given territory, and as belonging to a specific racial stock. Such groups became the subject matter of study of the anthropologists who came to these societies as a consequence of colonization. In this sense, tribals were also described as non-Western cultures.

Initially these students of 'Other cultures' came to the non-Western societies and studied those small groups that were remotely located as 'Little Communities', cut off from civilizational societies and pursuing primitive economic activities in settlements that were cradle-to-the-grave arrangements.[2]

Problems arose when countries like India were colonized. Described as an indigenous civilization, India got divided into the civilized and uncivilized sections, but belonging to the non-Western part of Human Civilization. In India, the original inhabitants got pushed into the remote tribal tracts by the groups that migrated from abroad at different phases of its history – as nomads and pastoralists, as invaders who became conquerors of parts of the vast territory of India. Many such groups who came from the Middle East, Eastern Europe and Mongolia came as adventurers or nomads and gradually got assimilated with the local populace; this involved initial confrontation, accommodation and finally integration into the main stream. Historians of the nineteenth century – mostly foreign, and primarily administrators or military officers of the Raj – called all such migrating groups as tribes – because of their common origin and a distinct identity. But they also acknowledged the process of their gradual assimilation into the Hindu fold.

It is important to note that there is no indigenous word for tribe in any of the Indian languages. In Sanskrit, there is a word *Atavika Jana*, which was used to denote agglomeration of individuals with specific territorial, kinship and cultural pattern. Prior to the colonial period, they were also commonly referred to as a Jati – caste. But the colonial administration began calling them as tribes, and differentiated them from the other groups as animists. In this category, some food gathering groups and shifting cultivators were also included, though they lived closer to the villages. In the censuses they were first called 'forest tribes'. In the 1931 Census, they were named as 'primitive tribes'. In 1935, the British began calling them as 'backward tribes'. Without questioning the nomenclature, the anthropologists, both foreign and natives, took those groups as subject matter of their study which were officially designated as tribes. It is interesting that the 1931 Census, which had recorded castes for the last time, had given the listing of the tribes. But even in this Census, the groups that were identified by a distinct tribal name were classified in terms of their religion. Only those that were not converted to any religion – Christianity, Islam, Hinduism or Jainism – were called Tribals. Let me quote as an instance the Bhils and Minas of Rajasthan. The Bhils were classified into Christian, Hindus, Jain, Muslims and Tribals; similarly, Garasia and Mina were classified into Hindu, Muslim and Tribals. Classified this way, the Tribal Bhils constituted only 23.62 per cent of the total Bhil population in 1931. Among the Minas, the conversion rate was so high that only 3.35 per cent of them remained tribals despite the fact that the total population of both the Bhils and the Minas was more than 6 lakhs. See Table 4.1.

The 1931 Census suggests that only 19 per cent of the Bhils were reported as Hindus in the previous Census, conducted in 1921; that percentage rose within 10 years to 70. In case of the Minas the conversion rate was much higher. Both these groups are acknowledged by

Table 4.1 Percentage of tribal among Bhils, Minas and Garasias

Ethnic group	Total population	Tribal segment	% tribal
Bhil	655,647	198,005	23.62
Garasia	29,231	8,258	24.10
Mina/Meena	607,369	20,336	3.35

Source: 1931 Census.

the Census as 'original inhabitants' and yet they were taken out of the tribal category on the basis of their religious affiliation.

Regarding the 1931 Census as the basis for identification of castes and tribes, the Indian government named them in 1948 as *Adivasis*, ignoring the religious distinction of the 1931 Census, and thus increasing their size. When the new Constitution of India was promulgated in 1950, all the Adivasi groups considered as backward tribes were included in the Schedule for special privileges, and thus all groups included in the Schedule were named as Scheduled Tribes.

It must, however, be said that the Constitution of India nowhere defines the word Tribe. Article 342 of the Constitution says just the following:

The President may with respect to any State or Union territory, and where it is a State, after consultation with the Governor, thereof, by public notification, specify the tribes or tribal communities or part or groups within tribes or tribal communities which shall for the purposes of this Constitution be deemed to be Scheduled Tribes in relation to that State or Union territory, as the case may be.

Article 366(25) defines the Schedule Tribes as follows:

'Scheduled Tribe' means such Tribes or Tribal committees or parts of groups within such Tribes or Tribal committees as are deemed under article 342 to be Scheduled Tribe for the purposes of this Constitution.

When the two articles are read in tandem, one discovers the tautological nature of these definitions. Left with such a situation, the Government of India prepared the list of those groups that were identified as tribes in the previous censuses. The 1951 Census listed a total of 212 Scheduled Tribes in India. But the moment the lists were made public, there were demands from the concerned groups to be included either in the category of Scheduled Tribes or Scheduled Castes. And those who could not be accommodated in either of the categories were provided with a separate category of 'Other Backward Classes'; for the later, a separate Commission – Backward Classes Commission – was set up under the Chairmanship of Kaka Kalelkar.

Responding to these demands, the lists have been significantly enlarged, and there continue to be additional demands for inclusion. The recent case of the Gujjars is a good example of this trend.

As was said before, the Constitution is silent about the definition, but is quite clear on one front, namely the eligibility for entry in the tribal fold. While in case of Scheduled castes it says that *'the castes, races or tribes, or parts of, or groups within castes, races or tribes'* could be notified for inclusion in the category of Scheduled Castes, the scope for eligibility in the category of Scheduled Tribes is limited only to *'the tribes or tribal communities, or part or groups within tribes or tribal communities'*. Implicit in the formulation is the point that *only* those groups that were included in the category of tribes in the Census of 1931, and in the following decennial censuses, qualify for inclusion in the category of Scheduled Tribes; no caste can be reclassified as a tribe, and yet we find that today the number of Scheduled Tribes in India has crossed the figure of 700, a big jump of over 500 from the 1951 Census. But this number has not increased because of conversion of castes into tribes. It has increased because each state in the Union of India has a right to declare particular groups as tribes. So the subgroups within a major group have now established themselves as separate entities.

Let me quote one instance from Rajasthan. In the 1951 list, only one category of Minas – namely Chowkidar Minas – was included who hailed from southern Rajasthan. As I said earlier, only 3 per cent of the Minas (out of a total of more than 6 lakhs) even in the year 1931 were classified as tribals. But the Meenas raised their demand for inclusion of all categories of Meenas and succeeded in getting the demand fulfilled. It is now alleged that the real tribals amongst this group continue to remain disadvantaged, and all benefits have been cornered by the advanced sections of this community that had long been converted to other religions and thus raised its political and social status.

The point I am making is that the 1951 list of Scheduled Tribes created several anomalies. For example, Bakarwal Gujjars were studied, prior to 1991, as a nomadic Muslim caste in Jammu and Kashmir; but now it is given a tribal status. A similar thing has happened among Muslim Gujjars in the State of Himachal Pradesh.[3] The Rabari are a Scheduled Tribe in Gujarat, but in Rajasthan they are included in the category of 'Other Backward Classes'. The old State of Hyderabad (Nizam) did not recognize Yenadis, Yerukulas and Sugalis as tribes, but the Andhra State has given them the recognition. Similarly, Gaddis are treated as a ST in Himachal Pradesh, but in Punjab, they enjoy this status only in the scheduled areas where they do not live. For a number of years, the State of Uttar Pradesh did not acknowledge tribal status for the Khasas of Jaunsar-Bawar and the Gonds and Cheros of the Mirzapur district; now they are included in the tribal category.

In 1967, a Joint Parliamentary Committee under the Chairmanship of Shri Anil K. Chanda was constituted to consider the claims of

ISSUES IN TRIBAL DEVELOPMENT

various communities for inclusion in the category of Scheduled Tribes. This Committee adopted the following five criteria for judging the eligibility of any group as a tribe:

1 Indication of primitive traits.
2 Distinctive culture.
3 Geographical isolation.
4 Shyness of contact with the larger community.
5 Backwardness.

The official documents nowhere provide any indicators for each of these variables to develop an objective index. Different people have interpreted each of these variables differently.

The Lokur Committee, which was set up earlier in 1965, also used more or less the same criteria. However, it was firm in stating that: 'care was necessary in drawing up the schedule in order to ensure that communities which had been assimilated in the general population were not at this stage invested with an artificial distinctiveness as tribes, and that communities which might be regarded as tribes by reason of their social organization and general way of life but which were really not primitive should not now be treated as primitive'. The Lokur Committee categorically stated (page 7) that 'in 1931 and 1935, as well as in 1950 and 1956, it was acknowledged that every tribe need not be regarded as requiring special treatment; the list of 1931 was of "primitive tribes" while the list of 1935 was of "backward tribes"'. It further said: 'we have considered that tribes whose members have by and large mixed up with the general population are not eligible to be in the list of Scheduled Tribes'.

Let us now look at the five criteria that the Government of India still uses in judging the eligibility of a group for the tribal status. Objectively speaking, the first criterion – namely indication of primitive traits – is broad enough to cover all the other criteria: the primitives are those that have a distinct culture of their own, live in relative isolation and therefore fight shy of contacts with the outsiders, and, as a consequence of their isolation, they have remained backward. What, then, are the additional 'Primitive' characteristics to be included in the first criterion?

It appears that the basic distinction, as is made in the context of USA, Australia and New Zealand, between the tribals and the non-tribals, is the criterion of 'indigeneity'. The tribals are the indigenous people, also known as 'autochthonous'. During the debates of the

Constituent Assembly – drafting the Constitution of the Republic of India – a tribal leader, Jaipal Singh, asked President Rajendra Prasad:

> I wish that you would issue instructions to your Translation Committee that the translation of Scheduled Tribes should be Adivasi (meaning original inhabitants or indigenous peoples). The word Adivasi has a grace. . . . Why this old abusive epithet of Banjati (forest dwellers) being used.

Even the SC&ST Commission, in its 1961 Report, stated that Scheduled Tribes are known as indigenous peoples under international law. There are people who believe that the word 'primitive' is antithetical to the universally recognized principles of dignity for, and equality of all human beings. These problems notwithstanding, the AnSI prepared an initial list of 6,748 communities in India. Of these, 461 were tribal, having 172 segments, comprising 8.1 per cent of the total population of the country. This number is much larger than the original figure of 212 given in the 1951 Census when the tribal population constituted around 6 per cent of the Indian population.

The new Tribal Policy document, issued by the Government of India in July 2006, acknowledges the redundancy of the five criteria. It boldly asserts: 'all these broad criteria are not applicable to Scheduled Tribes today. Some of the terms used (e.g. primitive traits, backwardness) are also, in today's context, pejorative and need to be replaced with terms that are not derogatory' (para 1.2). In para 20.4, it says that 'other more accurate criteria need to be fixed'. It is significant that the Tribal Policy acknowledged the need for a process of 'descheduling' so as 'to exclude those communities who have by and large caught up with the general population. Exclusion of the creamy layer among the Scheduled Tribes from the benefits of reservation has never been seriously considered. As we move towards, and try to ensure, greater social justice, it would be necessary to give this matter more attention and work out an acceptable system' (para 20.6).

The Chopra Committee, of which I was a member, expressed its inability to employ these criteria and pass a judgement on the candidature of Gujjars for the Scheduled Tribe status. In fact, it strongly advocated for a national debate on the issue to halt this process of what some people have begun calling 'reverse Sanskritization'.

The various references to the Commissions and Committees that I have made is to bring home the point that the social situation in India has drastically changed over the years with several forces of change – planned or unplanned, endogenous or exogenous, and there is no point of return. And the change has touched all sections of our society be they urban, rural or even tribal. If we stuck to our old definitions, then we should be prepared to take out those groups which earlier matched the definition but are now metamorphosed. To invent new definitions to suit the vested interests of the concerned groups is an exercise of little value. If the intentions of our Constitution makers were to include only the backward among the tribes in the Schedule and make specific provisions for them so that their backwardness is removed, then we should develop objective criteria for descheduling the groups that have shown improvement; and at the same time disallow entry of fresh groups on false pretexts. To insist on retention of the primitive traits is nothing more than conspiring to keep certain groups backward for all times. In today's context, tribal areas of the past can also easily be classified into urban, rural and even tribal. In many groups the claim of being tribal is of historical significance only. Many individuals or families who belonged to these groups but who have changed their personal and social profile by acquiring good education, a better employment, or a political stature should voluntarily opt out rather than wait for their ouster as a 'creamy layer'.

Today, it is more relevant to identify the geographical areas that are suffering from development deficit and develop suitable strategies to reach development to all those who inhabit that region rather than be partial to certain groups in such areas. Poverty or illiteracy is the attribute that needs to be evaluated at the level of the family or the individual and not at the higher category of ascribed status – be it caste or tribe. Time has come when we need to reprioritize our actions and direct them to those specific areas that have suffered from neglect. The connectivity slogan befits that strategy which would create India as a country of interlinkages, of grids, and of communication highways.

Notes

1 Inaugural Address delivered at the National Seminar on Tribal Development: Status, Challenge, and Possibilities, Barkatullah University, Bhopal. 28–29 March 2008.
2 Robert Redfield defined *Little Community* in terms of four attributes as under:

1 Quality of **distinctiveness** where the community begins and where it ends is apparent. The distinctiveness is apparent to the outside observer and is expressed in the group consciousness of the people of the community.

ISSUES IN TRIBAL DEVELOPMENT

2 **Smallness:** So small that either it itself is the unit of personal observation or else, being somewhat larger and yet homogenous, it provides in some part of it a unit of personal observation fully representative of the whole. 'A compact community of four thousand people in Indian Latin-American can be studies by making direct personal acquaintance with one section of it'.

3 Community is '**homogenous**'. Activities and states of mind are much alike for all persona in corresponding sex and age positions; and the career of one generation repeats that of the preceding. So understood, homogenous is equivalent to 'slow-changing'.

4 The community we have in mind is **self-sufficient** and provides for all or most of the activities and needs of the people in it. The little community is a cradle-to-the grave arrangement.

3 Taking this clue, the Gujjars of Rajasthan also laid their claim to the tribal status.

5

SOCIAL SCIENCE INPUT TO MAN AND THE BIOSPHERE PROGRAMME (MAB) OF UNESCO[1]

The decade of the 1960s was the decade when the world began to suffer from the 'future shocks' – a phrase popularized by Alvin Toffler. Population explosion, fast depletion of natural resources, energy crisis and pollution of the environs, including damage to the ozone layer, had become matters of universal concern. It is in this context that slogans discouraging exploitation of scarce energy resources were raised. Simultaneously, need for appropriate technology, use of local resources and return to old and traditional ways of living, innovation of biogas and the like were advocated. For all the damages done to the environment it was Man, with a capital M, who was held responsible. Man was declared guilty of exploiting the nature. 'Save the environment' became the key concern. Since 'environment' is a broader term that includes both natural and man-made environments, environmentalists proposed the term 'biosphere for the natural environment.

It is in such a milieu that UNESCO's intergovernmental Programme on Man and Biosphere (MAB) was officially launched in 1970. It was oriented towards actual management problems arising from the interactions between human activities and natural systems. The official document on MAB clarified the orientation of the Programme in the following manner:

> Although Man's interactions with his environment have continually been undergoing change, it is the increasing scale and rate of change in many situations, which is threatening to exceed the present adaptive, and carrying capacity of the various natural and socio-cultural systems that collectively constitute the biosphere. MAB Programme is conceived for the analysis of change in Man's interactions with various ecosystems, or what are called physiographic units. Change in these

73

interactions has not only time and space dimensions but also social and scale dimensions. Changes occurring in the human populations, in the pattern of division of labour, in science and technology, and in the structure of attitudes and goals of societies, have affected the entire gamut of man-environment relationships.

It is obvious from the above that the concern for the environmental scientists is to put Man in the dock. The National MAB Committees set up by the Member-States had high representation of scholars from physical and biological sciences. Of the fourteen programme areas that were delineated for MAB, most research projects were again in the field of biological sciences.

Soon after joining UNESCO as its Regional Adviser for Social and Human Sciences in Asia and the Pacific, towards the end of 1974, one of the tasks of this author was to collect filled questionnaires sent to the various National Committees for MAB, which included social scientists, in the Asian region. Incidentally, this Programme was located in the Science Sector of UNESCO, and there was then very little communication between MAB programme officers and the Division within the Sector of Social Sciences dealing with environment-related issues. My visit to various countries in the Asia-Pacific region to enquire about the questionnaire yielded the expected result. Since there was no social science involvement in MAB, the committees had nothing to report. I took upon myself the task of encouraging social science input to MAB.

Trained in anthropology, and as a votary of interdisciplinary research, I found MAB to be an ideal starting point for my work in the Asian region. It was also a rare instance where funds for social science programme were contributed by another sector. I rediscovered the fact that most MAB Committees focussed on the biosphere and neglected the *social* dimension. I was confronted with questions such as these: what contributions can social sciences make to MAB? Are there any social scientists who have researched on biosphere? Are techniques available in social sciences for the investigation of this terrain? Can social scientists participate in a joint research team with natural scientists? And, to cap it all, are social sciences really scientific?

MAB was never intended to be a preserve of the natural scientists alone. It was conceived as a programme of research aimed towards 'developing the basis within the natural and social sciences for the rational use and conservation of resources of the biosphere, and for

MAN AND THE BIOSPHERE PROGRAMME

the improvement of the global relationship between man and the environment'. Inclusion of social sciences in MAB was to bring Man into prime focus, for what if the environment is saved and Man – and his product, *Culture* – disappeared?

The reason why social sciences did not partake in MAB was partly related to the dominance of the natural sciences in the national committees on MAB, and partly to the indifference of the social scientists themselves. To be sure, environment has been the concern of all sciences – be they social or natural. But in social sciences it did not have the central significance.

Man's environment can be divided into natural and cultural. Adding time dimension, we may talk of the past, present and future of these environments. Confronted with the responsibility of promoting MAB in social sciences, I evolved a paradigm that I would like to present here. The disciplines dealing with the different aspects of the totality of environment are easy to identify. For example, the past of the natural environment is investigated by geology and palaeontology, and the past of the cultural environment is handled by prehistory, archaeology and ancient history. Similarly, the present of the natural environment is the focus of physical anthropology, physical and biological sciences and geography; whereas the present of the cultural environment is studied by history, social psychology, public administration, political science, economics and sociology/social anthropology. But when it comes to the future, it is the newly emerging discipline of futurology – combining concerns both of the physical and biological sciences and social sciences – which is at the forefront. See Figure 5.1.

It is clear from the above that the question of environment has been studied from the perspective of individual disciplines. In anthropology, for example, we have been defining culture as a product of interactions between Man and Nature, Man and Supernatural and Man and Man – constituting the triumvirate of economy, religion and social structure and polity. Ethnographies have devoted considerable attention to habitat. Primitive economies have been heavily dependent on the natural surroundings, and therefore man–nature relationships were seen primarily from an economic angle. Anthropologists were the first to question the deterministic role of the environment in relation to culture by offering examples of different cultures in a similar environment, and similar cultures in different environments. Their position was in contrast with those of the geographers.

What we needed in MAB was a truly trans-disciplinary perspective, culling out the important contributions made by different sciences and

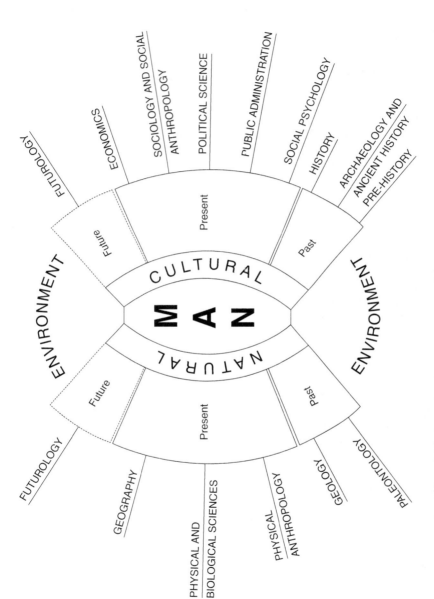

Figure 5.1 Academic disciplines dealing with various aspects of environment

MAN AND THE BIOSPHERE PROGRAMME

integrating them into a new paradigm. In such a perspective it would have been fallacious to simply raise a slogan either for 'saving the environment', or for 'saving the culture'. Both culture and natural environment are part of the surroundings of Man in society. We needed a strategy to ensure the survival of both – the environment and culture.

The interdisciplinary perspective in MAB required the fusion of the twin concerns of saving the environment and culture. An over-concern with environment to the total neglect of culture would mean disregarding the Quality of Life (QOL) question. Similarly, culture will not be able to survive and maintain, or improve the QOL if it did not have mechanisms to cope with the problem of environmental degradation. Anthropologists have shown concern about the ill effects of culture contact that were seen to be destroying the pristine character of tribal cultures. That was also a one-sided accentuation, which resulted in the criticism that students of tribal societies wished to preserve their subject matter as secluded communities living in the pristine milieu. A similar over-concern was being shown by the environmentalists to save the environment and preserve the ecological diversity. This one-sided accentuation was later toned down when the term 'sustainable' development was coined and adopted at the Rio Conference – the Earth Summit – in 1992.

When the slogan for the protection of environment was raised and given a universal colour, it was basically the problem of the developed societies who, through the development of new technologies and expensive life styles, had already begun damaging the environment. But the crisis of the North was generalized as the crisis for the whole world and environment was given priority attention. In the enthusiasm for the new concern it was almost forgotten that a basic distinction existed between the developed and the developing societies insofar as environment was concerned. The developed societies had the environmental crisis that was the outcome of the very process of development. Since the developing societies were far behind the race – with little urbanization and limited industrialization – they had not damaged their environment to that extent. Seen this way, the problem for the developed societies was to arrest the process of environmental decay, and to ensure de-pollution and rational use of the energy resources, along with a search for alternatives. In contrast, the problem for the developing countries was to have a second look at the development blueprints and to take prophylactic actions to prevent occurrence of the kind of crisis that the North was experiencing. The development model, adopted by most of the developing societies, was essentially the Western, capitalistic model, which was intended to initiate a process

77

of homogenization – a process that would gradually erase cultural diversity and create look-alike societies. The 1970s, thus, confronted a situation where ecologists were making a case for maintaining ecological diversity, and the developmentalists were undermining cultural diversity. All failures in development, for example, were attributed to tradition and to local culture. A dichotomy between tradition and modernity provided the base for the analysis of social and cultural change. Modernists were ready with their obituary to tradition.

In such a climate of opinion, quite naturally Man was declared the key culprit, and all focus of studies in the developing societies relative to MAB was seen in the context of adversative relationship between Man and his environment. While the city and the industrial townships did attract some attention, studies focussing on rural and tribal areas found one theme of great concern, namely *Shifting Cultivation*. In the several national meetings that we in UNESCO convened in Asia to develop a list of research topics, Shifting Cultivation was suggested as an important topic because this was seen as a practice that was damaging the forest cover and needed to be halted. When the 10th International Congress of Anthropological and Ethnological Sciences was convened in India in 1978, UNESCO sponsored a post-Congress symposium on this topic that was held in Bhubaneshwar (19–24 December 1978) with a view to developing a perspective on this age-old practice that engaged several tribal populations in large number of Asian societies.

The practitioners of Shifting Cultivation have always been viewed from the perspective of the outsider who either treated them as a different and a closed system, or viewed them as a satellite system having deleterious effects on their society and the surroundings. The first perspective led to the unintended consequence of 'leave them alone' philosophy, and the second to the missionary zeal reflected in 'change-them-fully' agenda. Both these perspectives are outsider perspectives and are biased against the people who lead the life in such an economy. The outsider treats the shifting cultivator as primitive and backward, and feels alarmed about the destruction of the natural environment of the neighbouring upland. The only option that the outsider has proposed was to move towards settled agriculture. The problem was never seen from an 'emic' perspective.

The English terms such as 'shifting cultivation' or 'slash-and-burn cultivation' had disparaging connotations, and indicated only some cultivation techniques and not the social system. It gave the impression that populations keep on shifting, and also that there are no other

MAN AND THE BIOSPHERE PROGRAMME

forms of economic activity in such societies. These are false notions and therefore anthropologists suggested to use the term 'swidden',[2] which is derived from the Old English swithen (meaning to singe, burn the top). Swidden refers to a diversity of agricultural systems in which fields are cleared and prepared using axe, adze or sword, and fire, and are cultivated for a short period and then fallowed for a period to allow fresh vegetation. Thus swidden is characterized by a cycle of clearing, burning vegetation, planting cultigens, weeding, harvesting and fallowing.[3]

Practised for millennia, in the tropical ecosystems with high rainfall and poor soils, Swidden was perhaps the best suited but it had constantly been condemned. The congregation of the anthropologists at Bhubaneshwar had a close look at the problem and raised very pertinent questions:

1   Is swidden a practice peculiar to the primitive tribes? In Sri Lanka, it is practised by Sinhala speaking people; in Korea, it is practised in the northernmost mountainous part by those people who escape to the mountains for political, economic or religious reasons.

2   Is swidden to be viewed only as an economic activity, or need it to be studied in specific historical and socio-political contexts? Is it not the case that the tribal has been made a refugee in his own habitat?

3   Is swidden really uneconomical? Does it destroy the environment, or is it the simple fire phobia of the non-tribal that regards this form of cultivation as bad?

4   Can there be a positive policy towards swidden cultivation? Rather than condemning it as bad – without proper assessment of the extent of damage caused by it to the biosphere – would it not be advisable to improve the methodology of shifting cultivation so that yield is increased and any damage to the environment is minimized?

In the interaction that I was able to initiate between the natural and social scientists, in the framework of MAB, it was accepted that any situation of man–environment relationship is basically exploitative in the sense that, in order to survive, Man has to exploit the resources of his surrounding environs, be they plants or the animals. Therefore, saving the environment at the cost of Man and his culture is an untenable proposition. The injection of the concept of 'sustainability' tried to bring balance in our approach vis-à-vis the biosphere.

The concept of 'sustainability' is still differently defined; the basic idea is that we have to have a development that can be sustained. This is how Agenda 21 of the Earth Summit held in Rio de Janeiro, Brazil, in 1992 (3–14 June) interpreted this concept. The road from Rio to Copenhagen, where the World Summit for Social Development was held in 1995, further refined the concept by adding that the development has to be humanly sustainable. While the Rio Summit talked of maintaining ecological diversity – by ensuring that the endangered species of plants and animals must be prevented – the Copenhagen Summit brought back *culture* to the centre stage and suggested that the common problems that the world confronts do not have common solutions. We have to look for culture-specific solutions.

I mention this to emphasize the point that the worry about the environment should be seen in a proper perspective. Such a perspective ought to de-emphasize one-sided concern for environment, and the solutions for the impending crises ought to be sought in the context of cultures. Culture should be a variable in all our development planning. The untested recipe of replacing all tradition with the so-called modernity – understood as practices of the North – has not always worked. The review of development results towards the end of the last century indicated that economic development bereft of concerns for the social and cultural spheres is hazardous. This acknowledgement prepared the ground for a plurality of models for development and progress while highlighting the crises that the entire humanity faces. Certainly, environmental crisis is one that is of universal concern but it needs different corrective actions in different social and cultural settings. Strategies and solutions that may work in a given society may not always be the appropriate ones in another setting.

The admission of this social reality secured a place of prominence for the social sciences in development dialogue, but only in the last decade of the last century. Until then, it was economics that ruled and the role of culture remained unrecognized. For the first time in the history of the United Nations an open invitation was issued to the social sciences. It was accepted that economic development has to subserve the cause of social development. Poverty, unemployment and socially disruptive tendencies need a holistic social science approach and not mere economic development.

This is certainly a matter of celebration for us, the social scientists; but we should not oversell our bill of goods. It would be wrong to use this opportunity to reintroduce the cultural bias to the total neglect of the biosphere. We have to ensure the survival of both nature and culture, and this is possible only through maintaining diversity in both the fields.

Diversity does not mean insularity. In a world on the path to globalization, one cannot prescribe a halt to interactions. We have to learn to live together in a symbiotic relationship. What the 'primitive' tribes did in the past vis-à-vis their biosphere has now to be remodelled where different cultures in a common biosphere evolve a symbiosis to ensure sustainability both of the environment and of the culture.

This is not an easy affair. If we have seen in the past decades the end of the Cold War, and the collapse of communism, we have also witnessed rise of ethnicity and ethnic and communal violence. If we have marvelled at ourselves for making tremendous advances in science and technology, we have also suffered from unintended negative consequences of such development on our environment and on our populations. Therefore, while emphasizing the importance of culture in our calculations for development we must not minimize the gravity of environmental crisis. As Gro Harlem Brundtland – Chairperson of the World Commission on Environment and Development – said, 'Our Common Future' requires us to move from one earth to one world. This one world of many cultures and many voices faces severe environmental problems that were created with the rise of human civilization. During the period of 900 days of the work of the World Commission on Environment and Development – from October 1984 through April 1987 – following major disasters occurred, all caused by human mismanagement:

- The drought-triggered environment-development crisis in Africa peaked, putting 35 million people at risk, killing perhaps a million.
- A leak from a pesticide factory in Bhopal killed more than 2,000 people and blinded and injured over 200,000 more.
- Liquid tanks exploded in Mexico City, killing 1,000 and leaving thousands more homeless.
- The Chernobyl nuclear reactor explosion sent nuclear fallout across Europe, increasing the risk of future human cancers.
- Agricultural chemicals, solvents and mercury flowed into the Rhine River during a warehouse fire in Switzerland, killing millions of fish and threatening drinking water in the Federal Republic of Germany and the Netherlands.
- An estimated 60 million people died of diarrhoeal diseases related to unsafe drinking water and malnutrition; most of the victims were children.[4]

All the examples cited by Brundtland convey the disastrous consequences of industrialization and urbanization. The fear is that if such development advances to cover the hitherto untouched rural and tribal areas they would equally be entering the danger zone. The blurb of the book, *Our Common Future*, serves notice that the time has come for a marriage of economy and ecology, so that governments and their people can take responsibility not just for environmental damage, but for the policies that cause the damage. Some of these policies threaten the survival of the entire humanity.

As we entered the twenty-first century, we witness the growth of two trends encouraged by our review of past development efforts: namely the environmental movement and the campaign for the protection of the indigenous populations. Both these movements have activated many NGOs and social activists. On surface, these movements appear reasonable; but discerning eyes also detect political subtexts in them. Studies of these movements in social scientific terms, without subscribing to any particular bias, would indeed be a welcome move.

Similarly, it is the concern with cultures of the indigenous peoples expressed in the development reviews that prompted the United Nations to declare an International Decade for the Indigenous People in 1995. Upon its conclusion, a second decade has also been dedicated to it which began in 2005 and concluded in 2014. This gives us – anthropologists – a new stimulus to return to our original interest, that of the study of the tribal societies. But while doing so, we must accept the point that today's tribes are not the same as those described in the ethnographies of the nineteenth century and the early twentieth century. Present-day tribes would defy the traditional definition of the tribes as primitive, exotic, backward and isolated groups. A great deal of change has occurred in them. Although there are pockets of underdevelopment in tribal areas, the people treat their educated and urbanized compatriots as positive reference groups. In such a situation, the attitude of charity or mercy by the 'outsiders' would not be very welcome. Of course, the indigenous people have begun asserting their cultural identity, and reviving their lost tradition, but would hesitate to re-enter their primitive past. A judicious mix of the tradition and modernity is needed and is happening as a result of their interactions with the wider society.

We must admit that in many of the tribal societies the 'insider' scholarship is now contesting 'outsider' reconstructions of knowledge of their respective societies. At the same time, there is a real danger to the tribal cultures in the sense that they might disappear as forces of

MAN AND THE BIOSPHERE PROGRAMME

modernization and globalization become more potent. There are people and agencies that express worry about profound loss of indigenous peoples and their knowledge about the natural world constructed by generations from their intimate ties to their locale. They allege that their practices and beliefs are marginalized and neglected because these are regarded as inferior forms of knowing compared to the Western scientific tradition, presented as universally applicable.

There is growing interest in incorporating indigenous knowledge systems, including traditional ecological knowledge, into truly participatory approaches to development. Moreover, it is also being emphasized that such knowledge might not only be relevant and useful at its place of origin but also have wider applications. It would, however, be wrong to over-argue the case of indigenous knowledge. The new fund of knowledge that the humanity has accumulated in different cultural settings over the millennia is part of the world heritage and not a monopoly of any single society. To deny entry to such fruitful knowledge and live in a cloistered world is an unacceptable prescription. It would be a disservice to insulate these communities and deprive them of the available stock of knowledge. If new medicines have been discovered to prevent debilitating diseases hitherto unattended, these must be made available. Glorification of past, or of prevalent practices, should not lead to ethnocentrism. We need both indigenization of the outside knowledge and universalization of parochial wisdom that is advantageous to the wider humanity.

One major worry of the many enthusiasts of indigenous knowledge systems is the commercialization and museumization of tradition. This is a fact to be reckoned. The challenge is manifold: how to preserve and record for the posterity the originality of the modes of production of artefacts and pieces of art of the indigenous people? How to ensure a quality life of the indigenous people? How to ensure that the local artists do not get pauperized and marginalized, and their skills are not stolen and used through mass medium of duplication?

As students of culture, we know that no culture is static. Changes in them occur both from within and without. It involves a process of attrition and accretion. Through non-use, or reduced use, cultural traits move towards the periphery of the culture and may even undergo hibernation. Similarly, new traits may enter either through invention or discovery or as innovations from abroad. Their acceptance is thoroughly screened by the cultural monitors. Thus, one should not repent over the disappearance of traits in any living culture, nor should one lament over arrival of new traits. Let cultures exercise their resilience.

MAN AND THE BIOSPHERE PROGRAMME

It would be wrong to approach the question as an outsider considering either the desirability of preserving the culture, or of changing it wholesale. We must also not think that it is only the underdeveloped who are responsible for damaging the environment alleging that they are thoroughly ignorant. The wisdom contained in folk culture ought to be recognized and spread beyond the confines of the culture of its origin; similarly, doors must be opened for entry of good and useful wisdom produced in other cultural contexts. Concern in MAB was oriented towards the future. As anthropologists we are also now invited to move from the paradigm of the 'primitive and the past' that prompted many to propagate a policy of preservation – interpreted as anti-change – to a policy of envisioning the future that would develop a protocol for conserving the desirable and discarding the damageable, on the one hand, and innovating and importing the traits and technology considered necessary for fashioning the future, on the other.

Anthropology in the twenty-first century faces new challenges. To meet them, its interdisciplinary orientation will have to be preserved. Breaking the discipline in watertight compartments of specialities – as is the current trend – is taking away the strength that has characterized it. Let us remind ourselves that anthropology has been defined by our predecessors as the Study of Man – at all levels of cultural development; we are obliged to honour that commitment.

Notes

1 Delivered as a Keynote Address at the National Conference organized by Anthropological Survey of India in Nagpur in 2007. Published in the *Journal of Social Anthropology*, 2009, Vol. 6, No.1–2, pp. 11–22.
2 In the three UNESCO volumes that I edited, this term has been used. It was first used by K. G. Izikowitz in 1951 in his book *Hill Peasants in French Indochina*; EthnografiskaMuseet. Eilert Ekwall has given the rationale for the use of this term in his article 'Slash-and-Burn Cultivation', in *Man*, 1955, 55 (144), pp. 135–36.
3 See Harold Conklin, *Hanuno's Agriculture*. FAO, Rome 1957.
4 *Our Common Future*, Oxford University Press, New York, 1987, p. 3.

6

SUSTAINABLE RURAL AND TRIBAL DEVELOPMENT[1]

I belong to that generation of social scientists in India who were the first to pay attention to research in rural India. It was during my student days that anthropologists shifted their attention from the study of the tribes to the intensive study of the villages. Of course, tribal areas were also regarded as 'rural' areas, unlike today when the tribal areas, particularly in the North-East, have become stratified into urban and rural, and out-of-reach tribal areas. Tribes are transiting from remote areas to rural and the urban settlements, breaking their relative isolation. That was the time when the book view of the village and of the Caste in India were being replaced by the field view.

The book view was based on idyllic descriptions of village life or on prescriptive overtones of an ideal village life. The reality of villages as they functioned in the 1950s was anybody's guess. As students, we were encouraged to undertake field work in the villages and observe the village life with an open mind. The village was thus a laboratory for us. It also became a meeting ground for sociology and anthropology – sociologists moving from the towns and anthropologists from the tribes to the villages and both exploring the actually existing social reality. The initial move to the villages was guided by the concern that the winds of change will bring about massive transformation of village life. It was, therefore, considered necessary to document the 'present' of the village before it got engulfed in the throes of change.

Greater spurt to village studies was given by the Community Development Programme (CDP) introduced by the Government of India to initiate planned social change. CDP made demands on the Indian social science to assist the planners and policymakers in their mission for rapid social change in rural life. With such an orientation Rural Sociology became a very distinct subarea, and very different than the

85

one taught in the West. Village studies in India became part of the development studies.

It is this aspect that helped introduce the dimension of change in sociological studies; in fact, Western Sociology of those times had little to offer by way of theories of social change at micro level. The development component in village studies was a distinctive trait of Indian sociology. Those running the CDP sought answers to many questions for which social scientists were not prepared. In order to provide answers they sought time to first study the actually existing structures. Students and researchers were dispatched to villages in different parts of the country to study them. Even economists felt the need to go beyond the secondary data to answer as to why people reject an innovation that is technically superior and known to improve productivity. Social change at micro level began attracting attention. The minutiae of a process of change – as seen in the adoption or rejection of a new practice – became the focus, and case studies became the preferred mode of reporting.

When developmental studies began in India in the 1950s, soon after Independence, they followed the paradigm of westernization and modernization, treating the developed West as the positive reference group. While this paradigm related to change, the focus of the planners and policymakers was on planned change, and their worry was resistance to change offered by the target population. Naturally, social scientists in this country focussed on the forces that were not allowing change to occur. The dichotomy of Tradition versus Modernity prevailed and the scholars found the key culprit in tradition; they hurriedly offered recipes and medicaments to handle culture and tradition. The debates of those times revolved around this premise and argued for the promotion of education, good health and a broadened world view including the need for a participant political culture to ease the process of transition from tradition to modernity. As a result, what we had were studies of non-change or resistance to change without questioning the merits and demerits of externally induced elements of change and without recognizing the importance of culture as the gatekeeper screening all arrivals and scrutinizing all departures.

This accumulated experience via field research helped bring about change in our orientation. As Willy Brandt, Chairman of the Independent Commission on International Development Issues, acknowledged way back in 1982 that 'focus has to be not on machines or institutions but on people. A refusal to accept alien models unquestioningly is in fact a second phase of decolonization. We must not

SUSTAINABLE RURAL AND TRIBAL DEVELOPMENT

surrender to the idea that the whole world should copy the models of highly industrialized countries'.[2] I may remind you that this was the time when already the revolution of rising expectations that started in the 1950s was transforming into a revolution of rising frustrations. The gap between the countries of the North and of the South was widening despite the efforts of the United Nations system. At that time, the world was already in its Third Development Decade, and in the beginning of each decade, there was review of achievements and of failures of development exercises and, based on it, new directions were taken.

The world has received the warning from the Club of Rome about *The Limits to Growth* which hinted at the depletion of resources and the damages done by development efforts. To quote just one example, the massive anti-malaria campaign throughout the Third World meant excessive use of a chemical called DDT. The slogan that began as 'Spray DDT, no more Mosquitoes' had to be dropped because more DDT-resistant mosquitoes surfaced; the protagonists then said, 'mosquitoes will remain, but no malaria'. Today we have both and in ample measure. The Club of Rome found out that the waste submerging in the ocean was carrying all the discharged chemicals used in the factories and farms and was becoming a feed for the fish which either killed the fish or returned to the belly of the fish eaters as a killer. These were crude reminders that blind following of the Western model of development may, after all, not be useful in the long run. Hence, the Club wanted to put limits to growth. The unease of the Club of Rome sprang from two painful realities. It had become clear that the life-sustaining role of the biosphere was at risk from open-ended consumption of natural resources. It also realized that the urgent cause of environmental protection could not be isolated from the right of poorer countries to develop.

Similarly, in the 1970s itself the First and the Second World suffered from another resource crunch: the shortage of gas. The world was told that the excessive use of energy is depleting the gas reserves. The petroleum exporting countries formed a union and decided to hike the prices of the gasoline. With all the scientific knowledge available at that time, the geologists were not in a position to predict the shortages of fuel, because the fuel shortage was more political than natural. It gave rise to OPEC – Organization of Petroleum Exporting Countries – which started dictating its own terms rather than be subservient to the countries of the Developed World. It created a world crisis. It was at this stage that the West started prescribing a dual policy: continuing its fuel consumption, and asking the South to delimit it, and also to control its population growth.

The fear of environmental deterioration and of geometrical progression of the population became two key features of a newly emerging development strategy. It was realized that the industrial path of development may not be feasible because of depletion of environmental resources, rising environmental pollution and population explosion. It was at this stage that the people of the South participating in the developmental debate argued that population increase should not be regarded as a burden but as an important human resource for development.

Development, thus, became HRD. Even the Ministries of Education were renamed as Ministries of HRD. This reorientation regarded trained manpower as a resource and not a burden, because people are born not only with one stomach but also with two hands and a reasoning brain.

Simultaneously, a search for renewable sources of energy and their harnessing ensued. Response to this need by the Third World was mixed. On the one hand, they did realize the well-known dictum that while resources are limited the demands are unlimited – after all, this is the basis of the science of economics. On the other hand, the countries of the Third World argued that the countries of the First and the Second World are polluted countries because of heavy industrialization and urbanization, while countries of the Third World are underdeveloped in terms of these processes and therefore the approach of the West cannot be blindly followed. In the North, or the West – whatever label you may like to employ – the problem was that of tackling the already polluted levels, whereas the countries of the South were alerted to follow policies that would ensure development without polluting the environment. The intellectuals of the Third World already started detecting conspiracy of the North to keep the South behind in terms of development. How can economic development be ensured without exploiting the environment? How to decouple development from environmental deterioration?

This became the key question in development thinking. It was felt in some intellectual circles that the South should not become the victim of the conspiracy of the North, and the entire question of environment should be seen in a much wider perspective. For the North, what was important was to contain pollution and to economize the use of natural resources in order to maintain their pace of change; for the South, the need was to speed up the process of development

SUSTAINABLE RURAL AND TRIBAL DEVELOPMENT

while ensuring that the strategies employed would not pollute their environs, and that resource depletion would not occur. The sources of renewable energy – air, sunshine and water – will be maximally used to ensure that the experience of the North is not repeated by the South in its journey of development. The important point to remember is that while the North has technological knowhow and a machine culture, the South has the needed wherewithal to run them and also the market to buy their products. It has provided a competitive edge to the South to be an equal partner in negotiations. The South is not going to oblige the North by delimiting its journey towards modernization because of the fear of environmental pollution or depletion of resources because the environment in the South is still not that polluted, and the needed resources are also available in plenty. Most of the South is unable to visualize the global crisis in national terms.

A few years later, in the same direction, another change in our orientation to development occurred. The international community brought forth the concept of *Endogenous Development*. It was acknowledged that each country will have to devise strategy that suits her rather than blindly copy others. For example, that was the time when the US city of Chicago alone was consuming as much electricity as the rest of the Third World. Imagine how much of such energy will be needed if the entire world were to follow the pattern of consumption of one US city alone.

This is also true of military expenditure. The world was reminded that expenditure on military can be reduced to create a peace dividend that would solve many problems. From Will Brandt Report let me quote some calculations:

In the 1980s, the annual military bill of the entire world was approaching 450 billion US dollars while official development aid accounted for less than 5 per cent of this figure. The Brandt report says:

1   The military expenditure of only half a day would suffice to finance the whole malaria eradication programme of WHO.
2   A modern tank costs about one million dollars; that amount could improve storage facilities for 100,000 tons of rice. The same sum of money could provide 1,000 classrooms for 30,000 children.
3   For the price of one jet fighter – 20 million dollars – one could set up about 40,000 village pharmacies.
4   One-half of one per cent of one year's military expenditure would pay for all the farm equipment needed to increase food-deficit in low-income countries in 10 years.[3]

The emphasis on endogenous development in the 1980s was received by the developing countries with a pinch of salt. Some saw in it the design of the developed countries to withdraw development aid and thus leave the developing countries in lurch. Others saw in it a possibility to bring culture back in developmental strategies. This movement did not find many takers.

Towards the end of the twentieth century, the United Nations system decided to convene world summits to review the entire gamut of activities and assess the gains and shortcomings of the previous development decades. The Conference on Environment held in Rio de Janeiro adopted the slogan of *Sustainable Development* proposed by Brundtland Commission in its famous Report – *Our Common Future*.[4] The Brundtland Commission's mandate was to:

[1] re-examine the critical issues of environment and development and to formulate innovative, concrete, and realistic action proposals to deal with them;

[2] strengthen international cooperation on environment and development and assess and propose new forms of cooperation that can break out of existing patterns and influence policies and events in the direction of needed change; and

[3] raise the level of understanding and commitment to action on the part of individuals, voluntary organizations, businesses, institutes, and governments. (1987: 347)

The Commission focused its attention on the areas of population, food security, the loss of species and genetic resources, energy, industry, and human settlements – realizing that all of these are connected and cannot be treated in isolation one from another.

(1987: 27)

Obviously, the Commission was concerned with the deteriorating environment caused by pollution and depletion of energy resources. It was felt that over-exploitation of the environment needs to be stopped. This cry came at a time when there was huge criticism of the development strategies that were aiming at the homogenization of world culture. While on the one hand, environmental enthusiasts were talking of saving the environment, cultural specialists were concerned about saving the cultures. The latter argued that for Man to survive,

SUSTAINABLE RURAL AND TRIBAL DEVELOPMENT

it is necessary to exploit the environment; the former countered the argument by saying that if environment is destroyed humanity will not be able to survive.

Let me point out the fact that the United Nations system functions through specialized agencies such as environment, education, labour, health etc. While addressing global problems, these agencies willy-nilly take a narrow view in terms of their specialization. Thus, the agency devoted to environment – UNEP – focusses on environment and provides it a one-sided accentuation. UNESCO similarly focusses on Education and so on. But in the process, the interdisciplinary perspective is lost. The Brundtland Commission was asked to focus on the problems of environment and, therefore, quite rightly it pointed out the dangers of environmental pollution and depletion of natural resources and quite rightly blamed human activity for the present crisis. But in the process it forgot that global change is inevitable because of the presence of Man on earth. To be sure, population growth, economic growth, technological change, political and economic institutions and people's attitudes and beliefs impact on the natural environment, and it is inevitable. It is also true that human societies change because of internal processes but also because of their contacts with the outside world. It is this Reference Group orientation that makes human societies behave the manner they behave. If the West has electricity, and the gadgets that run on it such as ACs and refrigerators, the countries of South will also need to have them as denominators of development and as items of luxury.

Focus on environment has come to the fore as a result of Global climatic change that is going to affect not this or that society but all societies. We are told that the climate change is caused by greenhouse gases such as carbon dioxide, methane and CFCs (chlorofluorocarbons). These are affecting the stratospheric ozone layer. Under an agreement CFCs and halons were to be phased out by the year 2000 and methyl chloroform and carbon tetrachloride were also to be eliminated. But little progress in this direction has been made. What is more important is the point that one is not sure whether their elimination would solve all the problems associated with ozone depletion. CFCs that are already in the atmosphere are going to continually damage the ozone for several decades. Also we are not sure whether the chemicals that are being tried out as their substitutes will prove benign in the long run. In the 1930s when the CFCs were introduced, they were regarded as ideal. Now the new replacements such as HCFs (hydrochlorofluorocarbons) and HFCs (hydrohalocarbons) are already being doubted for their contributions to the greenhouse effect.

The second concern of environmentalists is increasing deforestation and loss of biodiversity. This concern is genuine. It is found that an area of tropical moist forest of the size of a Latin American country, Honduras, is getting deforested every year – and this was the situation according to a 1988 estimate. Similarly, there is extinction of around 18,000 animal species every year. At this rate both the botanical and zoological diversity is threatened.

It is such an alarming scenario that prompted the Brundtland Commission to appeal to the world to save *Our Common Future*. The Report proposes 'sustainable development' as the new policy directive and recommends change of politics in order to achieve it. This is how the Report defines this term:

> Sustainable development is development that meets the needs of the present without compromising the ability of future generations to meet their own needs.

The definition contains two key concepts: the concept of 'needs', in particular the essential needs of the world's poor, to which overriding priority should be given; and the idea of limitations imposed by the state of technology and social organization on the environment's ability to meet present and future needs. The important departure that it makes is in terms of its future orientation. Sustainable development is to be seen in the context of the future. Brundtland once remarked to the effect that we have not inherited our present from our ancestors, but have borrowed it from our children. So we must hand over the world to our children in a quality better than what we had received.

To put crudely, we need development that is sustainable. What it means is that a hasty development may have to be stopped if there were no resources to carry it forward, or if it killed the very basis of survival, namely biodiversity.

When the Social Development Summit was held in Copenhagen in 1995, the slogan carried from Rio added one adjective. Member states talked of Sustainable *Human* Development. On the one hand, this elaboration reminded that Human is important – what if environment remained and the humans disappeared? On the other hand, the adjective *Human* remained undefined. Was it synonym of 'social'? or of 'cultural'? And how to talk of sustainability in these terms? Human ingenuity came to the fore and it was proposed that like biodiversity,

SUSTAINABLE RURAL AND TRIBAL DEVELOPMENT

there is also a need for maintaining cultural diversity, and not homogenization of cultures. The concept is still fluid.

Let us face the facts. It is true that 72.18 per cent of our population, according to 2011 Census, still lives in villages. But our villages numbering more than 638,000 do not all look like the descriptions of the villages in the 1960s. There is better road connectivity, many villages are electrified, there are several urban traits in our villages and our agriculture is also witnessing change. In such a changing milieu when we talk of sustainable rural development, we will have to be clear as to our intention. Are we saying that the process of urbanization should stop and villages should remain villages of the type we found in ancient times? What shall happen to the villages that have become part of urban centres through the processes of suburbation and conurbation?

In order to prepare a new blueprint for change that would satisfy sustainability criterion we need careful and sustained discussion. The old idiom will have to give way to new streams of thought.

In India the new programme that was initiated at the intervention of our former president, Abdul Kalam, is named PURA – Provision of Urban amenities in Rural Areas. It is designed to address defects and incorporate new dimensions combining rural infrastructure and livelihood creation. It is aimed to create physical, electronic and knowledge connectivities to take the economy to a new level. I understand that this programme is being operated at pilot level in eight districts of India of which two are in the state of Rajasthan, namely Rajsamand and Jaipur. Here lies an opportunity for our social scientists to study this project intensively and evaluate its outcome.

The message that the Brundtland Commission Report (published in 1987 by Oxford University Press) gave while proposing the strategy for sustainable development is that 'environment' should not be perceived as a sphere separate from human emotion or action; similarly, 'development' is just not political or economic; it is to be seen in the context of environment. We need to understand the environment in relation to development and development in relation to the environment. The Brundtland Commission Report argues: 'the "environment" is where we live; and "development" is what we all do in attempting to improve our lot within that abode. The two are inseparable.'

There is no short cut to good research. Our young researchers should not shy away from good and solid field work. What the field can teach, no one else can in the confines of a classroom.

Notes

1 Keynote Address delivered at a National Seminar organized by ISS University, Jaipur, 2012.
2 *North-South: A Programme of Survival*. Pan Books, London, 1980, p. 23.
3 I might say in passing that these are 1980 calculations; today the same items cost much more.
4 The Report of the Brundtland Commission was published by Oxford University Press in 1987, and was welcomed by the General Assembly Resolution 42/187[6].

7

TRIBAL STUDIES
Need for reorientation[1]

I shall dwell upon three issues in this chapter:

1 Anthropology and tribal studies.
2 Need for a definition of the tribe.
3 How do we approach development?

I Anthropology and tribal studies

There exists a general image that anthropology is the study of the tribes. On questions related to tribes, the government agencies and the informed public look at the anthropologist for knowledge-based answers. However, the situation in this regard has considerably changed over the years.

If one were to visit the university departments of anthropology one would get the impression that anthropology is getting redefined as 'physical' anthropology and is coming closer to biological sciences. This is a trend significantly different than the one prevalent when people of my generation joined the anthropology departments. At that time, anthropology was almost coterminous with tribal studies. An anthropologist was the one who studied the primitive groups; physical anthropology focussed on the past – prehistory and palaeontology. Concerned with the origin of Man, and the evolution of cultures and civilizations, anthropology was then defined as the study of the 'primitive' and the 'past'; the anthropologist was trained to handle both these aspects. Since the 'past' of human culture was seen to be partly present in the so-called tribal communities that were vastly different, and distantly located from the so-called civilized societies, anthropologists of that era focussed on them to trace the missing links in human history. They contributed to the emerging science of ethnology – used almost

95

as a synonym of anthropology. Genetics, Racial studies, Eugenics, Prehistoric Archaeology, and Palaeontology were treated as subsets of this discipline. However, the public image of the discipline remained that of tribal studies. The names of Verrier Elwin, von Fürer Haimendorf, S. C. Roy, N. K. Bose, D. N. Majumdar, S. C. Dube, Sachchidanand and L. P. Vidyarthi – to name a few pioneers of Indian anthropology – had all worked on Indian tribes. None of them was known as a physical anthropologist although Majumdar did some work in that area; so did Irawati Karve (who had a doctoral degree from Germany in that speciality). Even those who chose to specialize in physical anthropology at that time carried out their initial field researches in tribal communities; for example, P.C. Biswas and Inder Paul Singh – both of Delhi University – have to their credit work in the area of social anthropology in the beginning of their career. Today's leading anthropologists in India, barring exception, are specialists in physical anthropology working in the area of human genomics, anthropometry, serology and dermatoglyphics. The scope of the discipline has been considerably redefined. Work in the tribal areas is carried out mostly by the AnSI; however, even there one notices a gradual shift towards physical anthropology and human biology.

Today, more than 37 years later, the scenario has vastly changed. University departments of anthropology are no longer the departments of an integrated and interdisciplinary study of Man. It is Physical Anthropology that dominates; social anthropology not only has become secondary or marginalized but is neglected to the extent that some of the departments do not even have permanent lecturers in that speciality. The fact that the Rajiv Gandhi Chair for Tribal Studies is located here at this university in the Department of Sociology is indicative of the trend. I recall an incident when I was invited to deliver a lecture in my former department – that too at the instance of the vice chancellor who heard me speak in a different seminar in the town and learnt of my old association with that university. After the lecture, I was informed that the lecture was boycotted by all the physical anthropologists in the faculty barring the Head (as she was the one who invited me and thus was obliged to attend). It was chaired by my colleague and friend of long standing – who incidentally joined the department as physical anthropologist with me in 1960. He had to suffer me for one full hour; later in private he told me that he did not understand what I said. Incidentally, I spoke on Changing Orientation to Change and began with evolutionary theories that have been the forte of anthropology of our times.

TRIBAL STUDIES

In 1973–74, as Research Director at the Indian Council of Social Science Research, I was engaged in the task of establishing afresh a set of priorities for research in various social science disciplines. For this task, the ICSSR involved noted scholars from various universities and also sought inputs through a mailed questionnaire from the working social scientists. The priorities recommended for the tribal studies by the expert team headed by Professor S. C. Dube included *restudies* of those tribes which had been studied previously – and mostly – by foreign anthropologists as the monographs produced by them have become dated and the communities studied have been undergoing substantial changes. Along with it the Committee also recommended new ethnographic studies of the tribes that were not covered, by encouraging younger teachers and anthropology students to carry out field work in them.

That exercise has also not yielded good results.

During my recent visit to Shillong I visited the library of the Regional Station of the AnSI. I looked for any new books – particularly ethnographies – on the tribes of the North-East, I did not find any restudies of the Khasis or the Garos, or any other tribes that were studied earlier by the British anthropologists and read by us as students. Of course, more specialized works are being produced; for example, there is an excellent study of the Angami Nagas done by N.K. Das titled *Kinship, Politics and Law in Naga Society* (1993). There was also a copy of the monograph by Vinay Srivastava on the Raikas of Rajasthan that earned him a PhD from Cambridge in the 1990s, but it also focussed on the religious aspects of this semi-nomadic tribe. However, these are exceptions. In general, it can be said that there are few restudies of the tribes, and very few new studies of the tribes in a holistic framework have been undertaken that has been the hallmark of anthropology in our student days.

A review of tribal studies for the fourth round of ICSSR Survey of Research in Sociology and Social Anthropology, carried out by Vinay Srivastava, brought out the fact that there is decline of interest in the conventional field of anthropology. Of course, during this period some encyclopaedias on tribal societies have appeared. Also the People of India Project of the AnSI covered the tribal communities. In addition, some good pictorial – in fact, costly coffee table – books done by professional photographers, in league with anthropologists, who provided the script, have also come to the market. But most research is reported as articles, and as communications in professional journals such as *Man in India* and *Eastern Anthropologist*. Even here, the number of articles on social anthropological aspects of tribals is

97

falling. The ICSSR Survey revealed that only 67.11 per cent of the articles published in *Man in India* during 1993–2002 and 18.9 per cent articles published in *Eastern Anthropologist* during the period 1988–2001 related to the tribals.

There is another development in regard to the study of the tribes. While interest amongst the social anthropologists is generally declining, people from other social sciences have begun taking interest in the study of specific aspects of tribes, particularly those related to development. Additionally, there is now emergence of what is called 'auto-anthropology' – studies carried out by indigenous scholars of their own society. Such scholars have not only brought in the 'insider view' but also challenged the very definition of the discipline of anthropology – as 'the study of other cultures'.

As an important growth point, what we must take note of is the fact that both insiders and outsiders, and scholars from various disciplines – and not only the anthropologists – are now getting involved in tribal studies. This is a definite change in orientation towards tribal studies, which would hopefully enrich our understanding of the changing Tribal India. The changing demographic profile of researchers doing tribal studies is also reflected in the themes covered. There are relatively few studies on tribal family and kinship, social structure and religion. There is growing interest in tribal demography, tribal economy in the context of national economy, tribal ecology, tribal languages, tribal women, politics in tribal areas and on indigenous knowledge. But the knowledge produced by these efforts needs to be properly consolidated and systematized.

I must hasten to add that in the 1950s there began a new trend of village studies in social anthropology, particularly in India. It is through this route that Srinivas came to social anthropology from sociology. Dube also established himself as a pioneer in village studies with his study of Shamirpet in Andhra Pradesh. He came to anthropology via political science and qualified as an anthropologist by studying the Kamars of Chhattisgarh. The village studies by these scholars distinguished from other such efforts by following the ethnographic techniques of investigation and presentation. Their work gave spurt to village studies; in the process tribal studies also received a certain setback. Today, even village studies of that genre are also on the decline. No new villages are studied following that paradigm, and no restudies are being carried out. I have recently paid visit to the famed Shamirpet village which earned Dube a worldwide recognition. The village that is portrayed in the *Indian Village* represents the past of the present-day

TRIBAL STUDIES

Shamirpet which is highly urbanized with a few vestiges of the old order. The Village of today in India, like the tribes of today, demands a fresh set of studies. The stereotype of the tribe does not match with the actually existing and rapidly changing social structures of these communities. The same is true of the village communities.

It should also be noted that while ethnographic studies of the tribes somehow became less attractive, several new actors entered the scene to carry out studies of specific aspects of tribes using techniques other than participant observation that required longer duration of stay, learning of the native language and living away from the comforts of the towns. Also, technology has provided new means to collect and preserve data. In an unpublished article on the field work among the Raikas, written by Vinay Srivastava – that I had the pleasure of reading – there is an excellent recounting of the hazards of field work in the 1990s. Compared to the 1960s, these are less painful, but nevertheless indicative of the disincentives for the young researcher. A camera, a tape recorder, facility for postage that helped the researcher mail his notes to his supervisor or to a safer place for storage and receipt of instructions and comments on the notes from the supervisor are definitely the new facilitators that were not available to a researcher some 50–60 years back. But today, many more are added – a laptop, internet connection in the remote areas and even mobile connections are now there for speedy dispatch and receipt of messages. Additionally, with the spread of literacy and education, educated locals are available for support; these are the new potentates. Vinay Srivastava has recounted some of the hazards associated with such available manpower.

To sum up, the profile of tribal studies has considerably changed over time. No longer is the anthropologist the only outsider collecting all sorts of data on the tribal life. Tribal studies are no longer the monopoly of the anthropologist. People from different disciplines, and even belonging to governmental and non-governmental agencies, are carrying out specific studies amongst the tribes. Different kinds of statistics are available regarding the individual tribes. The discipline of anthropology is changing because of the inner dynamics and academic politics. Practitioners of sociology in India who resisted the so-called intrusion or encroachment of anthropology in their domain are now providing a space for tribal studies while anthropology departments are virtually giving up their claim on social aspects of the tribes and concentrating on the biological aspects of the study of Man. On top of all this, our tribal communities are in the throes of change. These developments require a change in the paradigm for the study of tribes.

II The concept of Tribe

While investigating tribes, it must be remembered that there is no uniformity in the use of the concept of Tribe. Ethnographies written in the idiom of 'eternal present' regarded these population groups as non-changing. Since they attracted the attention of the pioneering anthropologists visiting remote areas as being very different and perhaps representing the earlier stage of their society's own evolution, they just dubbed them as 'primitive' and 'preliterate' without bothering to furnish a definition. As a consequence, anthropology became a study of 'other cultures' – cultures other than one's own. When Indian anthropologists started studying Indian tribes and villages, they somehow challenged that definition of the discipline because they were, in a way, studying their own culture – a multicultural outfit called *indigenous civilization*. Unstated, they regarded those as tribes which were studied by alien anthropologists, and those that were listed in earlier censuses as tribes. During those times it was convenient to classify India into urban, rural and tribal as three distinct population groups based on residence. Tribes were regarded as those that were isolated and distantly located in relatively non-accessible geographical areas.

When independent India adopted its new Constitution that made provision for the listing of tribes in a special Schedule, the officialdom took recourse to the Census and listed all the tribes registered therein. In doing so, they ignored the finer distinction made by the Census Commissioners by classifying them on the basis of their religion which excluded all converts – Hindus, Christians, Muslims, Jains etc. – and listed only the non-converts (or the animists) into the category of the tribals. Hutton (1961) went to the extent of saying that tribal religion represents that part which is yet to enter the temple of Hinduism! But the official listing included all those that bore the tribal name. Thus, a total of 19,116,498 (19.1 million), divided into 212 tribes, got listed as population of Tribal India, constituting 5.36 per cent of the total Indian population in 1951. In undivided India of 1941, this percentage was 7.8 but the deficit of 1951 represented that section which became part of Pakistan (both East and West). Today the number of tribes listed as ST has burgeoned to around 700, and represents a little more than 8 per cent of the total population. The increase in the number of tribes is attributable to separate state-wise listing of the same tribe and inclusion of several other groups which claimed a tribal status. In the process, a group bearing the same name, and claiming the same origin, has become a non-tribe in some states. But we lack anthropological evidence to justify such exclusions.

It is for the latter purpose, that of granting a tribal status to a claimant group, that the question of defining a tribe became significant. Unfortunately, anthropology did not provide an answer, as it did not bother to fashion one. Dube listed six features as descriptors of a tribe, but that was hardly a definition in the real sense of the term. The government took note of Dube's formulation and came up with a list of characteristics to judge the candidature of a group for the tribal status. We have analysed them earlier and argued that they are no longer relevant, and do not add up to a definition of tribe.

The criteria being employed by the government are too vague to judge the candidature of any group. Not only this, if these criteria were to be applied even to those groups that are already included in the ST category, they will be disqualified and many of them will have to be de-scheduled.

In the Indian context, a tribe is the one that is included in the official Schedule. This approach may be administratively convenient but is technically wrong, and allows undue political manipulation. There are cases, for example, where a tribe bearing the same name belongs to the ST category in one state, but is not included in that category in another state. Also there are cases of several new ones that are included as tribes in certain states but denied that privilege in another. A case in point is that of the Gujjars who were included in the tribal category in the State of Jammu and Kashmir, but not in Rajasthan where there is a mass movement pressing for its inclusion in the ST category. Students of tribal studies take up those groups which enjoy government recognition without bothering about a scientific definition that would be universally applicable. The implication is clear: academic research is carried out along political lines without raising crucial issues. It is, in my opinion, the task of the researcher to point out flaws in the policy and offer guidelines rather than toe the official line.

We need to insist that there cannot be a path reversal, of moving backward. It is the government policy that is putting breaks to halt the process of status change. Today's India cannot be classed into the neat categories of Urban, Rural and Tribal. While the first two are residential categories, the third one is an ethnic or a racial category. That is why tribes can also be classified into urban and rural; certainly sections of them that still remain less mobile – socially or spatially – may need special assistance to move out of their insulation, but this cannot be the case for the entire community.

It is in this sense, that the clubbing together of all statistics for the 8 per cent of the population designated as tribal serves little purpose.

In the late 1950s and early 1960s when I carried out field work in the villages of Rajasthan and Madhya Pradesh, I found presence of the tribal groups in the multi-caste villages – the Bhil in Mewar and the Gond in Madhya Pradesh. They were part of the village system and their families were treated as representatives of their respective castes. The Gond and the Bhil families spread in a number of contiguous villages in the two regions had structures identical to castes and were part of the interactive system of multi-caste communities. The ethnographic descriptions of Morris Carstairs or of Verrier Elwin were not at all applicable to them. Ajit Jogi, former chief minister of Chhattisgarh, claiming a tribal status has failed in his attempt to align with the same-name tribal group. But the Gond and the Bhil of the two villages of my study in two different states now enjoy the ST status on empirically invalid premises; there is no *golgadhedo* among the Bhils, and no *ghotul* among the Gonds, who share the residence with other castes.

A politically desirable continuity of the confusion should, in my view, not become the basis for objective portrayal of the existing reality. It is time that we, as social scientists, propose the definition of tribe as a *transitional* structural unit and also suggest the process of its transformation into a larger society as well as its assimilation as a subset in a larger social system. Indian society provides adequate material for such an exercise.

III Approach to developmental issues

A good deal of social science work in recent years is related to developmental issues. Broadly it can be divided into two types: (1) assisting the agents of development in evaluation and (2) articulating the concerns of the people affected by development.

Since research money is provided by the governmental agencies, the projects carried out as commissioned studies have performed the function of internal assessment highlighting both the achievements and shortfalls. Such exercises served the purpose of giving praiseworthy certification to developmental agencies and of offering recommendations and suggestions – mostly unsolicited. Detached scholars have raised doubts about such researches as they do not generally question the value premises of the development paradigm and follow the politically or administratively defined protocol.

Those critical of developmental policies have followed the usual path of finding fault with the process of modernization, and now of globalization, and showing concern for the gradual death of traditional cultures. It is the perceived ill-effects of development that provided the needed ammunition to such critics.

To my mind, both the approaches are somewhat lop-sided. Of course, we must acknowledge that the use of social scientists in developmental work, particularly for purposes of evaluation, is a welcome trend. It is also desirable that the civil society take up the cause of the 'downtrodden'. But this should not rule out the other role of independent assessment in an objective fashion so that the outcome is compared not only with the expected goals, but with the overall impact in terms of both anticipated and unanticipated consequences. At the same time, it is important to examine the premises on which the development paradigm is built and actions initiated. While working with the agency introduces certain biases, taking a protective stance for the cultures brings the social scientist nearer the NGOs who only see the bleak side of the picture. I must make it clear that I am not denying the importance of these roles; I am only suggesting that they are different roles than that of the researcher who ought to be unbiased and evaluate the process objectively – and not with the tainted glasses.

While lecturing in a seminar in these very premises and under the same auspices, I had raised the question regarding the manner in which we look at development. Development is criticized for (i) its failure in achieving the ends, (ii) its poor implementation and consequent wastage, and (iii) its adverse effects on culture and tradition. In seminars like this, we generally tend to adopt the advocacy role for saving the culture. Such a stance taken earlier by anthropologists earned them an allegation that they are conspiring 'to keep the tribals in a zoo'. Verrier Elwin (1942), who vociferously advocated the cause of the tribals, was equally eloquent in denying such an allegation. But the undercurrent of such ambivalence still persists. When we want to do something to take the people out of their backwardness, we are obliged to initiate programmes of change. And change involves departure from the present state to another one – higher or lower, depending on how we rate the states. It requires no particular skills to identify the areas that get affected by the processes of change – be they planned or self-evolving. Change – whether orthogenetic or planned – does result in the death or disappearance of certain cultural traits. This is inevitable. It is important to record all this, but not to repent. Should we endorse the plea for a halt to development? Are we favouring the cry for retaining anthropological zoos?

Criticism is also laid for the non-effects of change. A good instance is poverty. All these years of planning, since India attained its independence in 1947, have focussed on the alleviation of poverty, and yet this task is on the top of the agenda. How do we view this trend? Should we rest with raising our voices to convey our dissatisfaction and ask for more or for further acceleration of the pace? Or do we challenge the very premises on which the programmes are mounted?

Poor planning, bad administration leading to faulty execution, waste of resources and continuing plight of the target population are known talking points of any reviews of development exercises. The message that is generally conveyed is 'more of the same' or 'different of the same' is needed. For all this, sociological imagination is not needed. What it is that we, as social scientists, can do that is distinct and useful?

For the weaker sections of the society, defined in terms of ascriptive status, the government enunciated the policy of special treatment by according them a 'policy of reservation', and offering them a host of privileges. Originally divided into ST and SC, the weaker sections were given yet another category of the OBC. Hoping that special packages for them would bring them at par with the rest of the society in about 10 to 15 years, the policy and programmes were devised and implemented with considerable publicity and fanfare. More than 64 years have passed and yet we are nowhere near the intended goal. The number of entries in the three categories is constantly rising, and there is clamour for more inclusions. Such demands are raised not only by those who are really poor but also by the rich and the powerful, and numerically preponderant agricultural groups. What the policy has done is (i) to reinforce a vested interest in backwardness amongst those that are already in one of these lists and (ii) to encourage those who once hated being dubbed as 'lower' or 'backward' to gladly assume the designation of 'Dalit'. As long as there are categories of *Adivasis*, *Dalits* and of *Pichhada Varg*, their assimilation into wider society will remain somewhat suspended. The policy favouring them has initiated the process of moving backwards – some sort of *reverse Sanskritization*. It is difficult to say whether this is the intended consequence or an unintended one. Since it was not part of the manifest objective, one would believe this to be the Latent Function of the Policy. Rather than highlighting this, we tend to examine the policy and its effectiveness in terms of the official 'givens', and even join the chorus in support of other groups, and even non-Hindu communities, who are seeking relocation in these 'privileged categories'.

There is yet another anomaly to which regretfully social scientists have not paid adequate attention. SC and ST categories are based

TRIBAL STUDIES

on the principle of ascribed status – now also known as *Janma-Pradhan*. When a new category was invented to accommodate the newer groups in the privileged section, it was named as Backward *Classes* – classes and not class. Sociologically, class is distinct from caste and tribe, as it represents *achieved* status (*Karma-Pradhan*) and allows mobility of its constituents upwards or downwards. But what were listed into this category were *castes*, using basically the criterion of backwardness conceived in terms of poverty and other attributes as resultant of poverty. This subtle distinction is nowhere properly highlighted, and we have also willy-nilly allowed ourselves to fall in this trap.

I have elsewhere indicated that poverty exists at several levels.

At the level of the country or the region it expresses differently and is generally measured in terms of natural endowment or GNP/GDP. Strategies needed for removal of such poverty require a different orientation: creation of suitable infrastructure, better connectivity, rational use of the available resources and proper distribution mechanism.

At the level of the family and the individual we need a different strategy. Such poverty ought to be de-linked from group-based or region-based poverty. A single community – ethnic or religious – has both rich and poor families. Poverty or affluence does not get distributed equally amongst all its members. Perhaps this is the reason for the introduction of the concept of Below Poverty Line (BPL) at the level of the family. But to perpetuate the ambivalence, government is now collecting data both about the castes and the BPL. If the Constitution forbids identification of castes, and the base data about BPL provides all indicators for judging the poverty status of a family, why collect data on Caste? How do you abolish caste while using caste as a status indicator?

I am tempted to elaborate this point, but shall stop here and proceed towards the problem of tribal education which is the theme of the present Seminar.

I have heard speakers lamenting the poor state of education amongst the tribals, and following the same style of reasoning to which I have alluded earlier in this Lecture, they lament over the deficit. I found the argument along the expected lines. It is true that aggregated data on tribal education paint an unfavourable picture compared to the overall data for the entire Indian population. But there is another way of looking at these figures. Compare these figures with those of 1951 Census figures. At that time, our literacy rate for the country as a whole was dismally low – around 18 per cent, and most of it amongst the male and the young populace. Since the tribals reside mostly – as

TRIBAL STUDIES

much as 93 per cent – in rural areas, they were part of the share of country's huge illiterate rural population.

When the country got its independence from the British, the overall literacy rate was low and most of this percentage came from Men, with Women, in general, having a really very low – in fact dismal – literacy rate. Surely, the situation must have been pathetic in our tribal belt, and in rural India as a whole which constituted nearly 88 per cent of the total. Literacy then was typically an urban trait. In our tribal population, literacy rate in 1961 was as low as 9.51 per cent compared to overall literacy percentage of 28.30. Female literacy amongst the tribals jumped from 1961 average of as low as 3.16 per cent to 34.76 per cent in 2001. This means that Tribal female literacy in 2001 was close to overall Indian literacy rate in the 1971 Census. And the literacy rate among tribal males in 2001 was more than the 1981 average for the country as a whole. In the year 2001, our literacy rate further improved to reach 64.83 per cent, and in 2011, it now stands at 74 per cent. Today our literacy rate in the rural areas is as high as 68.91 per cent, more than the overall literacy rate for the year 2001. Even the female literacy today has gone up from a meagre 8.66 per cent in 1951 to 65.46 per cent in 2011. Literacy data for the tribals for the years 1961 through 2001 tell a revealing story; see Table 7.1. From a mere 8.54 per cent in 1961 it reached 47.1 per cent in 2001. And in 2011, it reached 63.1 per cent (males = 71.7 and females = 54.4).

One can rejoice at the literacy climb of the tribal component of our population. It is not a small achievement that female literacy amongst the tribals jumped from 1961 average of as low as 3.16 per cent to 34.76 per cent in 2001, and 54.4 per cent in 2011. This means that Tribal female literacy in 2001 was close to overall Indian literacy rate in the 1971 Census. And the literacy rate among tribal males in 2001

Table 7.1 Tribal literacy, 1961–2011

Year	Male (%)	Female (%)	Total (%)
1961	13.83	3.16	8.54
1971	17.63	4.85	11.39
1981	24.52	8.05	16.35
1991	40.65	18.19	29.60
2001	59.16	34.76	47.10
2011	71.70	54.4	63.1

Source: Census of India

TRIBAL STUDIES

was more than the 1981 average for the country as a whole. What is more satisfying is the fact that amongst tribal children (of the age group 6–14) the enrolment ratio is as high as 86.06 per cent (90.58% for boys and 81.10% for girls) – this ratio ranges from 60.90 in Nagaland to more than 108 in Kerala, Manipur and Tamilnadu, and as high as 114 in Sikkim. Recent statistics also indicate that as many as 539 ST girls are enrolled for their PhDs. The total number of tribal girls in Higher Education, including the Polytechniques, is as high as 142,280. These figures definitely indicate a rising percentage of literates, particularly among the young population of tribal women. Of course, this must be acknowledged that the overall average does not suggest the precarious condition in some tribal groups or in sections of particular tribes that still lead an isolated existence. But more than 80 per cent enrolment of girls leaves out only less than 20 per cent of them in the category of non-school-going population.

I have dwelt here only on all-India figures for the tribal population. They prove the point that literacy is spreading in our tribal belts. More important than this is the point that we have reached a stage where we need disaggregated data for individual tribes in different states, and regions within the states. Since tribal areas in certain states are also classified as urban and rural, it is important to locate the percentage of not only the literates but also the educated in them. I suspect the profile of literacy and education to be substantially different amongst the tribal groups of our North-Eastern region. Given such heterogeneous profile of our tribal communities it would be unwise to suggest a panacea – a common cure for all the tribes; this is time to think of community-specific strategies. For this, we need systematic investigation of individual regions that would enable us to draw dependable profiles and to prepare noteworthy research papers in place of those that fall into the category of journalism or NGO-type advocacies. No doubt, they are equally important, but they cannot be substitutes for an in-depth enquiry.

Then, there is a need for giving up over-emphasis to literacy and to primary education. Having attained 74 per cent literacy, using whatever yardstick, we are left only with 26 per cent of our population that need to move in the realm of literacy. In the 1950s, literacy in the entire Third World was at low ebb, and the world community, under the aegis of the United Nations, particularly UNESCO, assigned eradication of illiteracy a well-deserved priority. It is in that format that the countries devised their own programmes and action plans. The challenge was so huge that the government budgets allocated for education

107

were largely diverted to literacy and adult education programmes, virtually to the neglect of higher education. In the changed circumstances of today where countries are recording high percentages of literacy, it is necessary to rethink our priorities in the field of education. In saying so, I am not undermining the huge challenge that still bothers us with regard to removal of illiteracy. While percentage-wise there is a fall in our illiteracy rate, in terms of numbers, our 26 per cent illiterates account for around 240 million people – close to the population of India at the time of partition!! But with so many literates around, the task of spreading literacy has become a bit easier. There are some scholars who believe that the IT revolution has opened new windows through which people can be educated without their being literate. Even the literates are rendered illiterate because of *computeracy* – this is a new indicator and requires adequate attention to save people from remaining *incomputerates*.

In our enthusiasm to promote literacy and universalize Primary Education, we have continually undermined secondary and tertiary education. Despite mushrooming growth of our schools and colleges, and universities, we are not able to accommodate the burgeoning number of students knocking the doors of these institutions. That is why the sub-culture of coaching centres and other surrogate structures has developed. That is why the cut-off line for admissions to colleges is reaching 99 per cent. All those who have passed the examinations conducted by competent bodies do not get automatically admitted to higher classes. And in such a competing milieu, we have brought in the additional factor of reservation of seats for special categories of people for whom the cut-off line is also lowered.

The question is that of denying admission to the deserving irrespective of one's ascribed status. An educational status is an *achieved* status. One ascends the educational ladder through one's performance. At the point of initial entry – that is, at the nursery or kindergarten level – admissions can be made on the basis of the child's *ascribed* status; but once it enters the educational domain, it is the child's performance which should matter irrespective of one's caste or tribe. To carry the culture of partiality in a system that is built on the premise of performance is to render the education system defunct.

When we examine the situation of education among the tribals, we need to address to this anomaly in our policy. Surely, this cannot be the politician's cup of tea, and the bureaucrat, who is expected to execute the orders of his master, has no choice but to fall in line. Sadly, actors in the academe have also not properly articulated this concern.

I also notice a trend that supports the idea of reviving traditional system of education among the tribals on the ground that the modern ways of teaching are alien to them. This argument makes education synonymous with socialization and enculturation. It implies, in a way, denial of access to the world of knowledge that is larger than the knowledge sphere of a tribe. We must carefully examine such a recipe. The tribals themselves may see in it a conspiracy of the elite to deprive the tribals from the fruits of modernity.

For instance, witness the trend of reintroducing English at the primary level in many of the Indian states. In view of the fact that many of the IT-related companies are hiring people who have command over English leaders are seeking such a revision to facilitate the poor sections of the society who go to government schools and are not taught that language until they reach grade 6. The fear that a foreign language would earn supremacy over the native language is part of cultural awakening, but the attendant disadvantages are the concern of the families that are struggling to move out of deprivation.

Note

1 Special lecture delivered at the National Seminar on *Tribes and Their Education: Implications for Development*, Barkatullah University, Bhopal, 11 August 2011.

   I have been privileged to attend almost all the annual seminars on the Indian tribal scene organized by the Rajiv Gandhi Chair at this University in the past few years. I presume this to be the last in the Series as most of the aspects of Tribal India have been covered. This special lecture offers me an opportunity to consolidate my views and provide a perspective for tribal studies to be carried out in future. For this, I am grateful to Professor S. N. Chaudhary who did not accept 'no' from me for his kind and friendly invitation although I feel that I am over-exposing myself. Not without an escape route I am rendered helpless; and I apologize for inflicting yet another lecture on this august audience. I do admit that many ideas presented here, including my point of view, is repetition of what I have said elsewhere and reproduced in other essays in this collection. Had it not been a "collection of essays" this would be unpardonable offence, but I am sure the reader will pardon me for this inevitability which is in the form of reinforcing my point of view. Each essay in this book can be read independently – this prospect should minimize my deliberate repetition.

8

MARCH OF TRIBAL WOMEN[1]

The chapter title has two key concepts: *tribal* and *women*; and it has chosen to focus on the *march* – implying progress on the path to development. Depending on one's orientation, a person can read two different messages from the title of the Essay:

1   The forward looking might read the message in positive terms: the tribal women have remarkably changed over the years as a consequence of planning and development that is specially geared to improve the life conditions of the tribes that are regarded as 'primitive' and 'backward'.
2   The pessimists may read that despite all development efforts and the privileges granted to the backward sections of our society very little has changed and the people, especially the women, continue to suffer from deprivation and low status.

Those who follow the second line of reasoning are sure to find faults with our policy and its implementation and to suggest new measures to improve the situation. Those following the first line of reasoning might hail the developmental efforts, but they may still come up with special measures to achieve the unfinished agenda.

What has anthropology to say in this regard? Since tribal studies have been the forte of anthropologists, it is quite natural that we turn to anthropology when we discuss the questions relative to tribes.

Let me view the problem from the angle of an anthropologist. The discipline of anthropology has grown significantly over the years. In our student days, anthropology was understood as the study of the tribal people. But the attention began gradually shifting to accommodate village studies. The ethnographic tradition allowed

MARCH OF TRIBAL WOMEN

the anthropologists to undertake the studies of the villages in a holistic perspective. Excellent ethnographies of the selected villages were produced during the 1950s and 1960s. At that time, Indian society was demographically divided into Tribal, Rural and Urban India. The village studies did recognize the interactions of the tribal societies with Village India, and dwelt upon those tribal groups that have settled in the villages and were treated as a caste. For example, the Bhils of Mewar, who settled in villages inhabited mostly by Hindu castes, were known as *Gametis*. Ruled by the Maharanas, the princely state of Mewar had the state emblem showing a Rajput warrior on one side and the Bhil warrior on the other – this was a clear acknowledgement of the inclusion of the Bhils into the mainstream Mewar society.

Shifting focus on the villages, anthropologists and sociologists somehow lost interest in tribal studies. It is only the Tribal Research Institutes, set up in various states, and the stations of the AnSI, which continued to carry out studies on the various aspects of Tribal India. But these institutions also studied other backward groups. In fact, the AnSI carried out a massive study on *People of India* under the direction of Dr Kumar Suresh Singh. This monumental survey of the entire human face of India was launched in 1985. It was the first post-colonial survey that took more than seven years to complete, yielding forty volumes that give information on all castes and communities, and not just the tribal ones. Of late, the Tribal Research Institutes have become perfunctory. Some of them are headed by those officials who have no grounding in social research. As a consequence, tribal research has received a serious setback. I do not think that these institutes can satisfactorily respond to the concerns of the changing face of Tribal Women. The government should, in my opinion, take adequate action to revive these institutions or to close them as defunct organizations.

Anthropology in Indian universities is also now dominated by physical anthropologists; and the social anthropologists prefer to work nearer home in non-tribal areas. Also tribal studies are no longer a monopoly of anthropologists; social scientists trained in other disciplines – political science, economics, social work and public administration – have extended their scope to cover the tribal segment of our population and produced studies on various aspects of tribal society rather than ethnographies. In the circumstances, the old and classic ethnographic accounts of the various tribal societies that

111

were published up to the 1950s have become dated. Though written in the idiom of the 'eternal present', these accounts do not portray the actually existing social conditions of today; they have generated stereotypes which continue to perpetuate. Those accounts did not focus on change. They also did not isolate women as a distinct subject of their study, but only as role-players in the traditional system. However, there is enough in the ethnographies to cull out the manner in which women contributed to the functioning of their societies. But we do lack dependable evidence to assess change in the tribal societies, more so regarding tribal women.

It is, however, clearly demonstrated by the studies that our tribal segment is not homogeneous. The vast country of India has tribal groups that are matrilineal as well as patrilineal; monogamous as well as polygynous and polyandrous; those living a subsistence culture and those who practise shifting cultivation and settled agriculture; those who represent different religions and even animism. They, therefore, defy easy generalization. The statistics generated at an all-India level that lumps all of tribal population as ST is thoroughly misleading. ST and SC, so also the category of OBCs, are administratively convenient categories but they have led to somewhat distorted perceptions about their so-called status.

Added to this is the fact that the waves of change – both planned and those coming from abroad as a consequence of our interactions with the rest of the world – have significantly changed the profile of India. India of today is vastly different from the India that we inherited from the British Raj. The threefold classification into tribal, rural and urban is no longer valid. Even the tribes can be classified on the basis of habitation into urban, rural and tribal.

I must hasten to say that this is not a new development. The process of integration of the tribal communities into the mainstream India began long before we attained our independence. It was accelerated in the post-independence era, and has made today such threefold differentiation of our population obsolete.

But we continue to divide our population on the basis of tribes and religions. This is, in my way of thinking, uncritical acceptance of the colonial policy that followed the principle of 'divide and rule'. Our Constitution makers differed on that issue but finally regarded it politically prudent to make special provisions for our backward sections, namely the tribes and the so-called oppressed castes. To offer privileges and reservations, these groups were entered into two schedules,

MARCH OF TRIBAL WOMEN

one each for the tribes and the castes, respectively. However, the Constitution was clear that only the primitive and very backward tribes are to be included in the schedule, and not all of them. But this directive was sadly ignored and all those who were known as tribes by name were included in the list. The provision also encouraged many groups that were not included in either of the lists to seek the status of an ST or SC.

In a way this policy led to a reversal of social process. In the early part of the twentieth century, when the decennial censuses also enumerated names of castes and tribes many groups used that opportunity to change their status, to move out from a tribal category to a caste category, and to rise even in the caste hierarchy. In the post-independence India, those very groups are now clamouring for a lower status – the advanced agricultural groups want to be listed as OBCs, and those who succeeded in getting an OBC stand are now asking for a tribal status! In Rajasthan, the Gujjar demand for a tribal status is a case in point.

The mistake committed by the officialdom in the preparation of the schedule for the tribes is partly responsible for this. As an illustration, let me take the case of some of the tribes of Rajasthan. Way back in the 1921 Census, we find that the indigenous and autochthonous communities were nominally mentioned as tribes, but they were classified on the basis of their religion. Thus, the Bhils of Rajasthan were classified in the 1921 Census, and also in 1931 Census, as Christians, Hindus, Jains, Muslims and 'Tribals'. The implication was that those who had converted to other religions were no longer 'tribals'. Based on this, the Censuses showed a decline in the tribal population. The 1921 Census, for example, classified 19 per cent of the Bhils as Hindus but 10 years later, in the 1931 Census, that percentage of Hindu converts, amongst the Bhils, rose to 70. In case of the Meenas (eh.kk), the conversion rate was much higher. Thus, of the more than six lakh Bhils, and an equal number of Meenas, only 23.62 per cent of the Bhils and a mere 3.35 per cent of the Meenas were classed as tribals in the 1931 Census; the rest were put in other religious categories. These censuses indicated gradual assimilation of the tribal societies into other religious groups, and treated them as separate communities. But all this got reversed in independent India. The Meenas, who were regarded as 'tribals' in the 1931 Census, represented only about 3 per cent of the totality of that ethnic group, are in today's Rajasthan the largest group among the tribals and their status is hotly contested by the Gujjars who also want to be included in the Schedule.[2] Other real claimants of the tribal status are in minority and they still remain deprived of the many privileges extended by the government. This is the root of the current unrest that we witness today.

Such conversions, mainly into Christianity, were quite prominent among the tribals of the North-East India, during the British period. Thus, while Nagaland is inhabited mostly by the people of indigenous origin, the State is also divided into urban, rural and tribal – thereby meaning the areas that are hard of access and people live there in relative isolation.

It is demands for inclusion by groups who are presently classified as 'non-tribal' that have raised the question about the definition of the very term *Tribe*. I must confess that the ethnographers of yore were not interested in theoretical formulations. Their primary focus was on detailed description of the primitive cultures. As definition of the term 'tribe', they just provided an inventory of traits, not all of which were equally applicable to all such groups that were treated as tribals. Articles 342 and 366(25) of the Indian Constitution are also vague in this regard which only suggest that those that are designated by a State as tribes shall be included in the Schedule. But how will they designate? What shall be the criteria?

It is important to remind that the decennial Census of 1931 was the last that enumerated castes and tribes. The declining population of the tribals indicated in the 1921 and 1931 Censuses, because of their gradual assimilation into the mainstream society, registered a rise as a consequence of the faulty implementation of the provisions of the Indian Constitution by enthusiastic but ill-informed bureaucrats; one may even allege that the general policy of the British to 'divide and rule' inherited by the bureaucracy led to such reversal. What is more surprising is that the anthropologists did not question the process of scheduling and willy-nilly accepted the official stand. The increase in the number of tribes is due to the constitutional provision that grants every state in the Indian Union to designate groups for the different schedules. As a consequence, the same tribe living in two different states and recognized as tribe by both of them is counted twice. It has also happened that the group is granted a tribal status in one state but denied in another.

It should be noted that the very concept of 'tribe' is a colonial legacy. We do not have in any of the Indian languages a synonym for this word. The words *Janjati* or *Vanjati* are new concoctions, and even in them their separation from the caste, that is *Jati*, is denoted by the prefix *Jan* or *ban* or *Adi*. Even the 1901 Census called them as a 'tribal type' caste. Nowhere, the term Tribe has been sociologically defined. At best, there was enumeration of some common traits as one finds in the writings of Risley and other anthropologists. Thus, whichever group was designated as a Tribe was accepted as such.

The need for the definition arose when after the publication of the list of STs in the 1950s several other groups that were not included in the list started making a claim for inclusion. In response to this, the Chanda Committee, set up in 1960s, suggested the following criteria: indication of primitive traits, distinctive culture, geographical isolation, shyness of contact with the community at large and backwardness. These criteria are still being used while examining the candidature of any new group claiming a tribal status. But these are hopeless criteria; if employed rigorously, many of the groups included in the ST category will have to be descheduled, and certainly they are not applicable to many new claimants to the tribal status.

This is not the occasion to go into the implications of this; therefore, suffice it to suggest that we lack a rigorous definition of the concept and it is the task of the anthropologist to provide one rather than accept an off-beat and thoroughly irrelevant inventory of traits that govern today's decision-making.

For heuristic reasons, we accept the official definition even when we discuss here the condition of tribal women. This point needs to be emphasized.

Let me now turn to the other focus of the Seminar, namely *Women*. I must say that social science interest in the issues related to the status of women is relatively recent. During our student days, as part of the study of the Indian Social System – in the tradition of Indology – there used to be some discussion on the Status of Women in Ancient India. That was based on sacred texts and related only to the Hindus. In the discussion on marriage and family, and on inheritance, the gender aspect was certainly covered; and comparisons were made regarding the practices prevalent in various religious groups as well as in different tribal communities. But the ethnographies did not devote any special chapters on women. It was rare to find any full-length monographs on women. Even Leela Dube's PhD thesis on the Gond women remains unpublished.

The status of women became the prime focus in the 1970s, when the national preparations for the first ever World Conference on Women were initiated. The Government of India also set up a National Committee on the Status of Women. It is the work of this committee that gave spurt to several studies and reviews of existing literature relative to women. My assignment with the Indian Council of Social Science Research as its first Research Director gave me the opportunity to interact with this committee and to assist it in its research programme. In fact, the ICSSR commissioned a series of studies on different aspects of the status of women. I was personally involved in the designing of the national study that was undertaken by the committee.

The Indian effort to portray the status of women was, thus, a part of the worldwide effort. The designation of the International Year of Women (IYW) and later devotion of an entire decade to women by the international community occasioned a spate of studies and researches. The decade of the 1970s saw the rise of the feminist movement that influenced not only the politics but also the academia. By this time I had joined UNESCO as its Regional Adviser for Social and Human Sciences in Asia and the Pacific. One of my responsibilities was to promote women's studies in social sciences.

During my tenure as Director of the Regional Unit for Social and Human Sciences in Asia-Pacific (RUSHSAP) – nearly 19 years of my stay in that position – forty-five different studies on various aspects of women in different countries of Asia were carried out, resulting in twenty-five monographs, all edited by me.

In 1982, I convened a regional meeting in New Delhi to evaluate the present status of women's studies in social sciences and to develop an agenda for future. That meeting was an important landmark because the recommendations that were made by the Group resulted in a series of activities for our unit. Soon after that meeting, the then chairperson of the Indian University Grants Commission (UGC), Dr Madhuri Shah, wrote to all the universities in India to carefully read the recommendations of that meeting and offered UGC's support for creating Centres for Women's Studies within the universities. The response to her call was overwhelming; consequently, such centres were set up in a number of universities in India.

I would wish to stress the point that there cannot, should not be, a single perspective on women. Their problems should be seen from different disciplinary perspectives, as well as from an interdisciplinary perspective. There is, of course, a place for feminist approach, but that is not all. Social scientists should also resist the temptation of using the social sciences for promoting any ideology. It is all right for the social scientist to work on a topic that is regarded socially, politically or even ideologically relevant, but it is wrong to be influenced by an ideological or social commitment while researching that topic. The subject must be researched scientifically, maintaining objectivity and value neutrality. Social science is not journalism, nor is it a handmaiden of politics.

The word 'status' is a well-developed sociological concept. But in the context of women this has been employed in a very journalistic sense. And yet social scientists working in this area have never bothered to correct their lexicon. The activists have used status to suggest the low and oppressed state of affairs of women compared to men. That is a vulgar and emotionally charged usage. We know that not all women are oppressed, poor or powerless. We also know that women constitute only a category and not a class in the sociological sense. They derive their socio-economic status (SES) from the family to which they belong and, thus, share the SES index value with other members of the family – both male and female. In that sense, it will be hazardous to club all the tribal women into a single category.

In saying all this I am not suggesting that all is well. We need to take serious steps to eradicate illiteracy among women, remove all practices of oppression and discrimination and make women equal partners in the process of development.

The key question relates to the model that we ought to follow, or the scenario of the desirable that we must construct. It should be admitted that there does not exist any consensus regarding the desirable, because desirability is value loaded. Social scientists have the responsibility of providing dependable portrayals of the actually existing reality and of working out cost-benefit analysis of alternative strategies proposed by social reformers and activists. But when they indulge in fashioning the scenario of the desirable, they enter the realm of values and become committed. While there is nothing wrong in being committed to a set of values, such commitment should be differentiated from commitment to social sciences.

With that caution, let me now knowingly enter into the fray. With all the pitfalls of 'lumping together' all the tribes into ST category, let us see where the tribal women stand compared to the non-tribal women.

In this regard one good index is *Literacy*. When the country got its independence from the British, the overall literacy rate was as low as 16 per cent. Obviously, most of this percentage came from men, with women in general, having a really very low – in fact dismal – literacy rate. Surely, the situation must have been pathetic in our tribal belt, and in rural India as a whole which constituted nearly 88 per cent of the total. Literacy then was typically an urban trait. In the year 1991, our literacy rate jumped to 52.21 per cent (from 18.33% in 1951), and female literacy rate from 8.66 per cent to 39.23 per cent. In our tribal population, literacy rate in 1961 was as low as 9.51 per cent compared to overall literacy percentage of 28.30 per cent. Female literacy amongst the tribals jumped from 1961 average of as low as 3.16 per cent to 54.4 per cent in 2011. This means that tribal female literacy in 2001 was close to overall Indian literacy rate in the 1971 Census; in 2011, male literacy rate touched a high percentage of 71.7, with female literacy percentage of 54.1. What is more satisfying is the fact that amongst tribal children (of the age group 6–14) the enrolment ratio is as high as 86.06 per cent (90.58% for boys and 81.10% for girls) – this ratio ranges from 60.90 in Nagaland to more than 108 in Kerala, Manipur and Tamil Nadu, and as high as 114 in Sikkim. Recent statistics also indicate that as many as 539 ST girls are enrolled for their PhDs. The total number of tribal girls in higher education, including the polytechniques, is as high as 142,280.[3] I am sure this number is much higher than the number for the total population when the country became independent. These figures definitely indicate a rising percentage of literates, particularly among the young population of tribal women. Of course, it must be acknowledged that the overall average does not suggest the precarious condition in some tribal groups or in sections of particular tribes that still lead an isolated existence. But more than 80 per cent enrolment of girls leaves out only less than 20 per cent of them in the category of non-school-going population.

Another indication of low status is the inclusion of families – and not only of women – in the category of BPL families. Here again, the picture seems to be encouraging. By the standard of 1999–2000 count, there are 45.83 per cent tribal families that are BPL; incidentally, this was the overall percentage of BPL families in the general population in the year 1983–84, when among the ST families this percentage was as high as 63.81. Certainly, this is an indication of families moving out of poverty line. Again, I must add a caveat: situation may still be grave in certain areas and in certain tribal groups as a whole.

MARCH OF TRIBAL WOMEN

Improvement in literacy rate and a reduction of number of BPL families among the tribals must have certainly influenced participation of women in political life. But tribal women have also begun taking part in national politics and some have even occupied high positions, even that of a minister at the centre.

These stray examples should make us rethink our strategies and even our generalizations about the status of women in general, and of tribal women in particular. There is need to conceptualize the dynamic interrelationship between women and development.

I personally think that in the past, whenever we talked of women in development, we talked only of women as passive recipients. But this is not true. They are not only recipients of the fruits of development, but are also agents of social change and development. It will be a patronizing attitude to think only of doing something for them; we have to ensure their contribution to society's development.

Thus, the moot question regarding women and development is: is it a one-way relationship? Are we talking only of women contributing to social development? Or of women receiving benefits, or otherwise, of development? Or, is there still another way in which this relationship can be conceptualized?

There are no readymade answers, but certainly these are legitimate questions. There are people who equate development with modernization, and dissociate the latter from westernization. In the context of women, the question is: does liberation of women mean making women westernized? Or making women modernized? How do we conceptualize development to find out the ideal, the desired destination, for women? What does development really mean? What is the locus particularly of tradition in this development paradigm?

Recent researches have indicated that the dichotomy between tradition and modernity is false. Traditions are not all that bad; nor are all traditions obsolete. Sometimes traditions can also help us modernize. There is an element of modernity in tradition and we need to investigate it.

Notes

1 Keynote Address given at the National Seminar organized by Vigyan Samiti, Udaipur, Rajasthan, 6–7 March 2011.
2 In a recent court verdict a distinction was made between the *Mina* and the *Meena*. Only one group was acknowledged as ST. It may be mentioned that originally also one group was included but then the people bearing this

name and residing mostly in eastern Rajasthan succeeded in getting themselves the tribal status, thanks to the efforts of a prominent Congress leader from Bharatpur. These people were called *Jagirdar Meenas* as against the *Chowkidar Meenas* who mostly reside in Southern Rajasthan.

3 These are figures based on the 2001 Census. Definitely, 2011 Census figures are expected to be higher than this figure, as literacy rates amongst younger age groups is rising faster.

9

CONCERN FOR INDIGENOUS KNOWLEDGE

Sometime towards the conclusion of the last century, when the world community was taking stock of the achievements of various development decades since the setting up of the United Nations, there arose a demand to attend to the needs of the indigenous populations. As a consequence, the United Nations decided to observe the decade of 1995–2004 as the International Decade of the World's Indigenous People. Since the agenda of the decade required more time, a second decade has been declared in continuation of the first decade. The Second Decade that began in 2005 concluded in 2014.

The overpowering processes of colonization that followed the Industrial Revolution influenced all the non-Western societies, including the tribal communities. It is during that process that the science of anthropology grew. Missionaries and political administrators were the first to reach the tribal communities who lived in comparative isolation and led a life that was quite distinct from the colonizers. These societies were characterized as queer, exotic and primitive, and their strange ways of life became the subject matter of many descriptive accounts published for the Western audience. Later, it was realized that a deeper understanding of their cultures and behaviour was necessary for an efficient administration of the area. Thus, anthropology entered the training curricula of the administrators chosen to rule these colonies. Concern with the past of the mankind also led to evolutionary theories that put these societies at lower levels of development and the Western societies at the top of the pyramid. Implicit in this kind of exercise was the belief that there is a single course of evolution and that the practices of the primitives will have to be replaced by those evolved by the Western societies. That was the prescription to make the primitives civilized. Opposed to this approach were many anthropologists and social workers who felt concerned about the ill-effects

CONCERN FOR INDIGENOUS KNOWLEDGE

of cultural contacts with the outside world that were destroying their distinctive cultural traits and subjecting them to the exploitation by outsiders. Their plea for the preservation of tribal cultures was eloquent and forceful. But it was misunderstood by others who alleged that these were treating tribals as 'anthropological zoos' to obstruct their progress.

It can safely be said that construction of knowledge about, and for, the indigenous people was made, during that period by the non-indigenous people. The 'outsiders' took on the role of understanding the 'other cultures'. That is how the discipline of anthropology came to be defined. It is this definition that also facilitated studies of communities other than the tribal that belonged to indigenous civilizations. India, thus, offered a good site for research to those anthropologists who extended their scope beyond the tribes to cover indigenous civilizations. However, in such non-tribal societies, nay the civilizations, the insider scholarship contested the social constructions by the outsiders. Of course, such contestations were part of a nationalistic sentiment that grew with the freedom movement. Now a similar reaction is in evidence in case of other tribal communities which have among themselves a good number of literates and highly educated people, including those trained in anthropology. These insiders question outsider reconstructions of knowledge of their respective societies. Moreover, much of what was written about them in the late nineteenth century, and the first half of the twentieth century, has already become dated.

Written in the idiom of the 'eternal present', as if the societies were non-changing, those ethnographies do not correspond to the actually existing realities of today. The Gonds of Bastar today are very different than those described by Verrier Elwin. The image of the tribe has changed. No doubt there exist tribal habitats. There are large pockets of the illiterates amongst some of the tribal communities, but there are also tribal groups, particularly in the North-East which have very high rates of literacy both among males and females. This is also true that those tribals who live in remote areas continue with several age-old practices, including wearing the traditional attire and jewellery. But there are others who have attained national stature. Take for instance, the case of Mr Sangma who established high standards of performance as Speaker of the Lok Sabha. This tribal from the North-East is a national figure who, according to some, had the potential of becoming the President of India! His command over Hindi and English, his professionalism and his stature as a national leader are indeed worthy of praise and serve as an example for others. Back in his tribal

CONCERN FOR INDIGENOUS KNOWLEDGE

habitat he may still wear the traditional attire, but in Delhi he merges with modernity. Without loss of tribal identity, people like Sangma are changing the profile of their primordial cultures. His daughter – then in her twenties – became a minister at the Centre; she took her oath of office, to the surprise of many, in Hindi.

In the midst of all this, there is a genuine concern shown by many that the tribal cultures might disappear as forces of modernization and globalization become more potent. There are people and agencies that express worry about the profound loss of indigenous peoples and their knowledge about the natural world constructed by generations from their intimate ties to their locale. They allege that their practices and beliefs are marginalized and neglected because these are regarded as inferior forms of knowing compared to the Western scientific tradition, presented as universally applicable. Foreign scholars pigeonholed indigenous knowledge in the scaffolding of their knowledge systems. That procrustean method of accommodation of alien knowledge led to several misrepresentations and quite often wrong interpretations and assumptions.

Our past development efforts, in which we laid emphasis on exogenous change, have taught us that introductions of innovations without regard for the recipient culture has, in many cases, led to costly failures, including erosion of biological diversity. Advocates of human rights have gone to the extent of attributing violation of human rights in those cases where the participation of local communities has not been secured in development projects. Neglect of traditional knowledge amounts to ignoring available and relevant information. They allege that foreign experts only indulge in transplanting their institutions and practices rather than finding local solutions to local problems. It is the review of past practices that have suggested that we must think globally but act locally. This prescription does not suggest *insulation* from the outside; it only broadens our vision and strengthens our foothold in our roots. Mahatma Gandhi also asked to keep all the windows open to let in the wind from all sides, but he never wanted to be swept away by them.

It is the over-attachment to the so-called modern that has caused deficits in our development profiles. Of course, it was an easy route for the analysts to blame all our developmental failures to our so-called 'insensitive' cultures and traditions. We wrongly believed that the modernity is to be built on the ashes of the tradition. Time has come to realize that while different societies might have common problems to combat, there are no common solutions. Since a common problem may be the result of one or more of the factors, its solution has to be situation specific, and not a generic prescription.

We had mistakenly written premature obituaries to our culture and tradition. For the first time, the World Summit for Social Development, organized under the auspices of the United Nations System in the year 1995 in Copenhagen, Denmark, declared that we have to give culture a place of centrality. Like biodiversity, we need to preserve cultural diversity. The world of tomorrow will be a world not of a common homogenized culture, but a world of rich cultural diversities.

There is a dramatically growing national and international interest in incorporating indigenous knowledge systems, including traditional ecological knowledge, into truly participatory approaches to development. Moreover, it is also being emphasized that such knowledge might not only be relevant and useful at its place of origin but have wider applications. We are familiar with the debate about the patent for *Haldi* (turmeric) that we have been using not only to colour our curries but also for medicinal purposes. The cure for the deadly dengue fever exists in the traditional system – the juice of two green papaya tree leaves it is believed, can perform this miracle. There is also a claim for an herbal 'Viagra', and of several other aphrodisiac herbs – such as Ginseng of Korea – that belong to the non-allopathic pharmacopoeia. Already in India we are now witnessing a trend towards increasing use of Ayurvedic medicines, available in modern packages at the chemists' shops. Swami Ramdev's *yoga* movement is gaining worldwide following.

One major worry of the many enthusiasts of indigenous knowledge systems is the commercialization and museumization of tradition. This is a fact to be reckoned. The challenge is manifold: how to preserve and record for the posterity the originality of the modes of production of artefacts and pieces of art of the indigenous people? How to ensure a quality life of the indigenous people? How to ensure that the local artists do not get pauperized and marginalized, and their skills not stolen and used through mass medium of duplication? The central government has involved the National Institute of Fashion Technology in developing a Geographical Indication Project to study traditional handicrafts in the Bastar region and have them patented. This will be done first for the bell metal artefacts known as *Garhwa Kala*.

Here we may discuss the fear for the disappearance of tradition. As students of culture, we know that no culture is static. Changes in them occur both from within and from without. It involves a process of attrition and accretion. Through non-use, or reduced use, cultural traits move towards the periphery of the culture and may even undergo hibernation.

CONCERN FOR INDIGENOUS KNOWLEDGE

Similarly, new traits may enter either through invention or discovery or as innovations from abroad. Their acceptance is thoroughly screened by the cultural monitors. Thus, one should not repent over the disappearance of traits in any living culture, nor one should ever worry over arrival of new traits. Let cultures exercise their resilience. We must also admit that as we cannot prevent death of an individual, despite all medical intervention, we may also not be in a position to prevent all attritions in a given culture.

Take language for example. While there are around six to seven thousand languages spoken all around the world, there are only eight that are spoken in several cultures. More interesting is the point that 96 per cent of the currently live languages are spoken by only 4 per cent of the world's population, and 80 per cent of these languages are confined to single countries. In Africa, more than 200 languages have fewer than 500 speakers each and may soon die out. The death of these languages is inevitable, and soon the total number of world languages may be reduced to half the present number. For the linguists, this should be a serious situation. But the recipe of their revival seems impractical. What the linguists might to do, as a service to posterity, is to record these languages and ensure their archival. Even with the reduction in the number of languages, cultural diversity has not been eroded, and this is a fact to be rejoiced.

The AnSI is now engaged in a massive project on what it calls Traditional Knowledge – TK for short. Any such exercise, to my mind, can be prompted by several considerations.

First, in the 1960s, for example, there was a movement in favour of what was named as *Urgent Anthropology*. The supporters of that movement had argued that we are living in an era of rapid social change, under the influence of which there is a real danger of disappearance of not only several cultural traits but also many small primitive communities – that may not survive or get submerged into larger entities losing their own identity. The movement, therefore, focussed on the 'dying' cultural traits and cultural communities and wanted them to be studied and recorded for posterity, and for the professional interest, before it was too late. Not studying them now, they argued, would mean never studying them as they would disappear from the world scene. This genuine concern for recording important aspects of human civilization is understandable. It was motivated by sheer academic interest, and not by any ideology that celebrates the past and the primitive. Work on TK or IK can, thus, be a fulfilment of the objective of Urgent Anthropology.

There can be, secondly, a set of people who sincerely feel that the primitive way of life is ideal and deserves to be preserved. This is what the proponents of anthropological zoos in fact intended; of course, some alleged that they were more eager to save the subject matter of their study rather than the welfare of the people they studied. This charge was countered by the likes of Verrier Elwin who thought that uncontrolled contacts with the outside world have led to the unfortunate exploitation of the tribals, who were rendered homeless in their own homes.

Third, there are others who think that the vast canvas of human civilization has been enriched, in a variety of ways, by the multitude of cultures. There is a need, according to them, to give due credit to each society and culture for its contribution, and that learning should not be a one-way process where the tribals are at the receiving end and the so-called modern societies are at the giving end. There is much good in the traditional knowledge that can be used for the general good of human society as a whole and should not be neglected simply because of its origin. This may relate to, for example, tribal pharmacopoeia, and even treatment of some ailments. In the general field of agriculture and horticulture, such knowledge may be immense and vastly scattered which needs to be collected and catalogued. It would, however, be wrong to plead that such TK can replace all other modern knowledge, or that modern knowledge has no place in the tribal setting. Acknowledgement of the multiplicity of cultures and, therefore, plurality of the TK bases should disallow cultural chauvinism. Anthropology's strength has been the emphasis on *cultural relativity*.

We need to come out of the either–or kind of dichotomy.

The social situation in India has drastically changed over the years with several forces of change – planned or unplanned, endogenous or exogenous, and there is no point of return. And the change has touched all sections of our society – be they urban, rural or even tribal. If we stuck to our old definitions then we should be prepared to take out those groups which earlier matched the definition but are now metamorphosed. To invent new definitions to suit the vested interests of the concerned groups is an exercise of little value. If the intentions of our Constitution makers were to include only the backward among the tribes in the Schedule and make specific provisions for them so that their backwardness is removed, then we should develop objective criteria for descheduling the groups that have shown improvement; and at the same time disallow entry of fresh groups on false pretexts. To insist on retention of the primitive traits is nothing more than conspiring to keep certain groups backward for all times. In today's context,

CONCERN FOR INDIGENOUS KNOWLEDGE

tribal areas of the past can also easily be classified into urban, rural and even tribal. In many groups the claim of being tribal is of historical significance only. Many individuals or families who belonged to these groups but who have changed their personal and social profile by acquiring good education, a better employment or a political stature should voluntarily opt out rather than wait for their ouster as a 'creamy layer'.

One thing that is definitely needed is for the scholarship to return to the tribal habitats. The old enthusiasm of studying the tribal groups is waning out despite the growing number of departments of anthropology in the universities and colleges. It is a matter of great worry that such departments are overwhelmed by physical anthropologists.

The time has come when the fruitless debate on tradition versus modernity needs to be closed. Historians of knowledge generally fall into two categories: the *adumbrationists* who attribute everything to the past, to the tradition and do not acknowledge any novelty of innovation; and the *palimpsests* who refuse to acknowledge the shoulders of the past on which the novelty is mounted. Let us accept that we cannot recreate our past and live in it, and also that the present and the future require the foundations of the past. It is the amalgam of the old and new that defines our present and would fashion our future.

In fact, this was the policy towards the tribals that was formulated during the Nehru era. Enunciating his *Panchsheel* for the tribal policy, Pandit Nehru said:

> I am alarmed when I see . . . how anxious people are to shape others according to their own image or likeness, and to impose on them their particular way of living . . . I am not sure which is the better way of living, the tribal or our own. In some respects, I am quite certain their's is the better. Therefore it is presumptuous on our part to approach them with an air of superiority, to tell them how to behave or what to do and what not to do. There is no point in trying to make of them a second-rate copy of ourselves.

However, Nehru made it clear that he was not in favour of an isolationist policy. In the Foreword to the book *A Philosophy for NEFA*, authored by Verrier Elwin, he remarked:

> We cannot allow matters to drift in the tribal areas, or just not take interest in them. In the world of today that is not possible

or desirable. At the time we should avoid over-administering these areas and, in particular, sending too many outsiders into tribal territory. . . . We should rather work through, and not in rivalry to, their own social and cultural institutions.

This is an excellent summary message, and continues to be relevant even today. However, it should not be over-interpreted as a plea to keep the tribals in a shell.

10

TRIBAL UNREST, STATE POLITICS AND EMPOWERMENT IN CONTEMPORARY INDIA[1]

Post Second World War, the world scene was characterized by three processes: Reconstruction of the West, Decolonization and Development of the so-called Third World. These processes not only affected the polity and economy of various societies but also significantly influenced the growth and development of social sciences. Societies and communities of the Third World that were the subject matter of study by scholars of the developed world attracted more of these scholars to carry out research not only on the existing structures and organizations of the primitive, traditional and indigenous societies but also on the newly initiated processes of change. These were joined by native social scientists, who not only added to the trained manpower but also expanded the scope of inquiry and initiated a change in the orientation of anthropological research. Finding pitfalls with the methodology employed by the expatriate researchers and limitations of the so-called theory generated on the basis of limited experience of Western societies, there arose a demand for indigenization of social sciences. Such demand coalesced well with the movement for decolonization; to release the 'captive minds' – to use the phrase employed by late Professor S. Alatas of Malaysia.

The twin processes of *Decolonization* and *Development* began operating simultaneously in the post-independence era with equal enthusiasm. But they carried an ambivalence which went unnoticed. Decolonization was meant to demolish colonial structures of power and colonial ethos, and as such it was inherently critical of, and opposed to, the elements that were external in origin, and particularly those that were directly related to England in our context. Development, on the other hand, was a second name for 'westernization' which later was replaced by a more generic term 'modernization'. The newly independent nations exhibited certain hurry in 'keeping with

129

the Joneses', treating the West as the positive reference group. Decrying the West for the colonial rule and at the same time treating it as a positive reference group for change is a good example of ambivalence. It is this ambivalence that characterized our planning, and also its criticism. A common criticism was that the forces of westernization and modernization are killing our culture and civilization. The promoters of change also held tradition as a key culprit for the failure of externally induced changes. There was support for change and yet there was anguish against change.

That was the period when people started talking about rising revolution of expectations, but with constant failures of externally induced changes and deficit in achieving the targets, very soon scholars coined the counter-phrase of 'rising revolution of frustration'. The various development decades, following the establishment of the United Nations Organization, went on changing and readjusting their future course in the light of past achievements and failures. It is as a consequence of development that in the latter half of the twentieth century 'indigeneity' became the central issue. The demand for the rights of the indigenous people came to the fore. It is estimated that such people are found in about seventy countries of the world and number around 370 million, and are seen as the most disadvantaged, being dispossessed of their land or uprooted by powerful migrants. In fact, all tribal communities are synonymous with indigenous people, forgetting the distinction between those who belonged to a particular region for ages and those who migrated from elsewhere and settled even before colonization. The clearly identified indigenous populations are in the Americas and in Australia and in New Zealand.

The point that I wish to make is that despite the definitional crisis NGOs and anthropologists alike take a supportive view favouring the plight of the people who are variously called tribal, indigenous or autochthonous. Historically they have often been dispossessed of their lands by outsiders – moneylenders or rich cultivators, or by the outside invaders and colonizers. Indigenous people are generally regarded to be the most disadvantaged people in the world. In the context of India, following the adoption of the new Constitution in 1950, people included in the category of Scheduled Tribes (ST) are regarded as indigenous, or *Adivasis*, although there are people who contest this by arguing that other groups are also old inhabitants. Tribal India is regarded as backward, and the state policies and programmes are specially geared on a priority basis to develop the various areas inhabited mostly by the tribal people.

TRIBAL UNREST, STATE POLITICS AND EMPOWERMENT

The policy of 'divide and rule' pursued by the colonial administration in India tried to fracture the Indian unity in terms of 'depressed' or 'oppressed' groups, minorities and tribes. It is this policy that succeeded in dividing India into two nation-states – one of which on the basis of religion. It also created conditions for further rifts in the remainder of India. So clouded was the vision of our national leaders that despite denouncement by leaders like Gandhi and Thakkar Bappa the Government of free India continued the policy of tribal isolation, and of giving special consideration to groups that were described by the British as constituting the 'Depressed' classes. While the idea of separate electorates was thwarted, the recognition of groups as deserving of special protection did create conditions for divisive and potentially dangerous tendencies in the democratic polity of India. I regard casteism and communalism as a product of such steps taken with good intentions but without proper assessment of the likely dysfunctional consequences. The exhibition of unrest, not only in Tribal India, but also in other regions and caste groups, that the country has been witnessing is a consequence of, in my view, wrongly crafted state policy.

Provisions of reservation are governed by the spirit of charity. And charity creates 'dependence' and 'parasitism'; it perpetuates the hierarchical relationship between the host (giver) and the recipient where the latter benefits and the former harmed. Dependence does not empower, it makes the recipient a non-doer and a perennially demanding entity. The policy of disempowering one in order to empower another is a policy of discrimination; it cannot generate equality. Such a policy may quieten unrest in one section but generate unrest in another.

This long preface is an invitation to fellow colleagues to rethink our role as social scientists. Somehow I have the feeling that most action researches carried out in this country are biased; they are either carried out in support of the government policy or the programme – particularly when they are funded by the state – or done with an ideological bias to challenge the status quo. I have attended many such seminars where the undercurrent is the demonstration of dissatisfaction with the development strategy.

The first point that I wish to make is about the very definition of the term 'Tribe'. On several occasions, I have raised this issue and I still feel that it must be reiterated. Despite the fact that anthropologists are seen as students of tribal communities, the discipline of anthropology does not provide a commonly agreed definition of the concept. In the Indian context, we regard a group tribe which is recognized by the Government of India as a tribe based on questionable criteria. Here again, one finds that the same group is regarded a tribe in one state while not in other states. The initial list of Scheduled Tribes in 1951 had 212 entries; it has grown now to around 700 while the proportion of tribal population vis-à-vis has remained more or less the same. We also learn from the writings of N. K. Das that the North-East region alone has 'diverse tribes and some other communities speaking over 250 languages and dialects'. Obviously, there is not clear understanding about their inter-community relationships.

Second, when we prefix the word 'unrest' with 'tribal', we talk of the unrest amongst the people who are covered by this category irrespective of the type of unrest. It is likely that the tribals may also express their anger against government policies as any other group. But perhaps here our concern is about that type of unrest which is limited only to the tribal populace. Again, such unrest may be limited to a single tribe or a region, and thus may not be unrest amongst the entire tribal population. Your Note also refers to the so-called analogous communities such as the Ahoms and the Gujjars. The Gujjar case is interesting. The Islamized Gujjars of the state of Jammu and Kashmir have only recently been granted entry into the list of STs. Inspired by this the Gujjars of Rajasthan are demanding a similar status. Since they are not yet granted that status, their unrest perhaps cannot be called 'tribal'. But the voices raised against such demand by the Meenas of Rajasthan and other tribal leaders from various parts of India can be interpreted as forebodings of tribal unrest. The Gujjars are claiming such a status comparing their past and the present social structure with that of the Meenas; and the Meenas are opposing their entry. Gujjar demand is twofold: give us entry or oust the Meena. As a member of the High-powered Committee appointed by the then Government of Rajasthan in 2007 to examine the Gujjar claim, I have deeply studied the problem. But this is perhaps not the time to elaborate on that issue. Suffice it to say that such demands for inclusion or exclusion are also part of the unrest syndrome. In this case, unrest is caused by the demands of a group that wishes to be included in the ST category. The demanding group employs all tactics to run down the system – strikes, blocking roads and railroads and arranging huge rallies that get uncontrolled and violent.

My third point relates to the process of social transformation. When does a tribe cease to be a tribe? History of human civilization suggests that the creation of civilization occurs with the merger of several groups into a bigger stream. At one stage or another, ancestors of each of us must have been members of one tribe or another, but today we

TRIBAL UNREST, STATE POLITICS AND EMPOWERMENT

are treated as non-tribals. Col. James Tod's *Annals and Antiquities of Rajasthan* uses the words 'tribe' and 'caste' interchangeably because no finer distinction could be made. This suggests that tribe is a transient category. In the twentieth century when India was divided into urban, rural and tribal categories, it was a spatial categorization, but perhaps at that time those living in the tribal belt were all, or mostly, tribals. Today, that classification is no longer tenable. The tribal region itself can be divided into urban, rural and tribal (for the lack of a better term). Nagaland or Arunachal Pradesh or any other state in that region will have such spaces, and yet the entire state is called tribal. The old ethnographic accounts of the various tribal groups hardly correspond to the changed way of life of these groups. While the government still continues to call all those groups tribes as they were listed in the 1931 Census, many of such groups or sections of them would disqualify if the criteria employed by the government for consideration of the new claimants are also employed for them. The idyllic view of the tribals is no longer tenable. The Census authorities of the British times had already introduced a measure to de-list sections of tribal population that had converted to other religions and employed the adjective 'tribal' for those who did not convert and remained animists. But this distinction was ignored by the officialdom of independent India while listing the groups in the ST category.

It is also interesting to note that those groups which used the census enumeration to move upward in the Hindu caste hierarchy by changing their caste names right up to the 1930s are now, as a consequence of reservation of quotas for STs and SCs, reasserting their lower status. What Srinivas called *Sanskritization* – encapsulating the trends of that period – is now giving way to the process of reverse *Sanskritization*. Now that the decision is being taken to reintroduce caste as a variable in Census enumeration, the groups will have the opportunity to reclaim their lost status as 'oppressed' though their situation might have improved considerably as a powerful community. The Gujjar demand is not yet settled and we now have in the neighbouring state of Haryana an identical movement by the Jats. Government policy has, thus, promoted a process of self-denigration, for which they even invoke or concoct their history, and emphasize their *Dalit* or backward status. Sociologically speaking, these are the unintended consequences of a well-intentioned policy of upliftment via the route of positive discrimination. A step taken to eradicate caste has strengthened caste loyalties; and the political parties have transformed these social entities as vote banks by helping them reassert their primordial

133

TRIBAL UNREST, STATE POLITICS AND EMPOWERMENT

ties. Rather than promoting their assimilation into the common pool, such policies have helped erect insulators and even blocked the existing apertures of interaction.

I regard this as failure of social engineering that has widened the gulf and created new pockets of negative discrimination. I feel that an answer to negative discrimination is not the positive discrimination, because this perpetuates discrimination while the profile of sufferers and beneficiaries change. Such happening was predictable, but as social scientists we rode the bandwagon and sang songs of praise for the ill-conceived policy. Even today, our assessments hinge on this redoubtable premise and we go on suggesting more of the same. We become party to excite unrest or to justify it, at times using the provisions of human rights.

It should also be stressed that clubbing all the tribals into a single category and call them Tribal India is erroneous. The heterogeneity of the tribal population is a well-established position. In terms of race, dialect, level of economic development and the type of contact with the 'civilized' sections of the neighbourhood, there exist differences. That is why it has been erroneous to think of a common strategy for tribal development. Obviously, responses to development, or the consequences of development, have also varied. But we notice that both anthropologists and tribal enthusiasts have taken pains to recount the adverse consequences of development which are summed up in one phrase: *Cultural Degeneration*. The tribals are described as 'victims of civilization' who have lost their religion and their dialects, who now suffer from landlessness and alcoholism which has forced them to beggary. And all this has been caused by culture contact, impact of Hinduism and Christianity, Forest Acts of 1865, migration, industrialization and urbanization, development projects, NGO intervention, consumer culture and advancing globalization. Such criticism gives the impression that development has done nothing positive and, in fact, development efforts have further worsened the life of the tribals. Implicit in it seems to be the plea that the process needs to be halted almost instantly. Such a position makes an interesting copy for a political statement, but also misguides the common man.

We need to ask: what kind of future do we envisage for our tribal brethren? Do we want to keep them out of the general run of the polity, and away from the modernizing and globalizing trends? Are they really getting restive because of these developments or that the changing environs have equipped them to situate in the new surrounding and to raise issues as intelligent citizens of the broadened polity of India?

134

TRIBAL UNREST, STATE POLITICS AND EMPOWERMENT

It must be stressed that even during the British regime, some sections of Tribal India did revolt against the government policy. The Kol rebellion of the 1830s, the Santhal rebellion of 1855, the Birsa Munda movement of the 1890s and the Naga rebellion of the 1940s and beyond are known examples of such unrest. Of these, the first three revolts were against the increasing control of the East India Company over the tribal areas and impositions of taxes and challenge to the customary practices. These were somehow quelled by the powerful forces of the colonial masters.

The Naga rebellion was of a different sort. With the arrival of Christianity and spread of literacy and education, they had already broken their cultural isolation though the difficult geographical terrain helped them maintain their physical distance. The British reluctance to grant independence to India found expression in encouragement of all secessionist forces so as to weaken the emerging entity. Talking of the NEFA region, Verrier Elwin explicated the reasons for the British Policy of 'Leave Them Alone'. The policy was influenced 'partly because the task of administration, especially in the wild border areas, was difficult and unrewarding, partly from a desire to quarantine the tribes from possible *political infection* (emphasis mine), and partly because a number of officers sincerely held the view that the people were better and happier as they were' (Elwin, 1957: 45).

It is the policy of 'Leave Them Alone' guided by three different orientations pursued by the British guided the new 'philosophy for NEFA' and was extended to other areas as well. Following the stand of the pioneers of anthropology, later generations also became advocates for the tribal people and opponents of change. All culture contacts were seen as agents of cultural degeneration. When critics of such an approach hinted at the hidden agenda of anthropologists to preserve the tribes as anthropological zoos, it was vehemently denied. Elwin admitted that he advocated this only as a temporary measure and in specific instances where he suspected real danger. The poet in Nehru which helped him discover India was inspired by the idyllic beauty of tribal lands. It now seems that Verrier Elwin used Nehru's dilemma of culture versus development to formulate a policy for the tribes in such an ambivalent frame. *A Philosophy for NEFA* (Elwin, 1957) had influenced me as a student and I must admit that at that tender age I was not able to read in between the lines. But now I feel that what is attributed to Nehru was in fact the viewpoint of Elwin and his British compatriots; assigning Nehru its authorship the policy found

135

TRIBAL UNREST, STATE POLITICS AND EMPOWERMENT

unquestioned acceptance. See how Nehru acknowledges this influence in the Foreword to this book:

> Verrier Elwin has done me the honour of saying that he is a missionary of my views on tribal affairs. As a matter of fact, I have learnt much from him, for he is both an expert on this subject with great experience and a friend of the tribal folk. I have little experience of tribal life and my own views, vague as they were, have developed under the impact of certain circumstances and of Verrier Elwin's own writings. It would, therefore, be more correct to say that I have learnt from him rather than that I have influenced him in any way.
>
> (Nehru's Foreword to Elwin's book, 1957)

The only point that I wish to make from the above observation is that our tribal policy is a continuation of the policy pursued by the British and thus it is succeeding in its hidden agenda of keeping various sections of society divided in one way or the other.

Let me now turn to the issue of tribal unrest in the present context. The issue of tribal unrest is a complex one. We need a typology of it, which I hope will emerge. We must make one basic distinction, however. The demand for secession and the demand for rights from the government are two different kinds of measures. While the first set of demands are indicative of negative orientation to the system – to move out of the membership domain, the second set of demands are within the membership domain. We need to employ Reference Group theory to understand these varied orientations.

It is the first set of demands that are really problematic for the system as they affect the very character of the social group – be it a nation or a society. The system responds to it by taking all actions that help it prevent its dissolution or diminution to retain what belongs to it. The challengers to the system do just the opposite – to weaken the system, to make use of the vulnerable points in the system to break its insulation and develop an external orientation. An alternative to the process of secession may be the dissolution of the existing structure and its replacement by another scheme of things. This does not encourage people to secede but to revolt against the existing system of rule and establish a new regime.

The second type of unrest is a natural product of any living social system. A society is defined as 'cooperation crossed by conflict', to use

136

TRIBAL UNREST, STATE POLITICS AND EMPOWERMENT

the phrase employed by MacIver and Page. It is natural to expect unrest in any living social system. Every social system also develops its own system of social control to bring back normalcy. But it is the disturbances in the system caused by dissatisfaction among some or most of its members, or caused by the arrival of outside elements, that pose a challenge. These disturbances herald the process of change which may, or may not, be functional. We also know that quelling a storm of unrest does not rule out upsurge of other forms of unrest in other quarters or in the same quarter. The system's radars have to keep constant vigil on such disturbances and activate its agents of social control to tame them in time or to prepare the system to accommodate them. In other words, there is need to view unrest not only in negative terms but as a natural occurrence with wide-ranging consequences. As anthropologists we were trained to study the so-called primitive societies as if they were non-changing entities. But the ethnographies written in the idiom of eternal present by our forerunners can hardly be used to understand the changed profile of the tribal groups who have provided leadership not only to their own communities but to the nation as a whole. It will be futile to reverse this course and advocate a policy of return to their shells.

In this regard, we need to raise the question: what do we mean by development? The very fact that the development exercise is an *exogenous effort* to bring about culture change, and what we are doing here is also an *outsider review*, can we talk of insulation from culture contact? Or, are we advocating complete stoppage of any outside influence and a return of the primitive to his pristine purity? If we are concerned about his health, his poverty and his limited world view and wish to provide him with better nutrition and Medicare, improved means of earning a livelihood and widened cognitive horizons, how do we do it? Do we still wish to keep him in the proverbial 'anthropological zoo'? Is the tribal leading an idyllic lifestyle worthy of our emulation? Or do we intend to bring him out of poverty, and of isolated existence? Should the tribal be deprived of the fruits of modern civilization, of advancements in science and technology? Should he remain where he has remained all through, or need we help him develop empathy to relate with the wider world?

Clearly, there is ambivalence regarding development. We detest development and we demand development. There will be no one in this audience who will not wish a better life for the tribals living in remote areas and pursuing a primitive way of life. And yet there will be many amongst us who would also wish to eulogize tribal cultures and the

137

traditional stock of knowledge they possess, advocating not only its preservation but also its promotion.

We need to come out of the either–or kind of dichotomy.

Note

1 Keynote Address to a national seminar organized by the Anthropological Survey of India and the Indira Gandhi National Museum of Mankind, Bhopal, 21–23 March 2012.

11

ANTHROPOLOGICAL PERSPECTIVE TO STUDY YOUTH IN ASIA[1]

Over the years, since I was inducted into the profession, anthropology has changed its course. Up to the 1980s, anthropology in India still meant study of the tribes, although village studies became the new concern since the late 1950s. Today, when I visit anthropology departments in the country I am struck by the fact that most of these departments are heavily dominated by physical anthropologists, though their concern from the fossils and prehistoric archaeology has moved towards human genetics and genomics. They are contending with human biologists and distancing themselves from social anthropologists. In the process, anthropology as an integrated science of Man is given a backseat. This is somewhat disheartening.

I might dare say that even social anthropologists are losing their grip over tribal and village studies, while people from other sister disciplines have begun approaching these sites, of course with a different perspective, to assess the impact of development programmes and identify major bottlenecks in bringing about culture change in a planned manner. Tribes are, thus, no longer the exclusive preserve of anthropologists.

It is somewhat worrying that despite better connectivity, compared to the olden times, few anthropologists in this country now visit the tribal areas, and even fewer of them conduct field research on them. The ethnographies, although written in the idiom of the 'eternal present', have become dated in the sense that they do not correspond to today's 'actually existing social reality' – this is how the emphasis of social anthropological research was described in our student days. The idyllic description of the tribe is no longer applicable to many of the groups that were earlier studied as tribes. Thus, there is both a change in the priorities of anthropological research, and the tribes themselves are in the throes of change. It is in such a changed milieu

139

that anthropologists have to prepare their future agenda of research. The focus on the youth and the elderly is indicative of such a transition. Old ethnographies can provide very little guidance for research in this relatively new terrain.

It is also disconcerting to note that anthropologists have not taken care to define the concept of Tribe – the main subject matter of our study. 'This is somewhat understandable if we went back to the beginnings of the discipline of anthropology. When societies were classified into civilized and uncivilized – as savage or barbaric – the task was simpler. All uncivilized societies were *preliterate*, meaning thereby the absence of writing in them. That meant that the transmission of culture was through oral tradition, and the history of the society went as far back as human memory could take it. Beyond this was prehistory. Absence of history, oral transmission of society's knowledge pool to the younger generation, elementary technology, greater dependence on nature for survival and faith in the supernatural described their way of life. Living in small hordes, and unaware of the world outside the narrow confines of the community, the geographically and socially isolated communities defined themselves as residents of a given territory, and as belonging to a specific racial stock. Initially the students of *Other Cultures* came to the Non-Western societies and studied those small groups that were remotely located as "Little Communities", cut-off from civilizational societies and pursuing primitive economic activities in settlements that were cradle-to-the-grave arrangements' (Atal, 2012:336).

The situation is different today and certainly in a country like India. As an old and indigenous civilization the Indian society has been multicultural and has a long history of culture contacts with various racial and ethnic groups and the autochthones. But when alien anthropologists first reached the unreachable areas and found the groups living in comparative isolation, they regarded them as tribals and made them as subject matter of anthropological study. They did not feel the need to define as to what is a tribe. The need was felt when the country became independent of the British rule and its new Constitution made a provision for special treatment to the tribes and for which their separate listing was required for a Schedule. Rather than assigning this task to anthropologists, the government in its hurry asked the bureaucracy to compile the list. It took the easy path of referring to the 1931 Census, when the enumeration also included castes and tribes, and listed all those who were under the category of tribes. In that hurry the bureaucracy missed the point that the Census authorities

ANTHROPOLOGICAL PERSPECTIVE TO STUDY YOUTH

classified each tribe by the religion it pursued and kept the name tribe only for those who were practising animism. As a consequence, those subgroups among each of the tribes who came out as a consequence of culture contact and change of religion to improve their social status were again hurdled into the tribal category.

Rather than questioning such listing, anthropologists, instead, unwittingly accepted whatever definition the officialdom had given. That listing included 212 tribes in the year 1951. Today, this number is anywhere between 650 and 750 tribes! It gives the impression that today we have more tribes than before whereas the fact is that some of the groups succeeded in getting themselves listed as tribes through petitions and campaigns; in addition, the same tribal group got divided into as many groups as the states in which its members now reside. What is disturbing to me is that even today there is no effort to provide an anthropological definition of the tribe that is not culture-bound. We need a sociological definition for the concept of a tribe, the one that regards tribal status of a society as a phase in its evolutionary career.

There is another reason to feel disturbed. For judging the candidature of any group for the tribal status, the Government of India has been using the following criteria: 1. Primitive traits, 2. Distinctive culture, 3. Geographical isolation, 4. Shyness of contact and 5. Backwardness. Leaving aside the point that these criteria are so vague and overlapping, I would argue that if these criteria were to be employed to re-examine the candidature of those groups that are already included in the category of Scheduled Tribes, many of these groups will have to be disqualified. One might add that the designations employed are somewhat derogatory.[2]

I am trying to bring home the point that Tribe is perhaps a category that applied to all human groups at the initial stage. But it is a transitional category. There comes a point where a tribe ceases to be a tribe. We can all trace our ancestry to one tribal group or another but we cease to be part of a tribe today. This is how civilizations came into being. And this process is still operative which is changing the tribal scene today.

Scholars like Robert Redfield talked of the folk-urban continuum to indicate that tribe is a transitional category. After all, the emergence of complex cultures and civilizations is the consequence of the process of change in the tribal characteristics. The same has happened in India.

In today's context, India can no longer be classified into three straight jackets as urban, rural and tribal, because even the heavily populated tribal belts have both rural and urban populations. It is, therefore, an anachronism to continue to use the tribal tag for the groups that have become rural or urban. In doing so, we are ignoring one sociological fact, namely the distinction between different categories.

In societies, there are some categories which are ascriptive, and some open-ended, based on the achievement criterion. The ascriptive ones are of two types: (i) completely closed categories – no doors to enter or to exit and (ii) partially closed categories – which have membership from within but which allow for an exit door. We have a third type which has both entry point and exit doors. *Gender*, for example, is a closed category – you are born a woman and die as a woman (sex change operations are likely to affect this example, of course). I regard *Tribe* as a semi-open category in the sense that a primordial group is identified as a tribe but with changes in its demography, habitat, way of living etc., it might move out of the tribal status – after all, in a sense all of us who now belong to the so-called civilized societies have our ancestors who must have lived in small hordes as tribals; but we cease to be the tribals, and there is no going back. We must acknowledge that at some stage a tribe ceases to be a tribe; that it exits out of the tribal shell and becomes part of the bigger entity.

In contrast to this, *Youth* – the theme of this Inter-Congress – is an ascriptive category of the third type; it has both an entry point and an exit door. Children attaining a particular age enter the youth category and, after a certain period in it, they move out as adults; the empty space of the youth is occupied by another set of members. Thus, the categories remain populated but the occupants go on constantly changing.

As against the ascriptive categories, the achieved categories have both the entry and exit doors. A person or a family, for example, may enter into a middle class leaving behind its lower class status, and through its achievements can still climb up the ladder; the reverse process is also possible – a rich man becoming a destitute for one reason or the other. In ascriptive categories such downward descent is generally not possible – a young cannot become a child again. Once a group gets merged into a wider group or gets itself enlarged and evolves a complex culture, it cannot technically return to a tribal status. However, the special privileges offered by the Government of India to the tribal groups, lower castes (called Scheduled Castes), and the Backward Classes are prompting interested parties to reclaim their primordial status. In the process, they are also concocting stories and highlighting their primitive indicators.

Unfortunately, these fine distinctions in the nature of social structure are not observed by many researchers who excel in descriptions (ethnographic details) but lag in theoretical constructs. When our task

ANTHROPOLOGICAL PERSPECTIVE TO STUDY YOUTH

was to reconstruct the past, perhaps such theoretical finesse was not needed, but as social engineers engaged in the task of improving the present, or fashioning the future, such distinctions assume special significance.

* * *

It is important to stress here that anthropological orientation has changed over time. Anthropology began as a study of the primitive and the past. Pioneering anthropologists and ethnologists devoted their time in the reconstruction of the past. But as colonialism came to an end our orientation shifted from *reconstruction of the past* to *the development of the present*. This change signified the importance of applied anthropology, and paved the way for research related to culture change. Today, as we are already in the early era of the twenty-first century, scholars are involved in the *fashioning of the future*. It is this orientation that has brought into focus the issues related to children and the youth, and it is our responsibility to build a future of their liking.

After such a long detour, let me now return to the focal theme of this Congress, namely the youth.

Anthropological research on children and the youth today cannot afford to focus on how these two categories were treated by various cultures in the past. The discipline called upon to investigate their present profile and to assist in designing a fruitful future for them. The perspective for the study of youth and children will have to be developed not with a view to reconstructing the past but with an orientation towards the future.

In this regard, past ethnographies may not be of much help. They did discuss the process of socialization and enculturation, and talked of the *rites de passage* treating the children and the young as categories filled by transitory population, and described the manner in which they were inducted into the society. In dealing with children and youth today, our concern is not to revisit those old practices of socialization and enculturation and to advocate their reinforcement. Instead, we are summoned to investigate how the winds of change are affecting new entrants to societies.

For this, we need a new conceptual framework and a new methodology for investigation and preparation of a blueprint for future.

* * *

Youth constitute an important segment of society. Yet, not much attention was paid to them until the 1960s. Very little by way of research was done, and the interest in them in the 1960s was aroused because they stirred a near revolution in the West.

It may be recalled that the 1960s witnessed widespread student unrest in Europe, which caused worry and drew the attention of the governments. Immediate steps were taken to resolve the crisis that was threatening to engulf the entire world. Treating the West as the reference group, students in other continents, including Asia and the Pacific region, also joined the protest movement against the political system, first to show their solidarity with the youth of the West, and then to express their disenchantment with the outcome of development exercises within their respective countries that failed to improve the social development profile – in particular, improving the prospects for meaningful employment. Faced with such angry protests, international agencies were forced to put youth on their priority agenda.

It is important to note that while it was the student population that staged a revolt in the West, the international agencies mounted the programme for the youth as a whole so that it becomes inclusive, and does not become student-specific.

This must have been for two reasons: (i) in the West, where literacy rates were, and are, in the top deciles, the categories of youth and the student are almost synonymous; and (ii) youth was a neutral category compared to the students who were spearheading the protests. The leaders of society felt the need to stem the growing alienation among them.

Programmes were devised to involve the youth in development and to channelize their energies in constructive work. Development programmes for the youth meant both: those addressed to the problems of youth, and those that involved the youth in development projects of the society. Care was taken to emphasize, however, that the youth are not a *problem* but indeed a *potential force*. Quite naturally, all programmes were action-oriented. They showed the concern of the non-youth, and had a hidden patronizing agenda, in the same manner as programmes related to poverty elimination, which are designed by the non-poor for the poor, the latter being at the receiving end.

While the programmes relative to youth were designed by the international agencies mainly in response to youth unrest in the West, they were implemented worldwide. Youth became a major target group for all developmental work.

When the United Nations announced the year 1985 as the International Youth Year (IYY) it gave further push to the youth agenda.

* * *

ANTHROPOLOGICAL PERSPECTIVE TO STUDY YOUTH

Youth is a demographic concept that has both biological and sociological aspects. It relates to an age group that is transiting between childhood and adulthood. Sociologically, it is a *category*, not a *group*. This category may, of course, consist of several groups – a youth club, a school or college class, an NGO etc. As a category, represented by certain biological attributes, youth are found in all societies, but the roles and expectations associated with them differ from culture to culture. The region of Asia and the Pacific is so vast and so culturally diverse that no generalizations can be made regarding the youth at the regional level without stating their limitations. Countries such as Australia, New Zealand and Japan, also Singapore and the Republic of Korea resemble in their youth profiles the countries of Europe and North America with high rates of literacy. In these countries youth and students are overlapping categories. But other countries with low literacy rates and high percentage of population still residing in the rural areas have relatively small percentage of the student population compared to illiterate and the rural youth. People in this category did not, in fact could not, treat the students of the West as reference group. They were not party to the student unrest movement of the 1960s. But that did not mean that the non-student youth in Asia or Africa did not have their own quota of problems.

The point that needs to be emphasized is that youth in Asia are not a homogeneous group. Problems of the youth in developing and developed countries within the Asia-Pacific region are also widely different. The dissimilarities in the youth situation within the region can be related to different political and economic scenarios of the countries. In the countries where, for example, filial piety and joint family are the guiding principles of family and kinship organizations, the socialization of the young is of a different order compared to societies such as Australia and New Zealand where the concept of Joint Family does not exist. In the latter societies, the young leave their families of orientation to live separately, and thus attain relative freedom from parental care and control. But in the South Asian countries, ties are not broken even after separation, and the family of orientation continues to meet the obligation of providing financial support for education, and during the period of unemployment. The functional jointness, even where there is physical separation, offers the kind of social security that is not available to the societies that follow the nuclear family norm.

The multi-ethnic character, and the presence of a large number of students from other Asian and European countries in Australia, pose peculiar problems. The 1985 study on Australian Youth, carried out

145

by G. Smolicz, tells us that age structure of the population in Australia was not steady, and the migration of people of all ages in that country caused an overall decline in its youth population. Youth here were concerned more with the problem of setting up their own houses, and were preoccupied with problems connected with employment, socio-economic advancement and education. New Zealand, on the other hand, was preoccupied with the problem of ethnic inequalities. The Republic of Korea faced the problem of militant student movement, but this was generated by factors other than those that caused student unrest in Europe in the 1960s; Korean students were protesting against the dictatorial regime and for the introduction of democracy.

These illustrations suggest that the problems encountered by the youth in these different social settings are very different. The dissimilarities in the problem profiles of youth in the countries are caused by differential impact of the processes of modernization and globalization, and by the economic and political structures. To mount workable programmes for youth development, it is essential to focus on the national variations rather than on the commonality of the youth status.

It is, however, not suggested that the non-student youth in Asia or Africa did not have their own quota of problems and challenges. In today's world, education itself needs to be seen in a different perspective. In the late 1940s, when agencies such as UNESCO were launched, their primary task was to eradicate illiteracy and promote primary education. Today, while the actual numbers of the illiterate is around 795 million[3] – which is nearly two and a half times the population of India of the year 1947 when it gained her independence from the British rule – the percentage of illiterates has certainly gone down. Today the illiterates of the world constitute around 11.5 per cent of the world population which is much smaller than the percentage of illiteracy in the 1950s. Moreover, many school surrogates have come up to perform the task that was earlier the unique domain of the schools. As a consequence of the revolution in the field of Information Technology (IT Revolution) literacy – understood as three Rs (Reading, wRiting and aRithmetic) – is made a bit redundant, and *computeracy*[4] has become a new *sine qua non*. With TV and other gadgets, new knowledge can be learnt without taking recourse to the book. Mobile phones are now operated in remote villages and even in tribal belts by those who can traditionally be defined as illiterate. Maids and cooks use new kitchen gadgets without possessing a literacy grade. Old ways of judging modernization are, thus, gradually turning obsolete. If anthropology were

ANTHROPOLOGICAL PERSPECTIVE TO STUDY YOUTH

to address the concerns of past those models of enquiry were appropriate, but in today's context there is need to pose new questions and invent new tools for investigation.

A major difficulty in comparing the countries in terms of their youth profile is caused by the *differences in the definition of Youth*. The United Nations treats the age group of 15–24 as the core of the Youth category; Commonwealth definition relates to the 15–30 age group.

There are also wide-ranging variations in country-based definitions. Nepal, for example, has set the lower limit at 10 for this age group,[5] and India has stretched the upper limit to 35. Obviously, the people between the ages 10 and 15 and between the ages 24 and 35 have different problems compared to the core group. Even the core group can be subdivided between 15–20 and 20–24. The first subgroup of the core consists of those new entrants who are in the process of being recognized as youth and struggling to train themselves for their eventual entry into the adulthood with participation in the economy, and establishing their own family of procreation. The 10–15 age group should be seen as consisting of those preparing to enter the Youth category and experiencing major physiological changes, such as menarche in the case of girls. Similarly, the 24–35 age group may contain people who are already out of the education system and who are either waiting to be absorbed by the economy, or already in it, with different degrees of satisfaction.

A Google search somehow helped me dig out a table that gives information about the size of our youth population in the age group 13–35. This I reproduce in Table 11.1.

Table 11.1 Youth population in India, 2001 (in thousands)

Age group	Total	Males	Females
All ages	1,028,610	532,157	496,453
13–19	142,701	75,972	66,729
20–24	89,764	46,321	43,443
25–29	83,422	41,558	41,865
30–35	106,450	55,116	51,333
Total	422,337	218,967	203,370

These 2001 Census figures for India indicate that a total of 422.3 million population inhabit the ages between 13 and 35, defined as the Youth category. We also get a fair idea of those who have recently entered and those who are near the exit door. The problems related to

147

ANTHROPOLOGICAL PERSPECTIVE TO STUDY YOUTH

the first category are those of schooling and training and manpower planning; similarly, the problems of the youth near the exit door relate to their entry into the economy – in fact, some of them might have already entered into the economy. It suggests that exit from the Youth category is not coterminous with entry into the economy with gainful employment.

All these figures indicate that growth patterns differ from country to country; consequently, there are different problems relative to youth in each country. Larger size youth populations would require larger infrastructure for their training and a wider job market. We know that many Pacific island countries have witnessed higher suicide rates among the youth. But it still remains to be found out whether such incidence is caused by their larger size, or lack of opportunities, or any other psychological factors.

One point is obvious. People in the Youth category today in the Asia-Pacific region are as many as the total population of India in the year 1971. Just as the huge population of India is pluricultural – that is diverse in terms of several socio-economic and cultural indicators – so is the youth population spread in the various countries of this region. Just as no single policy can be formulated for India's youth, so is the case for the Youth in Asia and the Pacific. It is also significant to mention that the youth constitute today nearly 20 per cent of the world population, but only 3 to 4 per cent are to be found in the developed world and the remainder 17 to 18 per cent youth are located in the developing world of Asia, Africa and Latin America. This fact alone signifies that the problem profile of youth of the developed world is less relevant for the majority of youth. We need a more comprehensive and detailed study of the youth of the countries in the developing world to evolve suitable strategies for their development. With such a heterogeneity that characterizes the category of Youth, it is not possible to think of a single recipe, or a single package of activities, for all those who belong to this transient group. We must admit that this category goes on continually renewing itself, unlike the category, say of women, whose entry or exit from the category is caused only by birth and death. That is why youth profiles of yesterday are no longer valid for today.

Like the differences in the definition of youth, difficulties are also encountered in the identification and use of other indicators.

In the context of the Asia-Pacific region, the youth today – 15–24 age group as defined by the UN – constitute nearly 17.4 per cent of the population. This percentage has come down from 20.6 in 1990,

ANTHROPOLOGICAL PERSPECTIVE TO STUDY YOUTH

and is expected to settle at 15.4 by the year 2025. In terms of numbers, people in the core category of 15–24 were 258 million in the 1950s; in 1980, this number went up to 494 million, and touched the figure of 631 million in 1990. According to UN estimates, the youth population in this region today stands at 618,591,685. Of course, it may be noted that these figures are for forty-five countries that are now included in this region. The new countries that are included were formerly parts of the USSR, namely Armenia, Azerbaijan, Kazakhstan, Kyrgyzstan, Tajikistan, Turkmenistan, and Uzbekistan. The youth population in these additional countries stands at 25.63 million; the youth population for the rest of the region is 592.954 million. In terms of percentage of the youth population to the total population, the lowest is to be found in Tuvalu (11.9%), but its total population is less than 16,000. Other low-percentage countries are Australia (13.5%), Japan (12.8%), New Zealand (13.9%), and Singapore (12.3%). The highest ratio in mainland Asia is to be found in Bangladesh (23.5%) followed by Mongolia (20.7%), Iran (20.3%) and Vietnam (20.2%). As defined by the UN, Youth in India, Pakistan, Papua New Guinea, the Philippines, and Sri Lanka constitute around 19 per cent of their respective populations. China, the most populous country, has only 15.5 per cent in this category, so is the case of North Korea (14.6%). It is interesting that all the Pacific Island countries have youth population ranging between 20 per cent (Vanuatu) and 31 per cent (Tonga).

As I told before, these data are not exactly comparable in the sense that different countries define youth differently. While India, for example, defines people in the age group 13–35, Census data use 10 as the cut-off category, and we have no means to calculate the people between 13 and 15 years of age; of course, we can go to age-specific data and then calculate it ourselves. As a consequence, people use different age cohorts. One estimate suggests that the age group 10–24 (that means inclusion of those in 10–13 age group which is not regarded Youth by the Government of India, and excluding 25–35 age group which is regarded Youth by the same agency) has as many people as 315 million. Another estimate of people *below the age of 20* suggests that it represents 35 per cent of the Indian population. These statistics combine all children and a portion of the youth. It is based on such figures that some have made projections that by the year 2020 a total of 325 million will reach the working age.

Suffering from this constraint, researchers feel handicapped while making cross-cultural comparisons. In traditional ethnographic research we were not concerned about numbers; our focus was on the behaviour

ANTHROPOLOGICAL PERSPECTIVE TO STUDY YOUTH

patterns where 'apt illustrations' – to use the phrase Malinowski employed – sufficed. The study of behaviour patterns was useful in propagating the philosophy of cultural relativism, but in the present-day context of developmental change reference groups are located in other cultures and strategies for change are needed to be devised in the framework of changing global context. For example, scholars have estimated that in the developed countries, and also in China, in 2020 there is going to be a shortage of people in the working age. In four countries – namely USA, China, Japan and Russia – there will be a combined shortage of 42 million workers,[6] but in India there will be a surplus by then of 47 million. This has implications for manpower training and placement. The problem of the four countries mentioned above would be to find additional numbers to fill the vacancies; for India, the crisis would be of finding jobs for the additional workforce. India will have to look beyond the country and prepare the surplus workforce for other economies.

We need to continually update the data because of fast rates of entries and exits from the category. For example, in the years to come, more and more people in this category are expected to be literate and educated, leading to a convergence of student and youth status. Also it would mean gradual rise in the number of educated unemployed compared to the uneducated unemployed. It may also show migration of the educated young from the rural areas to the urban centres.

Both the significant rise in their numbers and the problems the youth cause – ranging from demands for education to demands for employment, and occasional deviant behaviour – suggest that the youth deserve to be carefully studied. The demographic transition from high to low fertility has given rise to a youth bulge, which may return to its pre-transitional stage in 30 years after the onset of fertility decline, and then it may take several decades to stabilize at 12 per cent level, as is the case with New Zealand, Australia and Japan. Such growth of the youth bulge implies delayed marriages and rising demands for school and college enrolment in the lower end subgroup of 15–19. This may also affect composition of the labour force. Planning for schooling, for health care, and for provision of employment opportunities are all likely to be affected by the dramatic demographic changes in the Asian region.

It may also be reminded that the decline in the death rate has affected the entire age pyramid, particularly in the middle reaches and the top of the pyramid. Increasing longevity has continually been enlarging in several societies the size of the people in the senior citizen category.

ANTHROPOLOGICAL PERSPECTIVE TO STUDY YOUTH

These changes in the demography have consequences both on the health front and in the employment market. We are already noticing that the retirement age is rising. My father was made to retire when he was 55; I retired at the age of 60; now the Indian professoriate continues in the profession till 65 years of age. The age of retirement in developed countries is considerably higher.

The prolonged occupancy means decline in the availability of vacancies for the new recruits on the one hand, and in countries such as Japan, it is marking the return of the stem family, and a second entry for women into the workforce. Children are now having the privilege of once again getting socialized by the grandparents.

On the health front, we already notice changes in the *burden of diseases*. Diseases associated with the old age now affect more people; the old also require care on the part of the family particularly in Asian countries where filial piety is emphasized and where sending the aged to the hospice is regarded as neglect of the old by the family, and thus meets with social disapproval. Similarly, the young engaged in new jobs in the corporate sector carry a different kind of disease burden. We now notice that alongside of the diseases generated by malfunctioning of the body, there are now several diseases generated by humans through their behavioural changes which include even psychosomatic ailments. Suicides, accidents, body hurts resulting at times into death by abnormal behaviour of some individuals using modern weaponry or drug addiction are the new additions to the ailment pool for which the health sector has to orient itself. Already in today's context health and hospital are no longer coterminous. Moreover, the intrusion of *Management Culture* in the hospitals has changed the worker profile of the hospitals with several para-medics, and even non-medics, on their payroll. The hospital now competes with hotels; the doctors increasingly behave as businessmen to cheat the patient and make extra money. One can easily see the difference in the orientation of the old and new doctors – the latter being both professionally more competent and economically more money-minded.

* * *

Over the past few years the profile of youth in Asia has undergone dramatic changes. Today the youth constitutes not only a sizable population but also a very high percentage of the literate and educated group in most of the developing countries. In the developed countries, of course, illiteracy among the youth was never a problem. Exposure to education has not only provided them with skills and information,

151

it has also raised their expectations and facilitated the articulation of demands. It is important to ensure that the 1960s that saw student protests do not get repeated. If the rising discontent among them can be detected through our intellectual radars and the observatory of indicators, timely action can be planned to avert such a calamity. It is a happy augury that the youth today are seen not only as a problem group but also as a potential resource for the country's development. Increasingly, governments are getting involved in programmes that are directed towards youth – for the betterment of their position and for the utilization of their skills. The youth are also no longer passive recipients of favours and privileges; they are busy carving out a role for themselves in the country's development process.

It is in this changing context that we should evaluate the situation of youth in this region.

In the changing scenario, education and employment appear to me as two areas that deserve careful attention while developing programmes and policies for youth. In today's world it has become extremely important to develop a culture of learning. The educational institutions are required to change their conservative role of reproducing social structures. In the midst of change they are supposed to equip their clientele in coping with it rather than follow the trodden path unquestioningly. They also have now new competitors in the form of surrogate schools, and mass media to inform, educate and prepare the young for the society of the future. The role of surrogate schools in the training of youth in the developing countries deserves to be studied.

Similarly, it is necessary to investigate the relationship between national income and education. Mark Blaug confirms that:

> After two decades of intensive research on the association between education and national income around the world, little more can be said then that a 10 per cent rate of enrolment in primary schools and a 40 per cent literacy rate is a necessary, but, alas, not a sufficient condition for rapid economic advance.
> (Blaug 1970: Chapter 3)

When the students of the industrialized world openly revolted against the education system in the early 1960s, it shook the complacence of those in positions of power, and those who administered the system of education. It was a clear indication of the failure of the education system to gauge the coming waves of change and to suitably modify their curricula to prepare their students for the new set of challenges. This caused, and still continues to cause, mismatch between supply and demand of manpower. It created what Veblen had called 'trained incapacities', and it generated so much of frustration with the prevailing system.

With some betterment in the system of education, a relatively higher percentage of the young today is literate and educated; although in absolute numbers the number of illiterates is still continually rising, and most of these numbers come from the young and the developing countries. The existing educational infrastructure cannot accommodate all those who are eligible and willing to go to school, and the economy is finding it difficult to provide the kind of employment that the educated young are seeking.

Unemployment is a universal problem. Not only the countries with low literacy rates have high degrees of unemployment, even the countries of the developed North have frightening statistics of unemployment. This simple datum suggests that the relationship between education and employment cannot be taken beyond a point. In the developing countries unemployment exists both among the educated and the uneducated. Moreover, the pattern of joint family system allows the children of well-to-do families remain unemployed until a job suitable to their training and social status is found. This means that the unemployed are not all poor or uneducated.

The World Employment Report 1998–99 tells that unemployment for young people remains at high levels. In some countries of Asia unemployment rates for the young people reach over 30 per cent in urban areas. These high rates are attributed to structural adjustment and privatization programmes. Unemployment is said to lower the household income and block the crucial development of skills that comes from work experience and on-the-job training. It is regarded as an obstacle to a smooth transition from adolescence to adulthood. Many analysts link joblessness to crime, drug abuse, social unrest and conflict. Had this been the case, then the countries of the North should have been free of these indicators of social disorganization. In fact, in this age of technology revolution, we find that crimes of more serious nature are committed by the highly trained people and not by the poor or the novices. The World Trade Center in New York was destroyed by the trained pilots with a *Jihadi* zeal! It is, therefore, hazardous, in my view, to accept the prevalent hypotheses of alleged links between crime and education, or education and unemployment, as proven facts. In my earlier essays on poverty I have questioned the link between poverty and unemployment, and education and poverty (Atal, 2002).

ANTHROPOLOGICAL PERSPECTIVE TO STUDY YOUTH

One common complaint is about growing alienation among youth seen in terms of breakdown of traditional values, family ties and adoption of Western style. We are fed with the common criticism day in and day out that exposure to the Western media is uprooting our young who are losing touch with their culture and leaving their motherland for much greener pastures abroad. Such criticism is palatable and yet questionable. Researches on migration supervised by me during my UNESCO days falsified many of these assumptions. Rather than focussing attention on what damage migration was causing to the place of arrival, these researches in a few Asian countries tried to assess the impact of these on the places of departure. Quite unexpectedly, it was found that migrations to the urban centres by the youth, or to the Middle East, brought back modern culture to the migrants' places of origin. Not only this, traditions got reinforced as family visits coincided with the celebration of a religious festival or a family function such as wedding. The repatriated money became a source for the improvement of the home and the habitat.

If one were to see the lifestyle of the so-called NRIs – the non-resident Indians living in distant lands – one would find that they have become carriers of Indian tradition, rather than fully lost to the alien world. The revolution in Information Technology has facilitated their links with the country of their origin. Watching cable TV telecast from India or other site brings India into their drawing rooms. The TV serials of the old mythological stories have reintroduced them to their glorious cultural past and reinforced their attachment to the values of their parent culture.

The youth in metropolitan India are evolving their new lexicon. As an example, I give below the new coinages that are increasingly gaining ground among the youth of Delhi – the capital of India. Some code words have recently become part of the vocabulary of the teens to outwit their elders. See Table 11.2 for a sample.

Table 11.2 Code words of the teens

FWB	Friends with Benefits: it is used for the friends of the opposite sex who fulfil needs without commitment, with no demands, and no problems
UMFRIEND	Boyfriend
LMAO	Laughing my Ass Off
ILU	I Love You
ITILU	I think I Love You

(*Continued*)

ANTHROPOLOGICAL PERSPECTIVE TO STUDY YOUTH

Table 11.2 (Continued)

THUD	Depressing
8	Oral Sex
SEXTING	Sexual Text Message
@@@	[SMS] Parents are nearby
C-P	Feeling Sleepy
BF vs. GF	Casual hugging of boyfriend, but not in front of your parents
PLENTY CHOICE	Multiple Dating
BASIC INSTINCT	*First Base*: Kissing; *Second Base*: Kissing and Hugging; Homerun = Sex

* * *

There is one more aspect on which I would like to draw your attention. Our discipline that has earlier been criticized for advocating isolation for the tribals, as if we wanted to maintain our anthropological zoos, provides enough material to the culture enthusiasts for condemning onslaughts of changes brought from abroad. As a student I was exposed to the criticism of development defined as 'westernization' and 'modernization'. It was regarded as continuation of the hegemony of the 'West' – a colonial hangover. Now, from the beginning of the present century, these two processes are replaced by the new coinage called *globalization*. While reading criticism of this process I do not fail to notice almost word-to-word resemblance with the criticism of dual processes of westernization and modernization. If the criticism is the same, then why do we call it by a different name? Moreover, the new process is still in its infancy and has not so much penetrated into our rural areas, much less into the tribal belts. There have been few systematic and deeper studies of this new process and yet zealots in the profession have joined hands with the activists and human rights protagonists to criticize the process. As a student of anthropology, I find this as a sad development. We need not give up the difficult task of field investigation in favour of cheap publicity. We must also, unlike our academic ancestors, pay adequate attention to conceptualization. Our being trained in anthropology does not, in my opinion, gives right to us to sell our personal values as profound sociological truths. Scientific objectivity requires us to keep away our personal values while making any generalizations based on empirical research. But there is always a temptation to offer 'coloured' advice to suit the government and the bureaucracy. The latter then use such doctored advice to push their agenda.

I have been cogitating about globalization to find a suitable manner in which to locate this process of change in our social lives. It occurs to me that, contrary to the general perception, anthropology has always been interested in change, though it focussed on societies that appeared to be non-changing. After all, we had been addressing the question as to from where did we start our journey and how did humanity reach where it is now. We used the word *Evolution* as the key to our discipline – be it physical anthropology or social anthropology. I suggest that we replace the word *Evolution* by *Development*. In my view, development has gone through the following stages:

1   *Non-dependent Development*: It can also be called orthogenetic development which implies development from within. This was the pre-colonial stage for the several tribes.

2   *Dependent Development*: With the colonization of the societies, the colonial masters decided the development strategy and brought elements of development from their own society. It was a one-sided effort with colonial masters as 'givers' and colonies as 'receivers'. This phase can be summed up as 'westernization' as most of the colonizers came from the West – which is now redesignated as North. I also call it *single aperture model*. The process of *acculturation* that our predecessors mentioned corresponds to this.

3   *Independent Development*: This is post-colonial development where former colonies started taking decisions independently (at least in theory; proxies are of course not ruled out) to choose elements from abroad, and not only from the former colonial masters but also from a range of modern countries. This corresponds to the term 'modernization'. I call this as *multiple aperture model*. Of course, in this case as well newly independent countries remain at the receiving end – a continuation of one-way traffic.

4   *Inter-dependent Development*: This is the present phase where the give and take has become mutual. We are not only at the receiving end but also at the giving end. To me, globalization for India means the presence of the Globe in India, and of India in the Globe. The use of the word *transculturation* used by our seniors seems to me to be closest to this. It is in this respect that globalization differs from the earlier processes. Also, it must be stressed that these processes do not constitute a ladder. While they follow

ANTHROPOLOGICAL PERSPECTIVE TO STUDY YOUTH

a time sequence – which may vary from country to country – they can, and do, co-exist in any given country. That is why when we criticize the role of hegemony, we still wander in phase two or three, and acknowledge that phase four is yet to arrive.

I would like you to examine this new paradigm for whatever it is worth.

To conclude, all over the world, there is a growing recognition of the need to involve youth in the process of development and to curb the tendencies towards alienation and frustration among them. It is a late, but welcome realization that the future belongs to them, and that the society should do everything possible to ensure a better future. Student demonstrations and youth protest movements contributed, no doubt, to enhance the urgency of the matter. They forced the world community to realize that it is perilous to ignore the youth. It has received the message that the present is not inherited from the past but is borrowed from the future. It is in the shaping of the future world that the countries are now eager to utilize the enormous youth potential, and the youth themselves are preparing to perform that role.

It is they, not we, who should decide the kind of future they want. It is they, not we, who would reject what they do not like in our heritage and the prevailing norms of behaviour. It is they, not we, who must make choices and fabricate innovations to suit the new scenario. We adults have to redefine our roles as co-partners with youth, rather than playing the proxy role as planners and decision-makers. We have to regard the youth not only as passive recipients of whatever the society offers but also as creative individuals capable of fashioning their future.

The new perspective is to see the youth not as a *problem group*, but as a *potential force*, and that programmes be designed to utilize them for the good of the society. For this, it is important that we develop a good research agenda. At present, there is so much talk but very little by way of research on youth with a social science perspective. We think of action and research when a situation becomes critical. That is a fire-fighting approach, and not a constructive one. Also when philanthropy and well-intentioned patronage guide our action, there are chances of misplaced emphases and costly failures. They are not, and cannot, be substitutes for solid research which provides a dependable basis for planning and evaluation. Close cooperation is needed between people of action and the research-minded social scientists. We need both independent studies on the various aspects of youth as well

ANTHROPOLOGICAL PERSPECTIVE TO STUDY YOUTH

as critical evaluation of existing programmes and activities carried out by the governments and the NGOs.

Notes

1 Address at the Plenary, IUAES Inter-Congress, Bhubaneshwar, Odisha, 29 November 2012. I am grateful to the organizers of this Inter-Congress for kindly inviting me to address this gathering of fellow anthropologists. It is indeed an honour. Since this is meant to be a speech at the Plenary, my tone is somewhat different.

I am reminded of my last visit to this town way back in 1978 when IUAES held its post Congress Symposium on *Swidden Cultivation*. Then, in my capacity as UNESCO's Regional Adviser for Social and Human Sciences in Asia and the Pacific, I financially supported that initiative of the Utkal University. As a follow up to that Symposium, I launched and directed a cross-cultural comparative study on *Swidden Cultivation in Asia* as part of the UNESCO activities involving scholars from India, Indonesia, Malaysia, the Philippines, and Thailand. That exercise resulted in three volumes under my editorship.

Happily, my present visit, again, is in connection with the IUAES activities after a lapse of 34 years.

2 For a detailed treatment of this problem, please see Yogesh Atal, 2012, Chapter 15 titled *Race, Tribe, Caste and Class*.

3 Over two-thirds of the world's illiterate adults (15+ population) are found in only eight countries (Bangladesh, China, Egypt, Ethiopia, India, Indonesia, Nigeria and Pakistan); of all the illiterate adults in the world, two-thirds are women; extremely low literacy rates are concentrated in three regions, the Arab states, South and West Asia and Sub-Saharan Africa, where around one-third of the men and half of all women are illiterate.

4 In my article on Asian Futures, published in the *Encyclopedia of the Future* (Macmillan, New York, 2006) I introduced this concept of *Computeracy*. Now I find its use in several writings. Computeracy has become a more salient feature than mere literacy.

5 In 2010, Nepal revised the lower limit upwards to 16. Population of 16–40 age group in Nepal now is defined as youth. This accounts for 38.8 per cent of the Nepalese population.

6 USA (17 million), China (10 million), Japan (9 million) and Russia (6 million).

12

ETHICS IN RESEARCH AND RESEARCH IN ETHICS[1]

Preamble

The question of ethics is relevant in all research, be it in the social sciences or in physical and biological sciences. With the emergence of science as a distinct field of enquiry, a different system of ethical practice has evolved. In the absence of scientific truth, societies trusted philosophical speculation; such speculation is continuously replaced by scientific truth as it unravels. But what is truth at a given point of time may be questioned later and may be replaced by new discoveries and inventions carried out with more sophisticated tools. Research, thus, basically handles two kinds of ethics: the ethics relative to particular cultures and the ethics of scientific research. The latter ethics can be subdivided into three categories: ethics related to investigation, ethics related to the scientific community i.e. professional ethics and ethics involved in consultant–client relationships.

To be sure, ethics is a cultural product. Anthropological research involves a confrontation of three cultures and, thus, ethics associated with them. The three different cultures are: the culture of the people being studied, the culture of the society of the researcher and the culture of the scientific profession. Ethical issues in anthropological research need, therefore, to be studied in such a perspective. Value-conflicts are inevitable in any research enterprise that involves humans both as 'subjects' and as 'researchers'. The success of the enterprise depends on how such conflicts are tackled and resolved without sacrificing basic tenets of scientific inquiry.

I Growing concern for ethics in the academia

Like all other sciences, the science of anthropology also began as the investigation of the hitherto unknown. Its initial interest was in the reconstruction of human history. From where did the Man – the *Homo sapiens* – come? How did we arrive at our present? Answers to these questions were provided to the curious, in the pre-scientific era, by one's cultural and religious tradition. They were obviously philosophical speculations, but had the backing of tradition and, thus, had unquestioning acceptance. These beliefs may be rational, irrational, or even non-rational. But they carry with them religious sanction and are, therefore, considered by the believers as 'above reproach'.

History of science tells us that researches that were instigated by philosophical speculations emanating from different civilizational sources led to new discoveries and fresh reconstructions of our past. That was the task of anthropology which arose as a complete science of Man, federating physical anthropology, prehistoric anthropology and social or cultural anthropology – with due accommodation in it of philosophical and psychological anthropology. However, with the growing specialization, the discipline began to disunite into narrow specialisms. This process began somewhere in the 1930s, but became more prominent in the last three decades of the past century so much so that specialists of its sub-branches became almost non-communicative across their narrow boundaries. While social anthropologists engaged in ethnographic research cannot disregard the question of ethics, other specialists dealing with the prehistoric and paleontological evidence did not regard ethical issue that very important.

New ethical issues are surfacing in biological sciences, and a new specialism called *bioethics* has come to occupy an important place. The revelations of Nazi experiments conducted during the Second World War highlighted the issues relative to bio-medical research on the human subjects. This concern further deepened with the technological advances in the field of medicine permitting organ transplantation when new questions were raised about the status of the donor, consent for donation and about withdrawal of care and the desirability of euthanasia. With the replacement of the cottage industry model of surgical practice by evidence-based surgery, ethical issues have come into prominence.

The academic world responded to these concerns and set up bioethical think tanks and developed even teaching curricula. This trend began somewhere in the 1960s but assumed global significance in later years, so much so that a *Universal Declaration on Bioethics and*

Human Rights was adopted by UNESCO on 19 October 2005. The UNESCO Note on this says:

> Since the 1970s, the field of bioethics has grown considerably. While it is true that bioethics today includes medical ethics issues, its originality lies in the fact that it goes much further than the various professional codes of ethics concerned. It entails reflection on societal changes and even on global balances brought about by scientific and technological developments. To the already difficult question posed by life sciences – How far can we go? – other queries must be added concerning the relationship between ethics, science and freedom.

It is not insignificant that the programme on Human Genomics was located within the Sector of Social and Human Sciences in UNESCO. As one who had worked for more than two decades in this Sector, I have been associated with the concerns of this Programme.

II Emerging ethical issues in research

Normative ethics

The philosophical aspect of ethics is the oldest one, having its roots in the divine, and in religion, and manifesting itself in terms of cultural values, transmitted through the processes of enculturation and socialization. This is what scholars term as *Normative Ethics*. In addition, there is a tradition of deontology that emphasizes the principle of right action. Philosophers like E. Kant and William Ockham propounded Formalism and Divine Command Theory respectively to suggest that the methods of ethics are generally opposed to consequentialist methods. In their view, the moral value of an action is wholly independent from the consequences of an action – good or bad. Rather than focussing on consequences, deontological methods emphasize duty as the basis of moral value. For Ockham, the source of duty is the revealed law of God. For Kant, the source of moral duty is pure reason itself. One finds an echo of *Bhagwad Geeta* in such a pronouncement: *Karmanye Wadhikaraste, ma Faleshu Kadachan* वाधिकारस्तु मा फलेषु कदाचन: – work is thy duty, reward is not thy concern.

ETHICS IN RESEARCH AND RESEARCH IN ETHICS

Scientific norms: positivism and value-neutrality

The onset of positivism and the attendant scientific enquiry introduced yet another set of ethical values, namely the values of scientific research such as empiricism, objectivity, value-neutrality and reliability and validity of data and findings. These distinguished research in the physical sciences, and were then emulated in the biological – natural history – sciences. The social sciences, which were late to arrive on the intellectual scene, pursued research following the norms of scientific ethics.

Questions have, however, always been raised in regard to the claim of social sciences to be 'value-free'. The debate is not yet settled as to whether social sciences can ever be value-free. Humans dealing with humans, it is argued, cannot remain value-neutral, and be objective. Those supporting the claim of being value-free insist on training the mind to refrain from imposing the values of one's own culture, and to collect and interpret data in objective terms through empirical research. The divide between deductive and inductive approach is partly characterized by these two stances. Question marks on the predictability of social sciences are constantly raised and answered by the twin logics of self-fulfilling and self-cancelling prophesy. In social science research it is the queer situation of 'Man Proposes and Man Disposes' – you do not need a God to do the disposal job!

The question assumed special significance in anthropology which came to be defined as the study of *Other* Cultures 'with an emphasis on the small-scale tribal societies of the world, and for many years the study of such a society was virtually the initiation ceremony which admitted a scholar into the ranks of anthropology'. It was argued that since anthropologists studied societies other than their own, they can remain objective and value-free. The counterargument was advanced to emphasize the point that the discipline was an outgrowth of the phenomenon of colonialism, and the researchers were working for the colonial government to strengthen its stronghold and to keep the colonies enslaved. Therefore, it is the handmaiden of the administration, and cannot be value-free.

The birth of anthropology occurred when the Industrial Revolution facilitated colonization, and when academic climate was getting scientized with the reining theory of Evolution and Darwinism. The travel into distant lands brought the scientists into close contact with the so-called primitive societies and exotic cultures. Interested in the reconstruction of the humanity's past, evolutionists regarded the

ETHICS IN RESEARCH AND RESEARCH IN ETHICS

'Primitive Contemporaries' as the remnants of humanity's past and began documenting their culture. In the absence of any written history, this was the only way to access the past. Physical anthropologists worked on the fossils and helped reconstruct the past on that solid evidence. Social anthropology adopted the path of going from the present to the past, while the physical anthropologists dug the past to reach the present via the paleontological route. Some others among them opted for biological investigations among the contemporary populations to contribute to racial distributions of human population, and willy-nilly got involved in value judgements about racist theories that were coloured by cultural prejudices. The 'Out-of-Africa' theory of the origin of Man, now emerging with the help of DNA research, will have to protect itself from any such value infiltration.

Investigation of the past of humanity had, thus, necessarily allowed conjectures to fill the 'missing links'; at times the conjectures were tried to be supported by false evidence. One may cite here as an example the famous case of the fraud committed by Dawson – a lawyer of Sussex, in league with a palaeontologist working on fish fossils (Arthur Smith Woodword), an anatomist (Arther Keith), and a brain specialist (Grafton Elliot Smith) – to claim discovery of the Dawn Man – Eoanthropus Dawsoni – best known as the Piltdown Man. The academic community was befooled for a long period of 43 years, from 1912 to 1955, when the alleged discovery of half-ape/half-man skull and jaw bone was finally condemned as a forgery.

Even in social anthropology, ideological positions infiltrated conjectures and placements of societies on the evolutionary ladder, despite claims to objectivity. Colonial ideologues used the key phrases from Darwin to put their society on the top of the world as winners of the 'struggle for existence' and 'survival of the fittest' and thus as evidence of 'natural selection'. There were researchers who claimed to have found in the tribal societies 'primitive form of Communism', and others who disputed such interpretation – both inspired by the Marxian writings. Max Weber and Edward Westermarck, similarly, collected enormous data from different societies to battle with Marxism and propounding their own theories.

The beginnings of the social sciences, thus, had a queer mix of positivism and ideological acrimonies, putting a big question mark on the possibility of a value-neutral social science. Justifying the anthropological approach, ethnologists introduced the concept of 'cultural relativism' to bring home the point that alien societies should not be judged by the cultural lens of the outside researcher. This was an ethical injunction.

Theoretical and ideological biases

In this regard I wish to briefly allude to the controversy surrounding Margaret Mead's work titled *Coming of Age in Samoa*. Highly appreciated by Franz Boas – her mentor – this classic work, published in 1928, was challenged in a 1983 publication by Derek Freeman. Boas found in her work a strong argument against the 'apostles of Eugenics' who floated the 'nurture versus nature' controversy. Boas was of the view that 'the social stimulus is infinitely more potent than the biological mechanism'. He regarded the eugenics movement as a 'pseudo-scientific cult' and said that 'racial interpretation of history [is] irremediably dangerous'. To quote Freeman: 'the extreme doctrines of the hereditarians, Boas pointed out, had set anthropologists and biologists at odds, and so much so that a "parting of ways" had been reached' (1984:5). Boas' students – Kroeber and Lowie – worked hard to propound a doctrine of absolute cultural determinism that excluded biological variables. Mead's work was refuted by Freeman on the ground that in her enthusiasm to take side with cultural determinism she somehow ignored the role of genetic factors, and thus misguided her audience by a faulty portrayal of the cultural reality of the Samoans. Freeman's book became in the US a 'seismic event' as it raised some key ethical issues pertaining to the writings of the world's most respected and highly acclaimed anthropologist.

This episode is important to see the changing relationship between biology and social anthropology, and also to understand the role of theoretical or ideological positions in ethical terms. The eugenics movement, inspired by Darwin, led to racism as is evident in the writings of Francis Galton. He was of the view that the differences between savage and civilized societies are due to the 'innate character of different races' and, using this argument, he proposed to develop elaborate schemes for hereditary improvement. Read this sentence of Galton, written in 1865: 'what an extraordinary effect might be produced on our race' [if it were the practice to] 'unite in marriage those who possessed the finest and most suitable natures, mental, moral, and physical'. A careful reader can detect the influence of non-scientific values on the so-called scientific writing of Galton. For years, people talked of racial superiority and inferiority until they were put to rest through a UNESCO intervention. The more prevalent view now holds the role of both genetic and exogenetic systems that are autonomous and yet constantly interacting among the human species.

ETHICS IN RESEARCH AND RESEARCH IN ETHICS

Insider-outsider controversy: the carriers of cultural biases

Controversies also arose regarding the relative merits of insiders and outsiders as researchers. The outsiders claim to be objective as they approach the society with a clean slate. They also argue that insiders have only partial understanding of the social reality as they see it from their particular vantage point. Countering this, the insiders allege superficial understanding on the part of the outsiders, and hint at the biases they carried with them.

That this debate has not died down is amply illustrated by the present controversy regarding the Oscar-winning Indian film *Slumdog Millionaire*.

The point of contention is that the outsiders see only the 'dark' side of the 'other' society. This argument is countered by the outsiders by citing cases of highlighting only the 'brighter' side. The key point is that both sides have only a partial view of the society and what you hide and what you highlight is dependent on one's perception and cultural conditioning.

By the 1960s, the insider-outsider controversy became quite prominent. Social changes brought about by the colonial regimes, and the freedom struggles fought by the natives resulted in enhancing awareness, improvement in the literacy profiles and assertion of national interests. Education among the non-Western societies also produced scholars, including those trained in anthropology. Newly independent governments also began insisting on clearing applications of outside researchers. Some governments insisted on 'joint' projects involving the locals. It was in response to this development that the outside researchers came up with the new coinage, namely *Participatory Research*. Strictly speaking, Participatory Research is not a *method*; it is an *approach* to meet the new exigency. Participation is being defined both in terms of joint research projects and involvement of the community leaders in defining the scope of the project and the strategy of research. The message conveyed through this approach is that the people are not merely the 'subjects of research', but are 'active participants' in the research process. In several Pacific Island countries this approach was adopted to expedite clearance of project proposals originating from abroad. But it remains to be seen how much of it is only a bureaucratic formality, and how much real is the participation of the locals. Its utility in policy-related, action-research projects is generally recognized as it attempts to build people's ability to understand their own situation and to take relevant measures to solve local problems.

165

There are, however, people who regard this as tokenistic to overcome bureaucratic hurdles and to please the local potentates who generally possess little competence to participate in research as equal partners. Obtaining informed consent in clinical trials is, in my view, an extension of the same approach and remains tokenistic, and a protective garb for the medical researchers.

III Role of the researcher

I wish to make the point that it is possible to do social science, and particularly participate in programmes of social change, without letting personal values or values of one's own culture to overwhelm. This is like the role of a social architect or a doctor.

An architect is a person who has expertise in designing buildings and other structures to meet the demands of the client. In developing a blueprint for a building, an architect is expected to give due regard to the values and preferences of the client. For example, the client may be guided by the principles of ancient *Vastushastra* which prescribe location of gates and windows, kitchen and bedrooms and the like. The client may belong to a religion other than that of the architect. In such circumstances, a value-free architect is the one who makes the values of his client as part of the plan of the proposed building, but refrains from inserting his own value biases. In this frame, a Muslim architect can be approached to design a Hindu temple; similarly, a Hindu architect can be quite competent to prepare the blueprint for a mosque. It is a different matter that any one of these architects may refuse to build a religious place for practitioners of religion other than one's own. But this refusal cannot be on the ground of the science of architecture.

The same applies to the profession of medicine. The religion of the medical practitioner is irrelevant when treating a patient of another religion. Religion may play a role in the prescription of diet, but not in the diagnosis of the disease or its treatment.

A social scientist can, similarly assist a society – his own or an alien – in terms of his social science expertise with complete disregard to his personal ideological predilections.

IV Inevitability of ethical conflicts

I have given sufficient evidence of the ethical concerns both in the biological and social sciences, and have suggested that these concerns are constantly changing. At the moment, any scientific researcher is confronted with four sets of value syndromes: the values of the society to which a researcher belongs; the values of the society which is the subject matter of his/her study; the values of the profession – divided into values related to scientific research and the values governing consultant–client relationships; and the personal (idiosyncratic) values of the researcher. Obviously, there is likelihood of conflict between the four sets of values and the researcher has to find a balance. The common agreement between nations to give due respect to the dignity of the human person and to observe human rights poses yet another constraint on the freedom of the researcher in choosing the topic of study, subjects for investigation and use of the research findings.

Technological advances in the field of organ transplantation, kidney dialysis, DNA and human genome research have posed new sets of questions. Many responsible governments have issued codes of conduct, particularly when government funding is involved. Similarly, professional associations have also issued Codes of Conduct guidelines for their members.

Professor John Gledhill, former Chair of the Association of Social Anthropologists, writes about the importance of ethics for anthropological research in this manner:

> Although all research on human subjects and their social and cultural life raises ethical issues, those posed by anthropological studies are especially wide ranging and profound. The intimate nature of the information produced by ethnographic research is only one aspect of the ethical dilemmas anthropologists habitually face, wherever they work. Our comparative, anti-ethnocentric stance is relevant to any kind of enquiry into human social life, as our subjects range from the (relatively) powerless to the (apparently extremely) powerful, and our 'sites' now range from the command and control centres of transnational corporations and multilateral agencies to the most fragile of human populations in geographically and socially marginal situations, with a very great deal of our attention focused on the no less ethically demanding terrain of social lives lived in between these poles. In a world in which "places" are increasingly seen as something that human beings construct within networks of flows and relations that often transcend national frontiers, the structure and dynamics of the power relations that make-up our world and the way we talk about it have become increasingly central to

anthropological concerns. With this concern comes a heightened sensitivity to the ethics of what anthropologists are trying to accomplish when they address controversial issues – be they, for example, the social impacts of science and technology or the roots of conflict, social discrimination, violence and displacement. . . . What the ASA seeks to do is to encourage anthropologists to think about the ethical implications of their work in a broader, more profound and continuous way.

(http://www.theasa.org/ethics.shtml,
accessed 15 March 2015)

Ethics, in the context of research, basically relates to two questions: what is the proper way to collect, process, analyze and report research data? And how should researchers relate with their subjects? The application of research to the solution of problems – social or personal – related to reforms or health care introduces yet another dimension for ethical consideration. With rising literacy many aspects of scientific activity, which were at one point of time regarded as the monopoly of the scientists, have become part of the public domain. The consumers have been given the legitimacy to question the performance of a practitioner and seek compensation for neglect or malpractices. Thus, not only the peer group within the profession but also the wider community demand pursuit of ethics. Obviously, this has encouraged the professionals both to defend themselves and also to make their practice transparent. Surgeons, for example, use evidence-based strategies. Surgery has come to be defined as 'managing of human biology', and the surgeons are expected to 'minimize defects in the processes of surgery and progressively reduce the morbidity of disease and injury'. This has become important as people appear to be withdrawing trust from the medical institutions and practitioners. Their being co-fiduciaries of their clients is now under doubt. The conflict between their fiduciary obligation and self-interest in remuneration has altered the older paradigm of 'one patient at a time' and 'my patient comes first' resulting into over-, under- or mistreatment of patients. The societal values of higher socio-economic status also influence the people in the medical profession. Doctors prefer to work in private hospitals which charge heavy fees from the patients. This results in the neglect of deserving and yet poor patients who could go only to badly managed government-run hospitals. Ethical issues of this sort were raised recently when our prime minister was hospitalized for a major surgery. While everyone welcomed his decision to go to the AIIMS,

ETHICS IN RESEARCH AND RESEARCH IN ETHICS

critics put the finger at the fact that the specialists were called from another town and from a private clinic, waiving the rule of disallowing outside professionals to perform surgery at the AIIMS. The same facility was denied to another ailing politician who had to move to a private hospital.

The increasing significance of these basic questions has led professional associations and governments and international agencies to develop 'codes of conduct', 'ethical guidelines' and adopt 'Declarations'. But these man-made instruments are never perfect, and newly emerging situations may demand their revision. Since revisions are made only intermittently, practitioners may evolve some *ad hoc* solutions and hope for their acceptance by the wider scientific community and the governmental agencies. The point is that what goes in the name of ethics is based on temporal definitions and is subject to non-adherence on personal or ideological grounds. For example, when any members of the Society for the Prevention of Cruelty against Animals raise issues, others point out to the fact of prevalence of non-vegetarianism among the members of the Society. How can non-vegetarians talk about prevention of cruelty against animals? When a similar question was raised about non-vegetarianism amongst Buddhists, the explanation offered was quite amusing: Buddhists eat the killed animal; they do not kill – it is done by others!

Practitioners, particularly those who treat people, face a peculiar dilemma. The authors of *Freedom at Midnight* tell us the story of the Hindu doctor attending Mohammed Ali Jinnah. The doctor knew that his patient was suffering from tuberculosis and was not going to live for long. Had this 'privileged information' been leaked out to his opponents, it is surmised, the partition of the country could have been prevented by just procrastinating the process of negotiations. So what should reign supreme: the professional ethic of keeping confidential the 'privileged information' or the larger national question of the integrity of the country? A similar crisis might arise for a researcher on sexually transmitted diseases. If his subject is found to be an AIDS patient and guilty of not sharing this fact with his/her sexual partner and thus causing risk, what is ethical for the researcher: to disclose this fact to the partner or to maintain confidentiality demanded by the norm of 'privileged information'?

Societal norms also differ as regards the definition of death. When the first heart transplant was made in South Africa, legal luminaries raised the question about the propriety of removing the heart from a cadaver on the ground that if heart was functioning normally, how can

169

the person be declared dead? When the renowned Gandhian Vinoba Bhave realized that his death was near and that he could not be saved, he withdrew from all medicine and stopped the intake of food – as is the tradition amongst the Jains – some activists raised the voice that the government should arrest him for the offence of committing suicide. There was a recent case in Mumbai where a patient was refused permission by the court to abort as the embryo was near-dead, and the embryo died in the womb. A few days back there was a report that the parents of a young person who died of cancer, but who had left his semen in a lab, wanted to have a grandson using the dead son's semen for *in-vitro* pregnancy; but the laboratory refused to oblige. Was it right? All these point at deficiencies in the ethical code.

As against this, there are innumerable cases – practically every day the media reports them – where practitioners violate the ethical code. Relying on my memory, I cite a few such examples:

1   A well-known heart surgeon is found guilty by a court of cheating his patients by charging for expensive foreign-made valves but replacing them by local and less expensive ones during the surgery. And at times charging for two valves but planting only a single.

2   Two brothers, without proper medical degrees, practising kidney transplant surgery in make-believe hospitals and operation theatres. They were found guilty of removing kidneys from poor patients, without their explicit permission, and planting them unto rich patients, mostly from abroad.

3   Trained human biologists who operate private laboratories and simultaneously sell samples of their clients to foreign laboratories for research, and make good money. It is similar to other instances of foreign researchers hiring local investigators for collection of data and taking it home for analysis for report-writing and not giving any credit to the locals.

4   Patients are getting wary of a volley of tests administered on them for common diseases. They allege that these are done either to use the samples to learn new techniques and operate new machines, or to make extra money. Doctors, in turn, privately admit that these are done to save their skin when cases of medical negligence are filed in the courts – as a prophylactic device.

All these instances relate to the arena of bioethics. The increasing incidence of such cases and their media reporting now necessitates

ETHICS IN RESEARCH AND RESEARCH IN ETHICS

research on ethics itself. Not only the ethical considerations are part of scientific quest and applications of new scientific knowledge in solving human and social problems, the violations of ethical norms themselves constitute a new field for research. In between these are issues that relate to the subject matter of anthropology itself. The modern advances in science and technology have ushered in an era of development and now of globalization. The fundamental feature of these processes is rapid transformation of human societies, involving the inevitable disappearance of some cultural traits, intercultural mixing and even the lurking danger of the death of some languages and some cultures. The concern to save them is reigniting the old debate about the 'anthropological zoos'. In the new format are now included even the representatives of such fast disappearing cultures who see in the plea of outsiders a conspiracy to keep them backward. The question then is: if the researchers are not in a position to prevent their death, what other scientific obligation do they have?

Conflicting ethical premises notwithstanding, the moral dimension in academic pursuits has, of late, assumed a critical significance. Granted that a consensus is difficult, and that positions taken by the profession at a given point of time may change over the years, it is necessary to keep the basic principles intact and to ensure the extent to which they could be adhered to. These principles relate to (i) avoidance of harm to subjects, (ii) undue intrusion into the personal life of the subject/the culture of the people being studied, (iii) obtaining consent from the subjects, and ensuring compensation in case of a hazard caused by research/investigation, (iv) maintenance of confidentiality and anonymity, (v) due credit to all participants in the research process [research team, field investigators, local informants], (vi) academic honesty and non-exploitation of researchers by their teacher-guides, and (vii) rights over data and publications. Non-malfeasance and beneficence, respect for persons, fidelity, honesty, trustworthiness and justice are the key values that constitute the core of ethics.

In conclusion

There is broad domain of ethical issues and it is becoming a very complicated territory. It is not enough to pontificate on the desirability of ethics. We must begin researching this terrain. There is need for a proper stocktaking of various ethical principles adopted by the different scientific professions, of the violations of these norms as well as

ETHICS IN RESEARCH AND RESEARCH IN ETHICS

the root causes of such an aberrant behaviour, and case analyses of ethical conflicts. Such data will be a useful input for programmes of training in ethics, and for policymaking.

Not only should we talk of ethics in research but should also do research on ethics.

Note

1 Special Lecture delivered at the Symposium on Population Genomics at Annual Conference of the Indian Society of Human Genetics.

It may sound strange to many to talk of ethics – a subject that is associated with philosophical thinking, and concerned mainly with values, rather than with what human biologists handle as data.

My only relief is the fact that the organizers of this Symposium, and of the Annual Conference of the Indian Society of Human Genetics, imaginatively titled the event to include Ethics and Culture alongside of Population Genomics. I am sure that this was not the ploy to forestall the criticism of one-sided dominance of the biological over the social and cultural. I regard this as an admission of the need to restore the holistic character of our discipline of anthropology by bringing back the key concept of 'culture'.

13

ANTHROPOLOGY AND THE FUTURE OF HUMANKIND[1]

Asking a question about Future to the student of anthropology may sound somewhat contradictory in view of the fact that this discipline is seen as a study of the Primitive and of the Past. Both the original concerns were primarily governed by the keen desire to construct the Humanity's past and, in doing so, it followed the evolutionary path.

How could such a discipline predict the future of Humankind? How could it provide guidelines for ushering into the future? In other words, how does the knowledge of the Past that anthropology has acquired over the years equip its practitioners to chart out a strategy for dealing with the Future of Humankind? That appears, in the first instance, a tall order. And hence my hesitation!

I

The word 'future' in the title of this chapter invites our attention to a crucial issue: what can anthropology contribute to the future of Humankind?

Hidden in this question are many queries: is anthropology in a position to *predict* the future? Can it fashion the future of our choice? Can it suggest the contours of a desirable future? Can we perceive one common future for the entire humankind? In other words, the theme invites us to look into our discipline's capabilities – in terms of our orientation, existing theories and prevalent methodology – to respond to this demand. We can only suggest what we, as anthropologists, perceive as the future of Humankind.

Let me briefly go back to the origins of our discipline. The circumstances that gave rise to anthropology were vastly different than they are today. The discipline was the product of industrialization and was also used initially as a tool for extending colonization by the countries

173

that claimed to be 'civilized' and 'superior' – both genetically and culturally.

It must be said at the outset that while being of practical use to the colonial powers, the discipline, as it grew, also developed its scientific protocol. But it must also be admitted that some racially minded – in fact the racists who nurtured colonial aspirations – scholars worked hard to develop a new science of eugenics. They even borrowed some key phrases from Darwin to prove the superiority of the white race: *Struggle for Existence, Natural Selection* and *Survival of the Fittest*. They used these Darwinian phrases to justify their biological superiority and their right to be the natural rulers of the less gifted. Using these two key words they tried to justify their colonialist expansion and the subjugation of the tribal communities as well as their superiority over Eastern civilizations. They built up theories of Unilinear Evolution based on prehistorical and archaeological evidence, and on researches carried out by palaeontologists and ethnologists. Reconstructing Mankind's past, anthropologists of yore built an evolutionary ladder in which they put the industrialized societies of the West on the top, and the tribal societies, particularly of the non-Western world, on lower ladders. The evolutionary ladder required all societies to climb up stair by stair, and follow the same path of development as their 'superior counterparts'. Thus, those reaching the middle layer of the staircase were considered late arrivals.

The curious lifestyles of these autochthones and aborigines provided good descriptive material for the reading audience of the so-called West. In their enthusiasm, initial researchers working in the remote areas of distant lands also showed keenness to preserve the pristine nature of these cultures, and to save them from the onslaught of advancing technological culture. The powerful advocacy for the preservation of tribal cultures was, however, interpreted as a plea to save the 'anthropological zoos'. Anthropologists were blamed for their self-interest in the advocacy for keeping the tribal societies 'aloof'; colonial administrators bought the plea to pursue their strategy of colonial expansion. As regards the future of Humankind, the early scholars thought that there is only a single path. The primitives of today represent the past of the civilized, and the present of the civilized was seen as blueprint of the future of primitives.

II

Initially, anthropologists came from the so-called developed world. They were, therefore, rightly designated as 'students of *Other Cultures*'.

ANTHROPOLOGY AND THE FUTURE OF HUMANKIND

Although social anthropologists are students of society and culture, they were treated as a group different from sociologists on the ground that the latter studied their own society, while the former focussed on our primitive contemporaries.

As the discipline of anthropology – a *Study of Man in his totality* – grew, it began to draw boundaries to fence its operations. Anthropology distinguished itself by being a 'holistic' study of a small society covering all aspects – prehistory, archaeology, palaeontology, sociology, economics, political science, religion, arts and oral literature. An anthropologist was regarded as a person whose 'skull was full of many skills'. As against this, sociology required only 'one skull, one skill'. Dealing with the non-literate people speaking difficult dialects, anthropologists relied more on the technique of 'Participant Observation' compared to sociologists who were identified as users of the technique of 'Questionnaire'. Boundaries between the twin disciplines – sociology and social anthropology – were thinly drawn on the basis of technique of study and the size of the society as well as it being the 'other' – not the one to which the scholar belonged.

While it took some time to gain an independent status for the discipline in the academe, it somehow remained short-lived. The discipline began to develop internal colonization in terms of narrow specialization. Within anthropology, specializations grew which took specialists in physical anthropology closer to biological sciences and social anthropology to social sciences. It is disheartening to note that the anthropology departments in Indian universities have become, in effect, departments of genomics and genetics, with the result that such specialists increasingly know less and less about the parent discipline and its unifying character, and are also simultaneously treated as 'second-class citizens' in the domain of biological sciences. These departments are increasingly losing the 'federal character' and are over-dominated by physical anthropologists, who seldom visit the tribal areas for study. Even social anthropologists have expanded their fields of study. Way back in the mid-1950s, anthropologists working in India – both expatriates and indigenous – moved to village studies although they followed ethnographic approach. Later, they became the first researchers in the area of planned culture change. Today, there are very few students of anthropology who prefer to work on the tribes, barring those who themselves are tribals and are now christened as *auto-anthropologists.*

It is also strange that other social science disciplines which abstained earlier from researching the tribal belts are also moving towards

175

tribal studies. Thus, tribal studies are no longer the exclusive domain of anthropologists. Social workers, development specialists and even political scientists are taking up tribal studies, albeit with different perspectives and using different methodologies of secondary data analyses, and of evaluation of projects. On the other hand, anthropologists are moving away not only from tribal studies but also from village studies as well. Since most of the new graduates are from physical anthropology, their study populations are also different. As for the social anthropologists, they are exploring the same social frontiers as the sociologists. The debate regarding the differences between sociology and anthropology has virtually died down in India notwithstanding some old practitioners still holding on to the decrepit platform. How does it matter whether you designate S. C. Dube, or M. N. Srinivas, or T. N. Madan as anthropologist or sociologist?

The concern for exploring new frontiers damaged the unity of the discipline. The common thing, however, between the two major divisions – social anthropology and physical anthropology – is that they are no longer confined to the studies of the tribes only; both are working on other populations, and both are now focussing on the Present of Humankind.

III

I disagree with the view that anthropology is anti-change. Change has been the central concern of anthropology and it still continues. What has changed is its orientation. In the beginning, anthropology was oriented to the Past and was attempting to reconstruct the pathway through which the humanity travelled from its distant past to the current present. When it moved to the study of the villages, it extended its scope to cover societies other than the tribes – recognizing the trend of assimilation of tribal societies in indigenous civilizations. Since the euphoria of independence from the colonial rule led the new nations to introduce rapid changes in their old cultures, anthropologists also changed their orientation to focus on the processes of change initiated to improve the Present. Of course, they focussed more on 'resistance to change' and gave added significance to 'tradition' by advising change agents to include 'tradition' as an important variable in the change process rather than to hasten to write its obituary.

The profile of anthropology has radically changed over the years. Despite further compartmentalization, the various branches of the discipline are covering additional subject matter and different population

ANTHROPOLOGY AND THE FUTURE OF HUMANKIND

groups. Rather than focussing on the reconstruction of the past, and description of the queer and the exotic in human cultures, they are now orienting towards the Present. Their help is sought now in the management sector and in technological development. Anthropology has entered the domain of the management sciences. The corporate world that is increasingly becoming multinational feels the need to understand the 'local cultures' to penetrate into them and also to obtain new workers on cheaper salaries. In fact, it appears as a redefined role of anthropology from being in the service of the *colonialist masters* to now serve the *corporate managers*. In other words, it is a new version of the old agenda.

But there is one major difference. During the colonial times, the anthropologists serving the cause of the administration were aliens. In today's context, the newly independent countries have produced their own anthropologists and they are called upon to assist in the process of planned development by analyzing cultural factors that help or hinder innovations – technological, bureaucratic and educational, to name a few. A new branch is being recognized as auto-anthropology. Previously, students of their own society were labelled as sociologists irrespective of the techniques involved, but they were distinguished by the type of social group they studied: those Indians who studied the tribes in India, but who were not the tribals themselves, claimed the title of anthropologists. Even when they moved to the study of the villages, along with American and British anthropologists, they answered that description as they were 'urban'. Nevertheless, the orientation to the Present was a major departure. Rather than raising the question 'from where and how did we reach here' they began describing the path adopted by the new dispensation to change for the better, comparing their lot with the so-called advanced societies of the North. Anthropologists of the Third World (the euphemism that has now lost its currency) became students of 'Nations-in-Hurry'. Obviously, this change in orientation necessitated methodological innovations, and guided new theoretical formulations.

In such a situation, it is dangerous to delimit the anthropological research to the study of tribes. However, let me hasten to add, it is not necessary to exclude the study of the tribes in the changing context which would require us to re-look at our methodology, revamp the theory of social structure and change and to continue to propagate cultural relativism. We will have to bid goodbye to the idea of anthropological zoos, and reinforce interdisciplinarity (i) to bridge the widening rift between its various branches created by the desire to develop specialization and (ii) to foster closer ties with sister disciplines including futurology – that focusses on the desirable, and just not on the probable and the inevitable.

As anthropologists we are expected to participate in the fashioning of the humanity's future and not only to document the *changing* present.

I believe that anthropology has a special contribution to make. It was the first discipline amongst the social sciences that focussed on change, be it the exercise of reconstructing the past or the microcosmic studies of culture change in the post-independence phase of development. It is this discipline that has challenged the homogenization theory of modernization and westernization, and has finally succeeded in convincing the international community of the desirability of 'bringing culture back' to the main stage. It is the only discipline that can forcefully argue the desirability of *cultural diversity*.

The impending departure of the twentieth century invoked scholars to shift their orientation from the Present to the *Future*. Scholars began to wander in this new terrain. From *speculating* as to what was humankind's remote past, the new challenge is to *predict* the likely future of Humankind. If investigating the past promoted our exploratory skills, predicting the future needed skills other than astrological.

In this context, let us ask: can our understanding of the past help in accurately predicting our future? Do the present trends indicate the likely contours of our future?

Initial thinking on this issue resulted in the distinction between (i) *Certain Future*, (ii) *Probable Future*, (iii) *Possible Future* and (iv) *Desirable Future*. The magic figure of the year 2000 prompted a threefold activity: reviewing the past to gauge the trends of change and to learn the lessons from past experience to improve performance by modifying or changing the strategy of Development; predicting the future shape of the globe in the light of emerging trends; and constructing the desirable images of future. This is the intellectual query kit of the emerging science of futurology.

IV

How do we, as anthropologists, approach the question about the Future of Cultures? Perhaps it may be better to ask: why are we concerned about the future of culture/s? Is it because we are interested in knowing the shape of things to come? Or are we worried about the 'fate' of cultures? The latter question implies that cultures, that

ANTHROPOLOGY AND THE FUTURE OF HUMANKIND

is, *traditional cultures*, will vanish with the onslaught of modernizing influences brought about by rapidly advancing science and technology. The key concerns regarding the futures of cultures are generally expressed in questions such as these: will economic and technological progress destroy the cultural diversity and bastardize our cultures? Will we witness a return of intolerant chauvinism that would make cultures retreat to their shells? Will there be a judicious fit between the old and the new? Where are we going? Can we change the course?

It may be said that Future Shift in intellectual orientation is, in a way, linked with the societal commitment to development. Began as a process of decolonization – which was negative in its orientation – development became, in the countries of the so-called Third World, an ideology for rapid, planned and directed culture change. Newly independent nations began to move in the predetermined direction with defined goals and targets and preconceived strategies. The planners and administrators took on the role of the 'fashioners' of Future. Developing countries got involved in the *revolution of rising expectations*. The West served as the reference group and even proxied many decisions. Westernization and Modernization became synonyms of Development.

But expectations have led to frustrations because of the mixed gains of development. It was a mistake, it is now realized, to blindly imitate the West. Development did not succeed in homogenizing the world. Traditions did not oblige their obituary writers. The process of development, in fact, created greater disparities, broadened the divide between the rich and the poor and falsified many tenets of modernization. Alongside of modernization grew the process of revival and resurgence of tradition and even of religious fundamentalism.

Those who take the pessimistic view of the future of cultures feel that all cultures will lose their pristine character through hybridization and will be reduced to their ornamental roles. The optimists, on the other hand, feel that cultural communities will plunge into their indigenous roots and come up with their own recipes for survival and advancement.

The narrow specialists of culture – the so-called culture people such as prehistorians, archaeologists, the traditionalists and the fundamentalists – are at best 'preservationists'. They have mostly engaged themselves in the rediscovery of the past and its glorification through sheer adumbrationism. They are worried about the dilapidation of the physical structures (such as monuments) because of their gross neglect, or about the damages done to them by natural hazards

179

or irresponsible human actions. Their guiding motto is: 'preserve', 'protect' and 'renovate'. 'Change' does not exist in their vocabulary; Culture, to them, is a mere museum of tradition. The first generation of anthropologists, for example, regarded all forms of culture contacts with the outside world as disruptive of the 'primitive' way of life and, therefore, they wanted the primitives to maintain their *status quo*; they were dubbed as advocates of *anthropological zoos*.

Their protests against culture contacts notwithstanding, what has happened even in regard to the tribal groups the world over is quite astonishing: no tribe has remained completely *insulated* from the outside world maintaining its unique and undisturbed exotic existence; and many of the material cultural traits of various non-Western societies have travelled far and wide to become showpieces in modern drawing rooms. There is a discernible trend towards, what may be called, *museumization* of the drawing rooms.

I hold the view that there is no going back to our cultural shells by isolating and insulating the cultures from each other. Cultural oysters are no longer possible. The opening out, the intercultural dialogue, and the cross-cultural fertilization have brought into play two seemingly contradictory processes of globalization and localization or *indigenization*. The coexistence of these processes is, in fact, indicative of resilience of cultures. There is a need to know how these twin processes relate and operate in different cultural settings and how new equations are worked out. The fact remains that while cultures are no longer completely *insulated*, their opening out of *apertures* has not uprooted them. They are able to maintain their core and retain their identity. How should that core be defined? How does a culture maintain its core? These are the questions that need examination.

There are three prominent strategies employed in the name of saving the culture, namely:

i Reservationist Strategy: Protection of sites, insulating people from outside influences, 'caging' the cultures in museums, or zoos. The policy of 'reservation' for STs, and even the anti-regime movement of the so-called Maoists-Naxalites also fall in this category.

ii Display: Putting the 'Culture' on stage; cultural performances for outsiders where they are torn out of context, and become a 'show'. Preservation and display in the museums of cultural artefacts are similar efforts. This may be called *Museumization of Traditional Cultures*.

ANTHROPOLOGY AND THE FUTURE OF HUMANKIND

iii Displacement: Through thefts of cultural artefacts, or their faking, some aspects of a given culture get displaced. Acquisition of these artefacts results into *Museumization of the Drawing Rooms* in other settings. Bereft of their cultural meaning, such traditional artefacts from other cultures become symbols of modernity in the developed world. In some sense, modernization partly involves 'transfers of traditions' – Western traditions of long standing (including Christianity) came to the non-Western cultures as part of the modernization package; and similarly, material cultural elements from the primitive and other non-Western societies enter the Western drawing rooms to modernize them. Modernization has, thus, displaced and dislocated traditions.

In the midst of sea change experienced by non-Western societies, one notices a reassertion of their respective cultural identities. The resurgence and revival of traditions are manifestations of this assertion.

One may ask: what is the function of Cultural Identity? Does it create solidarity among the people who belong to that culture? Or does this process lead to the emergence of sub-regional loyalties which may become secessionist? What happens when a person is sandwiched between dual loyalties – for example, religious identity vs. cultural identity? The Indonesian Muslims enacting Hindu Ramayana justify their action by saying: *Islam is our religion; Ramayana is our culture.* How does culture give identity to its people? Can newer identities be created by manipulating cultural symbols? Do identities really empower? Or are they fictitious?

It is not very easy to define and identify 'core values'. Nevertheless, cultural values are brought in as explanatory variables when evaluating the success or failure of an innovation. It is important to note that values of the outsiders are a major source for distorting the reality or misreading it. They are also used to condemn a reality. Both insiders and outsiders have their own angles to view reality and to judge its significance. What is good or bad depends upon these perceptions. What an outsider regards bad may be a highly cherished value amongst the insiders, and vice versa. So, whose values should or would prevail? Who should fashion the future – the outsiders or the insiders? Should a futurist impose his own ideological predilections while predicting or prescribing future? Or should he accept value diversity and acknowledge the powers of living cultures to find their own ways of moving ahead?

181

In this context, the concept of *Resilience* of cultures seems quite important in explaining the phenomenon of continuity in societies that are going through a phase of rapid transformation. The retention of cultural identities alongside of modernization can be explained in terms of resilience. But this concept is still vague and is used in a variety of ways; for example:

i   Accounting for the unchangeables in Society.
ii Capability of a Culture to 'withstand shock' so as not to allow 'deformation', 'rupture', 'fracture' of the cultural and social system. Resilience can be equated with the pliancy of the bamboo – 'bending with the storm but not breaking'.
iii As a synonym of 'homeostasis' or *Gaia*: springing back to former position: recidivism, cultural resurgence, fundamentalism, conservatism.
iv Adaptability, Integration, Accommodation, Plasticity.
v   Creative response to cope with Change: symbiosis, encapsulation, cultural reinterpretation, indigenization.
vi Opposite of stability.

It remains to be found out whether resilience occurs in all societies, or only in certain societies – for example, developing Asian societies. If the latter is the case, then what are the contexts that give rise to resilience? Questions also need to be raised in regard to the measurement of resilience, spheres of its manifestation, role of exogenous and endogenous forces in invoking resilience, types of processes through which resilience manifests itself and the manipulability of resilience.

V

There is a need to establish a relationship between the concepts of 'Change' and 'Future'. In my view, both concepts are diachronic, but Change is past-oriented and Future is forward-looking. One is rooted in history; the other is dependent upon our powers of prediction. Analysts of Change often indulge in the glorification of the past; prognosticators tend to exaggerate the glory of their vision of future or decry the prospects of an unwanted future. Those concerned with future either talk of *appropriating* the PAST, or of *displacing* the PRESENT, or of *colonizing* the FUTURE. Are our visions of Future, and their propagation, an attempt towards the colonization of the Future? And can we really colonize it given the existence of several variables that

ANTHROPOLOGY AND THE FUTURE OF HUMANKIND

tend to influence any cultural change? Who determines what is good or bad for a given society? The conspiracy allegation implicit in our critiques of the past and the present is based on our wisdom of the hindsight. How can we say that our imposition of the vision of the Future is not yet another conspiracy? There has been ample criticism of the West as a colonizer responsible for destroying Asian cultures; but the fact is that the West itself is disintegrating in some respects. Contrarily, despite a spate of changes in Asian cultures, their cores are still intact.

Change has now become a key concept and its inevitability is recognized. It is acknowledged that the desire for change is universal; all societies – big or small, modern or primitive, Western or non-Western – share this desire. At the same time, one also notices a new-found attachment to one's own culture; there is in evidence an effective assertion of cultural identity. No society would wish to lose its cultural roots. No culture would allow itself to be engulfed by another dominant culture. These two tendencies – desire for change and keenness to maintain identity – have resulted in increasing modernization of the societies, on the one hand; and revival and resurgence of tradition, on the other. Forces of change have not homogenized the globe into a common culture. The individual cultures have certainly changed and expanded, both in material and non-material terms, but they have not all become even lookalike societies. Religion and tradition have constantly tried to establish new equations with external forces of change. There is an accretion of new cultural elements – either invented within or innovated from the outside; simultaneously, there is also an attrition of some old cultural traits – deliberately or otherwise.

One may ask: does disappearance of certain cultural traits amount to the destruction of a culture? If the answer is in the affirmative, then we may pose yet another question: how does a Culture grow? Or, is Culture just another name for the deadwood? I would submit the point that changes occurring in the ambit of culture do not always erase its identity; it may, however, confuse its identification. Accretion and attrition are the processes that operate in all living cultures, that is, how cultures grow and express their vitality.

The phenomenon of cultural continuity has challenged the 'homogenization' hypothesis. While individual cultures are experiencing vast changes, they are not becoming similar, not even lookalike. Even their own homogeneity has suffered; they are becoming heterogeneous both in terms of their demographic composition and cultural constitution. The so-called World Culture's mono-cultural stance is no longer tenable. The plausible perspective is to view both culture and future in their plurality. No single future can be imposed on all cultures. Cultures have their ingenuity to respond to changes and bring about new equations between the old and the new.

In this sense we cannot talk of 'future' (in singular) of 'cultures' (in plural). Of course, there will be a single, empirical future of a given culture, but scholars may present alternative scenarios – these would be in the nature of 'prescriptions' and not as 'predictions'. Similarly, predictive futurists may sound optimistic or pessimistic depending upon the premises of their prediction. There is a need to use both culture and future as plurals. Plurality goes even further: most nation-societies are plural – both in terms of ethnic composition and in cultural constitution. Each society consists of multiple layers of Culture. At least three strata can be easily identified:

1   Universal, international (global) culture of science and technology, modern industry, bureaucracy, transport and communication, emerging Infosphere
2   Emergent national culture, deriving civilizational base and giving the country its cultural identity, and Regional and local, parochial cultures
3   *Sandwich Cultures* – cultures of migrant groups which emerge as a result of sandwiching between the forces of the parent culture and the host country culture.

Anthropological research has proved the falsity of the dichotomy between tradition and modernity. They are not polar opposites. There are elements of modernity in tradition, and modernization has helped in the propagation of tradition. The rise of ethnic restaurants, the modernization of the architecture of mosques and temples and the popularization of mythical epics through their televization are cases in point. Jumbo jets have not replaced the bullock cart as a mode of transport; allopathy has not made Indian *Ayurveda* or the Chinese acupuncture redundant; not only forks and knives are used by non-Chinese to eat Chinese food, chopsticks are, likewise, employed by the Chinese and the Japanese while eating Western cuisine. It seems that the co-existence principle has overshadowed the replacement and transplantation paradigm of Western development. There is a symbiosis of the elements of tradition and modernity, and since traditions represent a given culture's uniqueness, the symbiosis has resulted in different profiles of emergent cultures in different societies. Cultures

ANTHROPOLOGY AND THE FUTURE OF HUMANKIND

will not be dead; they will be different both from their past, and from other cultures. What is difficult to foretell is the exact chemistry of this difference.

What can be predicted, however, is the outcome of irreversible trends – trends that cannot be halted, and therefore what is inevitable to happen. For example, in case of Asia it can be said that it is inevitable that literacy levels will rise in the near future; that urbanization and industrialization processes will further accelerate; that information revolution will transform the styles of management – both of governments, and of private business; that environmental pollution and depletion of natural resources will increasingly become difficult to stem; that there will be more people inhabiting the region; and that there will be more scientism in our mode of thinking.

There is nothing strange in culture change. What a culture retains and what it gives up, or what it receives from the outside after a thorough cultural screening and redefinition, is a complicated process. Living cultures do not oblige spectators who would like to put the culture 'on stage', or make it a show piece, an anthropological zoo. It is common knowledge that tourists arriving in traditional societies to observe 'exotic' cultures have been primarily responsible for disturbing their status quo. But such disturbance may not be regarded as 'dysfunctional' by those who live that culture. Surely, their culture will not remain the same, but changes in it need not be symptomatic of an impending demise. And views may differ on what is good or bad; what the 'outsiders' may like to retain may be the one that the 'insiders' would like to discard, and vice versa.

It can be said that all cultures in future will look different from what they are today with changes in the profiles of their demography and literacy, and with the continuing onslaught of technology and its attendant ramifications. But they will remain, and remain different, with their own identities. Similarities in material culture – the externalia – will not obliterate differences in values and ways of life. Neither will there be a single future for the globe, nor will there be a single global culture.

Multiple cultures will have multiple futures. Heterogeneity will prevail.

Note

1 Presented at the Round Table, 2013 INCAA Conference, Kannur, Kerala.

BIBLIOGRAPHY

AASSREC. 1988. *Youth in Asia: Viewpoints for the Future.* New Delhi: New Statesman Publishing Company.

Abella, Manolo and Yogesh Atal (ed.). 1986. *Middle East Interlude: Asian Workers Abroad.* RUSHSAP Series # 15. Bangkok, UNESCO Regional Unit for Social and Human Sciences.

Atal, Yogesh. 1989. 'Outsiders as Insiders: The Phenomenon of Sandwich Cultures – Prefatorial to a Possible Theory'. *Sociological Bulletin* (India), Vol. 38, No. 1, pp. 23–41.

Atal, Yogesh (ed.). 1991. *Culture–Development Interface.* New Delhi: Vikas Publishing House.

Atal, Yogesh. 1996. 'Unemployment: Common Problems, Uncommon Solutions', Discussion Paper for the Fourth Olympiad of the Mind. Reproduced in UNESCO Publication: *UNESCO and the World Summit for Social Development*, pp. 148–52.

Atal, Yogesh (ed.). 1997. *Perspectives on Educating the Poor.* New Delhi: Abhinav Publications.

Atal, Yogesh (ed.). 1999. *Poverty in Transition and Transition in Poverty – Recent Developments in Hungary, Bulgaria, Romania, Georgia, Russia, and Mongolia.* New York and Oxford: Berghahn Books.

Atal, Yogesh. 2002. *The Poverty Question: Search for Solutions.* Jaipur: Rawat Publications.

Atal, Yogesh. 2012. *Sociology: A Study of the Social Sphere.* New Delhi: Pearson.

Blaug, Mark. 1970. *An Introduction to the Economics of Education.* London: Penguin.

Dube, S.C. 1990. *Tradition and Development.* New Delhi: Vikas Publishing House.

Elwin, Verrier. 1957. 'Do We Really Want to Keep Them in a Zoo?' *Indian Journal of Social Work*, Vol. 2, No. 4. pp. 438–48.

Elwin, Verrier. 1942. *A Philosophy for NEFA.* New Delhi: Gyan Publishing House.

BIBLIOGRAPHY

ESCAP-UN. 1989. *Review of Youth Policies in the ESCAP Region.* Bangkok: UN-ESCAP.

Gale, Fay and Stephen Fahey (eds). 2005. 'The Challenges of Generational Change in Asia'. Proceedings of the 15th Biennial General Conference of AASSREC. UNESCO RUSHSAP, Bangkok and Association of Social Science Research Councils.

Hutton, J.H. 1961. *Caste in India.* New Delhi: Oxford University Press.

Masini, Eleonora Barbieri and Yogesh Atal (eds). 1993. *The Future of Asian Cultures.* Bangkok, UNESCO RUSHSAP Series # 38.

Redfield, Robert. 1956. *The Little Community.* Chicago: University of Chicago Press.

RUSHSAP. 1980. *Youth Related Indicators* (ed. Yogesh Atal). Bangkok: UNESCO Regional Office.

Secombe, M. J. and J. Zajda (eds). 1999. *J.J. Smolicz on Education and Culture.* Melbourne: James Nicholas Publishers.

Siddh, Kaushal K. and Surendra K. Gupta. 1987. *Youth Profile: India.* RUSHSAP Series on Occasional Monographs #18. Bangkok: UNESCO Regional Office.

Smolicz, J.J. 1985. 'Greek-Australians: A Question of Survival in Multicultural Australia'. *Journal of Multilingual and Multicultural Development,* Vol. 6, pp. 17–29.

Smolicz, J.J. 1988. 'Tradition, Core Values and Cultural Change among Greek Australians'. In A. Kapardis and A. Tamis (eds) *Afstraliotes Hellenes: Greeks in Australia* (pp. 147–62). Melbourne: River Seine Press.

Smolicz, J.J. 1994. 'Multiculturalism, Religion and Education'. *Education and Society,* Vol. 12, pp. 22–47.

Smolicz, J.J., Hudson, D.M., and Secombe, M.J. 1998. 'Border Crossing in "Multicultural Australia": A Study of Cultural Valence'. *Journal of Multilingual and Multicultural Development,* Vol. 19, pp. 318–36.

UNESCO. 1972. 'Youth: A Social Force?' *International Social Science Journal,* Vol. 26, No. 2.

UNESCO. 1979. *Youth Mobilization for Development in Asian Settings.* Paris: UNESCO.

UNESCO. 1980. *Youth Prospects in the 1980s.* Paris: UNESCO.

UNESCO. 1995. *Our Creative Diversity.* Report of the World Commission on Culture and Development. Paris: UNESCO.

Veblen, Thorstein. 1928. *Theory of the Leisure Class: The Challenging Analysis of Social Conduct That Ironically Probes Misused Wealth and Conspicuous Consumption.* New York: Vanguard Press.

INDEX

acculturation process 156
Adivasis 67, 104, 130
adumbrationists 21, 127
Ahoms 132
Angami Nagas 17, 97
Annals and Antiquities of Rajasthan 133
AnSI *see* Anthropological Survey of India
anthropological research 1, 3, 12, 17, 25, 129, 139, 159, 167, 177, 184
Anthropological Survey of India (AnSI) 4–5, 8, 16, 18, 37, 43, 63, 70, 96–7, 111, 125, 138
anthropological zoos 2, 21, 44, 51, 62, 77, 103, 122, 135, 137, 171, 174, 177, 180, 185
anthropology 1–4, 6–28, 42–3, 74–5, 84–5, 95–101, 110–11, 121–2, 139, 155–6, 159–60, 162, 173, 175–8; beginnings of 10–13; cultural 13, 24, 160; departments 1, 4, 6, 8–9, 13, 26, 95, 99, 127, 139, 175; discipline of 2–3, 16, 18, 24, 98–9, 110, 122, 131, 140, 172, 175; general 11–12, 24–5; humankind, future of 173–85; ideological underpinnings of 3; tribal studies and 95–9; and youth, in Asia 139–58
artefacts, cultural 180–1
Asian cultures 183
auto-anthropologist 16
auto-anthropology 4
autochthonous, tribes 37

backwardness 19, 21, 37–9, 41–4, 46, 69–71, 103–5, 115, 126, 141
backward tribes 30, 33
Banvasi 33
Below Poverty Line (BPL) 105, 118
Bhils 30, 46, 66, 113
bioethics 160–1, 170
biological sciences 12, 25–6, 74–5, 95, 159–60, 175
biosphere 73–4, 79–81, 87
Blaug, Mark 152
Brandt, Willy 86
Brundtland, Gro Harlem 81, 82
Brundtland Commission 90–3

castes 2, 28–36, 39–42, 44–6, 64, 66–8, 71, 85, 102, 105, 108, 111–13, 115, 133; hierarchy 34–5, 113–14
Chauhan, Brij Raj 14
Cheros 68
children 81, 89, 92, 142–3, 149, 151, 153
Chopra Committee 64
Coming of Age in Samoa 164
Community Development Programme (CDP) 85–6
countries, developing 77, 90, 151–3, 179
creamy layer 44, 70–1, 127
cultures: anthropologists 12, 25; artefacts 180–1; change 9, 52; communities 22, 63, 125, 179; complex 141–2; constitution

189

INDEX

183–4; contacts 22, 47, 62, 77, 134–5, 137, 140–1, 180; degeneration 62, 64, 134–5; development 51, 84; development interface 22, 56; distinct 37–8, 69; diversity 14, 22, 78, 124–5, 178–9; environment 75; factors 8, 22, 53, 55, 58, 177; future of 22, 178–9; identity 55, 59, 82, 181–4; individual 59, 183; living 22, 83, 125, 181, 183, 185; museumization of 55; native 51–2, 56; primitive 52, 114; relativity 64, 126, 163; resilience of 180, 182; role of 57, 59, 80; students of 20, 83, 124; traditional 179–80; traits 22, 34, 53, 59, 63, 103, 125, 171, 180, 183; treating 59–60; values 161, 181

Dalits 104
Darwin, Charles 10, 27
Das, N. K. 17, 97, 132
de Cuellar, Javier Perez 56
descheduling process 43–4, 70–1, 126
development efforts 61–2, 87, 110, 134
Dhebar Commission 114
Draft Tribal Policy Statement 41–2

Eastern Anthropologist 18, 97–8
economic development 14, 51, 55, 80, 88, 134
education 4, 16, 38, 55, 86, 88, 91, 99, 105, 107–9, 118, 135, 145–6, 150–3, 165
Eggan, Fred 11, 12, 24
Elwin, Verrier 2, 64, 96, 102–3, 122, 126–7, 135–6
empowerment 129–38
enculturation 109, 143, 161
ethics 16, 159–61, 167–9, 171–2; in academia, concern for 159–61; conflicts, inevitability of 166–71; cultural biases, carriers of 165–6; issues 159–61, 164, 167–8, 171; normative 161; in research 159–71; researcher, role of 166;

scientific norms 162–3; theoretical and ideological biases 164
ethnic groups 14, 30, 56, 66, 113, 140
ethnographies 3, 18

female literacy 106, 118
Freedom at Midnight 169

Gaddis 39
Gairies 34
Galton, Francis 11
Gametis 111
Garasias 30
Garhwa Kala 124
Ghurye, G. S. 19
Gledhill, John 167
globalization 155
Gluckman, Max 11, 12, 24
Gonds 68
Gond Woman 6
Gray, Henry 12
Gujjars 16–17, 20, 29, 31, 34–5, 43, 45–6, 48, 64, 67, 70, 101, 113, 132

human societies 10–11, 64, 91, 126, 171
Hutton, J. H. 35

ICSSR *see* Indian Council of Social Science Research
illiterates 106, 108, 122, 145–6, 153
Indian anthropologists 18, 100
Indian anthropology 28, 96
Indian Council of Social Science Research (ICSSR) 3, 9, 17, 28, 97, 116; Survey 18, 97
Indian literacy rate 106, 118
Indian population 19, 37, 70, 100, 105, 114, 149
Indian sociology 7, 86
indigenous civilization 18, 100
indigenous knowledge 121–8
indigenous peoples 37, 70, 82–3, 123
Information Revolution 15

Janma-Pradhan 105
Jati caste 33, 66, 115
Jati vyavastha 35

190

INDEX

Kalelkar, Kaka 29, 67
Khasas 31
Kinship, Politics and Law in Naga Society 17, 97
knowledge, traditional 63–4, 125–6

Levi-Strauss, Claude 59
literacy 3, 52, 99, 105–8, 118–19, 122, 135, 144–6, 185
Lokur, B. N. 39
Lokur Committee 36, 39–40, 69

Majumdar, D. N. 6–8, 14, 96
management culture, in hospitals 151
Man and Biosphere programme (MAB) 73–84
Mandal Commission 42
Man in India 7, 18, 97–8
Mathur, K. S. 14
Matriliny and Islam 6
Mead, Margaret 164
Meenas 30–1, 64, 68, 113, 132
Minas 66, 68
modernization 2, 9, 52, 59, 83, 86, 89, 119, 123, 129–30, 146, 155–6, 178–9, 181–2, 184
monographs 6, 17, 25, 97, 116
multiple aperture model 156
Murdock, George Peter 27
museumization, of culture 55

Naga rebellion 135
natural environment 73, 75, 77–8, 91
Nehru, Jawaharlal 2, 127, 135
nomads 34, 65
non-tribal groups 47
normative ethics 161

On the Origin of Species 10, 27
oppressed castes 28–9, 112
orthogenetic development 156

palimpsests 21, 127
A Philosophy for NEFA 2, 127, 135
physical anthropologists 12, 25–6, 96, 111, 127, 139, 163, 175
physical anthropology 3, 9, 12–13, 15, 25, 27, 75, 95–6, 156, 160, 175–6

Pichhada Varg 104
pluricultural societies 56
policymakers 12, 24–5, 61, 85–6
population 19–20, 31, 61, 78, 81, 88, 90, 93, 100–1, 106–8, 111–12, 114, 145–6, 148, 176
positivism 162–3
poverty 46, 54–5, 62, 71, 80, 103–5, 137, 153
preliterate societies 65
preponderant agricultural groups 104
primitiveness, of community 10, 38, 45
primitive societies 3, 27, 137, 162
primitive traits 19, 37, 43–4, 69–71, 115, 126, 141

reconstruction, concept of 50
Redfield, Robert 44, 141
religious groups 30, 47–8, 113, 115
resilience 59, 83, 125, 180, 182
reverse Sanskritization 104, 133

Sandwich Cultures 184
Sanskritization 133
Scheduled Castes (SCs) 29, 32–3, 36, 39–40, 67, 133, 142
Scheduled Tribes (STs) 17–19, 29–30, 32, 36–7, 39–41, 43–4, 65, 67–70, 100, 104, 112–14, 130, 132–3, 180
SCs *see* Scheduled Castes
Sen, Amartya 55
Shah, Madhuri 116
shifting cultivation 78–9
Singh, Kumar Suresh 111
single aperture model 156
Smolicz, G. 146
social anthropologists 12, 15, 18, 25–6, 36, 98, 111, 139, 160, 167, 175–6
social anthropology 9, 12–14, 18, 25–7, 96–8, 156, 163–4, 175–6
social change 14, 86, 119, 165–6
social development 52, 54–5, 80, 119, 124
social development front 54
social sciences 2–3, 12–14, 16, 25, 36, 74–5, 80, 85, 116–17, 129, 159, 162–3, 166, 175, 178

191

INDEX

social scientists 18, 21, 26, 40, 43,
53, 74–5, 79–80, 85–6, 93, 102–4,
111, 117, 131, 134
socio-cultural dimensions 50–60
Srivastava, Vinay K. 17, 97, 99
state politics 129–38
STs *see* Scheduled Tribes
Sugalis 39, 68
sustainable rural development 54,
77, 85–93

TK *see* Traditional Knowledge
Tod, James 133
Traditional Knowledge (TK) 63–4,
123, 125–6
transculturation 156
Tribal Research Institute 1, 16, 111
Tribe-Caste Continuum 36
Tribe-Caste Question 46
tribes 1–3, 18–20, 28, 30, 37,
61–6, 68–9, 98, 105–6, 108–9,
113–14, 118–19, 126–8, 132–4,
142; backward 30, 33, 66–7,
69, 112; category 29, 31, 67–8,
101, 113, 133, 141; committee
32, 67; concept of 100–2; culture
of 2, 51, 122, 174; cultures 1–2,
28, 51, 61, 63, 77, 82, 123, 137;
definition of 21, 24, 36, 65,
101–2; development 1, 3, 20, 61,
85, 134; development, issues in
61–71, 102–9; female literacy
106, 118; Indian 8, 96; population

21, 30, 37, 70, 78, 106–7, 112–13,
118, 132–4; primitive 30, 33,
66, 69, 79, 81; status 17, 19–20,
29, 31, 37, 39, 45, 48, 68–9,
100–2, 113–15, 141–2; studies
1–2, 4, 8, 17–18, 20, 26–7, 95–9,
101, 109–11, 176; sustainable
development 85–93; unrest 129–38;
women 98, 110–19

unemployment 54, 80, 145, 153
Urgent Anthropology 63, 125

value-neutrality 162–3
village studies 14, 85–6, 98, 110–11,
139, 175–6

Weber, Max 163
Weltanschauung 16, 38, 46
Westermarck, Edward 163
westernization 52, 59, 86, 119,
129–30, 155–6, 178–9
women 106, 110, 112, 115–19, 148,
151; status of 115–16, 119
world civilization 59–60
world culture 90, 183
World Employment Report (1998–99)
153

Yenadis 39, 68
Yerukulas 39, 68
youth population 146–9
youth profiles 145, 147–8